RUSSELL SAGE FOUNDATION
1907–1946

In Two Volumes

VOLUME TWO

ROBERT W. DE FOREST

RUSSELL SAGE FOUNDATION

1907–1946

By

JOHN M. GLENN
LILIAN BRANDT
F. EMERSON ANDREWS

VOLUME TWO

New York

RUSSELL SAGE FOUNDATION

1947

WM. F. FELL CO. : PRINTERS
PHILADELPHIA

CONTENTS

VOLUME TWO

v

PART V

DEPRESSION AND WAR

CONTENTS

CONTENTS

APPENDICES

ILLUSTRATIONS

Eight Medallions Symbolizing the
Aims and Spirit of the Foundation

XXVI

SURVEYS AND EXHIBITS: 1918-1931

AFTER the war the content of the work done in the Department of Surveys and Exhibits gradually changed, until in 1931 its name no longer described its activities. By that time participation in surveys had become limited to consultation and the publication of material on survey methods. Work on exhibits had broadened to include various kinds of publicity techniques applicable to social work, and thence to study of the larger problem of interpretation of social work. The addition of Allen Eaton to the staff in 1920 as assistant to Mr. Harrison brought in a new interest—beauty as an element in social welfare—which by 1931 was represented by work that constituted practically, though not yet formally, a distinct department.

No other additions[1] were made to the permanent staff of the Department during this period, though several investigators were engaged at different times for temporary work on special studies. Mr. Harrison had increasing demands on his time from outside the Department. As acting director of the Division of Industrial Studies during Miss van Kleeck's absence in Washington, he became responsible in 1919 for the study of public employment offices, completed in 1924. His heavy responsibilities in connection with the Regional Survey began in 1921 and were not finally discharged until 1931. After his appointment as vice-general director of the Foundation in 1924 his administrative duties, together with obligations of a voluntary nature in connection with important new organizations,[2] cut down con-

[1] Except Mrs. Routzahn, on her return from Washington in February, 1919, but this was a formality rather than a substantial change, as she had been employed on special assignments almost continuously since 1912.

[2] Conspicuously the Social Science Research Council, organized in 1923, on which he represented the American Sociological Society. He was a member of its Committee on Problems and Policy, which made heavy drafts on his time, particularly during several of the earlier years when he served as its secretary. In 1929 President Hoover appointed him a member of the Research Committee on Social Trends, of which he became secretary-treasurer.

siderably the time he had for strictly departmental work. In September, 1931, he assumed his duties as general director of the Foundation, but continued "for the time being" as director of the Department.

COMPLETION OF UNFINISHED WORK

When the war interrupted the routine of the Department's work, Mr. and Mrs. Routzahn had in preparation a practical handbook for the aid of "people who may wish to use exhibits for promoting social welfare." Originally intended to be a pamphlet, it grew to book size, partly as a consequence of added experience and new devices developed during the war.[1] This was the first book ever published on the subject. When it was allowed to go out of print in 1935 its place was taken by a bulletin of the Social Work Publicity Council, Tell It with Exhibits, written by Mrs. Routzahn. It was also the first of a Survey and Exhibit Series, edited by Mr. Harrison, which made available the experience accumulated by the Department.

A second volume in the series was also under way before the war. For some time Mrs. Routzahn had been collecting information about educational campaigns on wheels, which toured a city, a county, or a larger territory in wagons, automobiles, trucks, trolley cars, or railway trains. Although this device had been used extensively for a number of years—by federal and state departments, agricultural colleges, and some private organizations—in the interest of better crops, better cattle and dairy products, better roads and houses, better health, and fewer accidents—there was no publication that brought together a description of methods and problems. Mrs. Routzahn had begun work on a manuscript before she went to Washington in 1917. In the summer of 1919 she took it up again. The resulting book[2] was based on accounts of about 75 tours of various kinds of vehicles besides her own observations and experiences. Mr. Harrison, in his Editor's Preface, called it "an anthology of practical experience thus far formulated."

[1] The ABC of Exhibit Planning, by Evart G. and Mary Swain Routzahn, 1918.
[2] Traveling Publicity Campaigns. 1920.

352

The plan for a Social Survey Handbook by Mr. Harrison was realized in essence by his summary volume on the Springfield Survey,[1] which included not only condensation of the nine reports on special topics and a description of the exhibit, but also a discussion of procedures and methods.

SURVEYS

Two relatively small surveys—one of a single topic, the other a "pathfinder"—were undertaken by the Department soon after the close of the war.

In December, 1918, following negotiations pending since the previous spring, a formal agreement was made by Mr. Harrison with Mayor Charles P. Gillen of Newark, New Jersey, on behalf of the Board of Commissioners, to take responsibility for a survey of the city's Department of the Overseer of the Poor (also called Poor and Alms Department) and its Almshouse. Mr. Harrison asked Francis H. McLean to make the study. With the help of two members of his own staff, Mr. McLean finished the field work within two months. His study necessarily involved examination of the relations of the public department to other social agencies, and his recommendations had to do with "the whole family-welfare problem of the city" and "the adjustments in various directions" that seemed to be needed. Copies of the printed report[2] were in the hands of Mayor Gillen on April 28, three days before the date stipulated in the agreement.

The pathfinder was a preliminary survey of the Negro colony in Harlem, New York City, which had grown during the war into one of the largest urban aggregations of Negroes in the world. The deplorable living conditions and serious social problems among them were giving social workers increasing anxiety. In May, 1921, the Foundation engaged George E.

---

[1] Social Conditions in an American City. 1920.

[2] The Poor and Alms Department, and the Almshouse, of Newark, N. J., by Francis H. McLean, 1919. The city of Newark paid the Foundation $1,400 for the survey; $400 was used for the printing of the report, and $1,000 was turned over to the Family Welfare Association in partial reimbursement for the time of Mr. McLean and his staff. The Foundation contributed editorial and statistical services on the report as well as Mr. Harrison's time.

Haynes[1] to make an exploratory survey under Mr. Harrison's supervision. He submitted a report in the fall and recommended an intensive survey of the district, for which later he drafted an outline. While this proposal was under consideration by the Foundation, the Federal Council of Churches decided to develop its Commission on the Church and Race Relations, and asked Mr. Haynes to become secretary of the Commission. With the approval of Mr. Glenn and Mr. Harrison he accepted this position, which seemed to offer an opportunity for promoting surveys in many places. His studies in Harlem were useful in various ways in his new work.

When in 1921 the Foundation initiated its general survey of the New York Region, Mr. Harrison naturally had important responsibilities for that project. No more surveys were undertaken by the Department, but it continued to keep its information up to date, to confer on plans for surveys, and to suggest persons competent to direct them.

Printed material on surveys had increased so much since the Department published the revised edition of its bibliography in 1915 that in 1918 preparation of another revision was begun. After Mr. Eaton joined the staff, the search for items and the laborious detail of preparing and classifying entries were mainly his responsibility. Publication was delayed from year to year, partly because of pressure of other work, but chiefly because of the large amount of material and several changes in plan of classification. When at length it was issued it was a substantial book,[2] listing 2,775 projects completed to January 1, 1928. An introduction by Mr. Harrison[3] reviewed the survey movement from its beginning, analyzing the trends that had taken place since 1907, offering "an attempt at a definition of the survey

---

[1] Professor of social science, Fisk University, 1910–1921; on leave of absence 1918–1921 as special assistant to the United States Secretary of Labor. Mr. Haynes had written on The Negro at Work in New York City for his doctor's thesis at Columbia University in 1912.

[2] A Bibliography of Social Surveys, by Allen Eaton and Shelby M. Harrison, 1930.

[3] Reprinted separately as a 42-page pamphlet, The Social Survey, in 1931.

and its purposes,"[1] and discussing "the significance of surveys as a means of informing citizens regarding community conditions."

While collection of data for the bibliography was in progress Mr. Harrison agreed to compile for the new Welfare Council of New York City[2] information about the studies made in New York City by or for social agencies during the previous five years. Mr. Eaton assumed the main responsibility for this. Material already in hand for the bibliography supplied a foundation. Additional search, and extension back over ten years instead of five, resulted in a list of 527 reports. Helpful indexes of subjects and persons were included. References to studies in progress or contemplated were also sent to the Council, and other information that would be useful in keeping the list up to date. The report was published by the Welfare Council in a pamphlet of 84 pages in August, 1926.

Incidental to its study of printed reports of surveys, the Department accumulated examples of symbols used on maps to represent social institutions. Such symbols were in common use but there was no uniformity as to their significance. Nineteen different figures for designating a church were found. When the Regional Survey began work it was anticipated that an accepted system would be in demand. Mr. Hurlin's help was enlisted in 1922 and gradually the project was transferred to the Department of Statistics.

There was a marked revival of interest in surveys after the war, not only in America but also in many foreign countries. In part this arose from activities of the Inter-Church World Movement, the Young Men's Christian Associations, the Young Women's Christian Associations, missionary organizations, and the American Red Cross, but it was also manifested by many and diverse independent agencies or groups. Requests for help and

[1] "In short, the social survey is a co-operative undertaking which applies scientific method to the study and treatment of current related social problems and conditions having definite geographical limits and bearings, plus such a spreading of its facts, conclusions, and recommendations as will make them, as far as possible, the common knowledge of the community and a force for intelligent coordinated action."

[2] Established in 1925. Its first executive, William Hodson, was a member of the Foundation's staff, and the Foundation contributed to its support.

information came to the Department in increasing volume. For a number of years it was estimated that the time given to advisory consultation was equivalent to the amount that would have been required by "at least one major undertaking" conducted by the Department itself.

Each year the Department was asked to conduct several surveys but was obliged to decline, because of other demands on Mr. Harrison's time. Some of them were beyond the scope of the Foundation, as they would have involved spending money to improve conditions in foreign countries: the Foundation was asked to send a commission to China to make a general study of social and industrial conditions; Mr. Harrison was invited to direct a survey of Prague. Advice was given freely to inquirers, through correspondence and office consultation. Plans were discussed, directors and other personnel were recommended, references to material were supplied and frequently copies of some of the material, and reports on file in the office were made available for study. In most years through 1929 help was given on surveys in 40 to 50 cities in the United States. In 1930 and 1931 the number fell below 30, presumably as a consequence of the depression. Consultation on surveys and exhibits outside the United States was at its height immediately after the war. In the three years 1919–1921 the list included 18 countries, from Sweden to South Africa on one side of the Atlantic, from Nova Scotia to Argentina on the other, and westward around the northern hemisphere from Siberia to Japan, China, and India. Ten years later the number had dropped to five.

In 1921 Mr. Harrison gave a course of lectures in the summer session of Columbia University on community problems and social surveys; and in the second semester of 1921–1922 a similar course in the New York School of Social Work. Each year thereafter through 1931 he taught for one term in the School. In eight of these years he also gave semester courses at Teachers College, and in two other years he conducted a five-session course at the National Training School of the Young Women's Christian Associations.

NEW STUDIES

In the spring of 1919, when conditions once more permitted planning for the future, Mr. Harrison proposed three new major studies to be made by the Division of Industrial Studies, of which he was still acting director, and the Department of Surveys and Exhibits. His proposals were made after a field trip in 1918 which took him into a number of important industrial districts, including those in and around Chicago, several in Ohio, Pennsylvania, New Jersey, and Delaware, and after conferences with leaders in business, industry, labor, education, public welfare, and social work in these and other localities, including Washington and New York City. On the recommendation of the general director, all three suggested studies were approved by the Trustees and special appropriations for them were made to supplement amounts that would be available from the budgets of the Department and the Division.

Two of the studies—the capture and recording of the experience of the United States and Canada in operating national systems of public employment offices and of experiments under way in the United States designed to increase the participation of labor in management—were planned in consultation with Miss van Kleeck and were entered upon as joint undertakings with the Division of Industrial Studies. The former got started promptly. By the time Miss van Kleeck returned to the Foundation in October, 1919, a large part of the field work had been completed. At her request Mr. Harrison continued in charge. On the second study nothing but preliminary collection of material was attempted before Miss van Kleeck's return and she then assumed its direction. The third study—of publicity methods for social work—grew out of the work of Mr. and Mrs. Routzahn in the Department and was carried through by them.

J. Bradley Buell,[1] of the Division of Industrial Studies, returned from service in the Army about the time the study of public employment offices was approved by the Trustees in

[1] Mr. Buell, one of Miss van Kleeck's students at the New York School of Philanthropy, had been added to her staff in January, 1918. He was drafted for military service the following August.

357

February, 1919. He and another member of the Division's staff, Miss Helen B. Russell, began work at once. In addition, three special investigators—Miss Mary LaDame, Leslie E. Woodcock, and Frederick A. King—took major parts in the collection of material and the preparation of the report. Miss van Kleeck was in close touch with the study throughout, and generous help was given by scores of persons in the United States and Canada, including such outstanding students of unemployment and pioneer administrators of public employment bureaus as W. W. Leiserson, Bryce M. Stewart, Charles B. Barnes, and Miss Louise C. Odencrantz.

Field work was completed within a year. It included observation of employment bureaus in operation, comparison of methods, collection of forms and other material, study of statistical and other documentary data, and interviews with many persons who had knowledge of placement work from various points of view. About 70 cities in the United States and Canada were visited. A preliminary draft of the report was ready by the fall of 1920. It was then submitted, in whole or in part, to a number of competent critics and revised in the light of their comments, the revision, supplementary studies, and publication taking four years.[1] The book was a review of the methods and agencies in operation at the time, with special consideration of the place of the public bureaus among them; a description and discussion of the questions of organization and administration of a national public employment service; and similar consideration of the work of a local office and of special types of service for special categories of workers.

In advance of publication various chapters of the report were placed in the hands of persons to whom it would be useful. Parts of it were put at the disposal of the Conference on Unemployment called by President Harding in September, 1921. A chapter based on the data was written by Mr. Harrison for a report prepared by the National Bureau of Economic Research for the

[1] Public Employment Offices, by Shelby M. Harrison in collaboration with J. Bradley Buell, Mary LaDame, Leslie E. Woodcock, and Frederick A. King. (Each of the collaborators had primary responsibility for a section of the report.)

Committee on Unemployment and Business Cycles appointed by Herbert Hoover, then Secretary of Commerce, following the President's Conference; and a memorandum of recommendations for the establishment of a nationwide public employment service was prepared for the same committee. At the request of Gifford Pinchot, then governor-elect of Pennsylvania, a report on the public employment offices of Pennsylvania was prepared by Miss LaDame from material accumulated in the study and was presented at a conference called by him in December, 1922.

EXHIBITS—PUBLICITY

There was no abrupt transfer of interest from the topic of exhibits to the broader field of publicity methods in general. Conducting an exhibit, as the Department conceived it, had always involved the use of newspapers, advertising, lectures, plays, and other media, as well as the designing and installation of graphic representations of facts in two or three dimensions. And interest in exhibits was not dropped when special attention was given to these other media and to the principles underlying effective use of all of them and their synthesis in a "publicity program." But after the war it was the larger problem and the interrelation of its elements that primarily engaged Mr. and Mrs. Routzahn.

Although after the war the Department did not undertake the actual direction of exhibits of social and living conditions as it had done in its earlier years,[1] Mr. and Mrs. Routzahn continued to keep in touch with developments and to study methods.[2] The amount of consultation, moreover, was larger than ever before. As in the case of surveys, the time spent annually in giving advice and information on exhibits was estimated as the equivalent of the amount that would have been required for "at least one major undertaking."

[1] The exhibits of arts and handicrafts developed by Mr. Eaton (see p. 369) were of a different kind and his concern was primarily with the subject rather than with the technique of exhibits.

[2] To the end of his life Mr. Routzahn delighted in discovering and experimenting with new materials and new ideas for exhibits. He also gave special attention to window displays, particularly for social agencies participating in community-chest campaigns.

Geographically help on exhibits was spread over as wide a territory as advice on surveys. Subjects covered a wide range and types of organizations were varied. Associations begun before and during the war and in the preparation of books continued with cumulative effect.

Among organizations seeking advice about exhibits after the war were the National Tuberculosis Association and a number of its state and local affiliates, the American Public Health Association, the Federal Council of Churches, the Inter-Church World Movement, the International Committee of the Young Men's Christian Associations (on plans for an elaborate exhibition at one of its triennial conventions), the Department of the Interior (on an exhibit of its activities held in May, 1919), the Health Service of the American Red Cross, the National Health Council, the National Safety Council, the Department of Agriculture (exhibitors at state and county fairs), 13 social organizations that exhibited at the Sesquicentennial Exposition in Philadelphia in 1926, and agencies that sent exhibits to Paris in 1928 for the First International Conference of Social Work.

Assistance included discussion of plans, suggestions for revision and new features, reference to material, and recommendation of persons who might be engaged to take charge. Charles J. and Walter Storey and Miss Stella Boothe were three of the freelance exhibit specialists who were frequently suggested. The Storeys had assisted the Routzahns in some of their early exhibits for the Department.[1] Miss Boothe prepared many exhibits for county fairs. With a great deal of encouragement and help from Mr. Routzahn, she developed a "suitcase theatre" of marionettes, which she used in health instruction for children.

In addition to material on exhibits, from window displays to world fairs, information was gathered about motion pictures and lantern slides, suggestions for illustrations for books and articles were filed. Scrapbooks of press releases and photographs of exhibits were prepared for the use of visitors to the office and for

[1] In the twenties Charles J. Storey also worked with Mr. Hanmer on his volume for the Regional Survey, and then for four years was on the staff of the Department of Recreation.

circulation. As the volume of printed publicity increased and improved in quality, similar portfolios were arranged of well-written and well laid-out articles and pamphlets. A list of specialists in publicity was begun. Data on methods used in money-raising campaigns were systematically collected.

Shortly after the war Dr. W. W. Peter[1] came back to America from China, where he had spent several years under the auspices of the Young Men's Christian Associations in teaching the Chinese about health with extraordinary success. Mr. and Mrs. Routzahn arranged a number of conferences for him and an address by him in the Russell Sage Foundation building in which he acted out his story of China as a man weighed down by a burden of disease and displayed the dramatic devices he had used to interest illiterate Chinese audiences in such subjects as cholera, smallpox, and typhoid fever. On the basis of this address and talks with Dr. Peter, in 1920 Mr. Routzahn wrote an account of his traveling educational campaign, including descriptions of his use of dramatic action and of mechanical devices on the platform.[2]

PUBLICITY FOR SOCIAL WORK

When the study of publicity techniques for social agencies was outlined in 1919, it was expected to occupy one or two years. The book was published in 1928.[3] The reason for undertaking it was the belief that, although spreading information and enlisting support were among the main purposes of social agencies, they had given comparatively little attention to evaluating methods or discovering the principles underlying effective presentation.

The plan was to hunt out the best examples of publicity in the field of public health—the areas related to social work in which most had been done in the way of popular education—in the expectation that these would provide models that could be presented as a guide. Austin Pierpont was engaged from February, 1920, as a special assistant in this field work. In 1922 he wrote

[1] Later associate professor of public health in the Yale School of Medicine.
[2] The Health Show Comes to Town, by Evart G. Routzahn.
[3] Publicity for Social Work, by Mary Swain Routzahn and Evart G. Routzahn.

a report on it. What he found was (through no fault of his) "too negative" to warrant publication. The search then was extended into practically all branches of social welfare, including the annual campaigns of the safety movement and of community chests.

While the study was in its early stages two developments took place that not only facilitated the collection of material but also provided forums for discussion and channels for spreading knowledge of improved methods.

At the National Conference of Social Work in 1921 the growing interest in publicity methods[1] led a group of members to ask Mr. and Mrs. Routzahn to organize a series of meetings at the next conference for the discussion of methods and technical questions. The success of these meetings in 1922—lively, practical, informal, held in the chinks of the official program and after the close of the evening sessions until lights were turned off—established the Committee on Publicity Methods and its annual program[2] as a feature of the National Conference.[3] Mrs. Routzahn was chairman of the Committee in 1924 and then became permanent secretary. In 1923 she began editing a News Bulletin, issued six or eight times a year, as a clearinghouse for ideas and reports on experiments.

Similarly, in 1921 and again in 1922 Mr. and Mrs. Routzahn conducted several sessions on publicity and educational methods at the annual meeting of the American Public Health Association. This led to the establishment of a health education section in the Association, which had its place on the program, its headquarters at the annual meetings, and its department in the monthly Journal. Mr. Routzahn was appointed editor of the department.

[1] Foreshadowed in informal discussions at the Conference in 1917 (see p. 196) and recognized more definitely in the official program of 1920 in a paper on "Elements of a Social Publicity Program" by Mr. Routzahn. This paper was reprinted as a pamphlet by Russell Sage Foundation in September, 1920.

[2] Including the "Follies," an entertainment of revues and songs satirizing social workers.

[3] Within two or three years the Conference added to its regular organization a Division on Educational Publicity, of which Mr. and Mrs. Routzahn were among the first chairmen. The Committee continued its own program as "an associated group."

Throughout the twenties Mr. and Mrs. Routzahn spent a great deal of time in helping to develop these two agencies for the improvement of educational methods and publicity. In each case meetings, exhibits, and consultations at the annual convention and interim bulletins were the chief methods. Many of the meetings were in the popular form of "clinics," at which examples of publicity were criticized by experts and discussed by the audience.

Relations between the Committee on Publicity Methods and the National Conference of Social Work included certain professional services to the Conference itself, which were also in the nature of demonstrations or practice work for members. In 1924 it conducted a publicity service for the Conference during the week it was in session. One feature was a daily story by delegates to their home papers. Later a committee directed and assisted in the general publicity program of the Conference, as well as at its meetings. Some advisory help was continued until the Conference employed a full-time publicity director.

The contributions of Mr. and Mrs. Routzahn to the Committee on Publicity Methods and the health education section of the American Public Health Association were by no means without reciprocal advantages. Their responsibilities for meetings, news notes, and contests brought to them automatically a stream of material and an acquaintance with persons that could hardly have been accumulated by any system set up for the purpose. All this was particularly useful while the book on publicity methods was in preparation.

Contrary to expectation, the early laboratory material collected by field workers as a basis for the book and the samples coming to hand in other ways not only were disappointing in quality but they did not disclose any well-defined standards or principles. The next step, accordingly, was to turn to such established forms of publicity as journalism, printing, advertising, and public speaking for techniques that might be applicable to the special problems of social work; and to the basic principles of psychology involved in attracting and holding attention, creating good will, and stimulating effective action. From the publications consulted a selection was made of titles that had some bearing on publicity methods in social work, though very few of them discussed that subject specifically. This list, circulated first in mimeographed sheets, was printed later as a pamphlet.[1]

For the parts of the book that discussed fundamental psychological principles and the use of newspapers and miscellaneous printed matter—more than half of the total contents—there were at least some accepted standards. For such subjects as public meetings, one of the commonest methods in use—plays, pageants, fairs, expositions, and intensive campaigns—the main reliance had to be on personal experience and observation.

Motion pictures and the radio, the revolutionary new channels of communication, were making great strides during the period that this book was in preparation, but little space was given to them. As to radio, there was not yet much conception of the tremendous importance it was to have as a medium for spreading information and influencing public opinion. As to motion pictures, the authors explained that there was "much experimenting and little specialization" in production of educational films (the silent variety) and that distribution was "in a chaotic condition." Since demands from social agencies for help in producing and obtaining such films were "growing more pressing" they thought "the whole problem should be studied." Another topic "deserving attention" was the organization of a publicity department within a social agency. This was the subject of the closing chapter of the book.

Advisory services and study of methods went hand in hand. During the greater part of the twenties study of publicity methods was rather concentrated on printed matter, the form of expression that had the most definitely formulated standards and techniques. Copy for leaflets, pamphlets, advertisements, and letters of appeal, sketches for posters, manuscripts of articles, annual reports, chapters of books, and entire books, were submitted to Mr. and Mrs. Routzahn for criticism. In the stream of material they could see a gradual improvement both in appearance and

[1] Publicity Methods Reading List, by Evart G. Routzahn and Mary Swain Routzahn, 1924. A mimeographed supplement was issued in 1929.

in quality of writing. Continued attention was given also to dramatic methods of presentation. Help was given on scenarios. Motion pictures and marionette plays were reviewed. To stimulate the writing of one-act plays, contests were sponsored by the Committee on Publicity Methods in 1924 and later. Awards were resorted to on many occasions and in many localities to rouse interest in publicity programs and bring talent to light. Mr. Routzahn served on many juries to select the best poster or window display, the best campaign. One of them awarded the prizes to cities of different classes for the best celebrations in 1928 of National Negro Health Week.

Continued Study of Methods of Interpretation

After the book was published special attention was given to the newer or less studied modes of spreading information. Radio programs were studied and help was given in preparing radio talks on social work. For some time Mr. Routzahn had been collecting notes for a contemplated publication on how to make meetings effective. Although one of the commonest means of publicity in use, there had been little examination of the relative success of methods employed in conducting them. Beginning in 1930 Mr. Routzahn worked for three years to improve the meetings of the National Conference of Social Work. He analyzed the factors involved in a successful meeting, devised an "observation record" for impressions produced on the audience, collected records through volunteer "observers" who were coached in advance on how and what to observe. Results of the studies were presented to the program committee of the Conference. In this connection attention was given to techniques of public speaking, in meetings and over the radio.

Money-raising techniques[1] were not made a subject of special study by the Department, though it received many inquiries about them and though it recognized that money-raising was one of the primary objects of publicity for social agencies. Its services

[1] How a department for that purpose should be organized in an agency, how much it should cost, the relative efficacy of various methods and of different fund-raising firms, how to elicit favorable responses from foundations, and so on.

in this direction consisted chiefly in collecting sample material for circulation and in urging such publicity as would attract an informed and convinced body of supporters. Its chief concern was to stimulate and help social agencies to give the public a more intelligent understanding of their work and of the social problems back of it rather than to supply them with formulas that would bring them the largest return in contributions per dollar spent in solicitation.[1] From this point of view many talks were given and many letters of appeal were criticized.

In December, 1928, a group of financial secretaries of social agencies in New York City asked Mrs. Routzahn to meet with them for informal discussion of some of their common problems. This was the beginning of regular monthly meetings. Mrs. Routzahn acted as chairman for several years and then served as a member of the steering committee until 1940. In 1930 Mr. Routzahn began a study of the publicity problems of the national agencies: how they might bring about a better understanding of their place in the scheme of social work; promote better standards of work in their respective fields; and help their state and local affiliates in their publicity programs.

All this work had for its underlying object the better interpretation of social work. In Mr. Routzahn's paper at the National Conference of Social Work in 1920 he spoke of the advantage of planned year-round programs of publicity over annual or sporadic bursts of activity. The subject was discussed in Publicity for Social Work. A symposium on "A Health Education and Publicity Program" was arranged for the meeting of the American Public Health Association in 1929 and printed in its Journal. To encourage social agencies to give more thought to planning their publicity, the Social Work Publicity Council in 1930 sponsored a contest for which the Harmon Foundation offered awards. Prizes were given for the best year-round programs presented by

[1] In the fall of 1926 Mrs. Routzahn helped the Welfare Association of Webster County, Iowa, plan a financial and educational program. After the campaign was over the executive secretary wrote: "It is true that we did not reach the amount of our budget, but we more than doubled our last year's income. . . . We discovered a lot of unknown friends and created a lot of new ones. We have given the organization a better standing in the community, and have given the community a wider realization of the thing we are trying to do; so of course it was a tremendous success."

agencies in three classes of places. The number of entries was disappointing but the winning programs provided excellent material for reference.

TRAINING OF PERSONNEL

To plan and execute effective publicity programs qualified workers are essential, and to insure a supply of such personnel there must be opportunities for systematic training. The Department's portfolio collection and bibliographies were useful educational material for students. Personal consultation had helped many. Mr. and Mrs. Routzahn had given many single lectures or groups of lectures of a practical nature in various places. In 1923 they offered a full course on publicity in the New York School of Social Work, and this course became an established feature of the curriculum with increasing enrollment. Later in the twenties they conducted five-session institutes for publicity workers at the State Conferences of Social Work in Ohio and Pennsylvania, which were followed in the next few years by similar institutes elsewhere.

In 1929 the Department projected a new major study, which had for its object to increase the supply of properly trained and qualified personnel for publicity work by promoting opportunities for training and determining what the content of such training should be. As a preliminary step Mrs. Routzahn got together information on the approximate number of publicity positions in social agencies in the United States and Canada; typical requirements of such positions; and the courses offered in colleges, universities, and schools of social work that might be useful in training for them. A tentative standard course of study was outlined.

At this time Mrs. Routzahn added a second course to her teaching in the New York School of Social Work, offering practice in writing and other forms of expression. She also, at the request of local executives, arranged an experimental course in public speaking under the auspices of the Social Work Publicity Council, which was taken over by the School in 1930–1931.

SOCIAL WORK PUBLICITY COUNCIL

It became increasingly evident through the twenties that the Department could not continue indefinitely to carry responsibility for the Committee on Publicity Methods. As the Committee grew in usefulness to its members it frequently interfered with the progress of research under way or projected in the Department, though, on the other hand, it supplied valuable material for studies and served as a laboratory and a record of current practices. It was contemplated that the Committee would in time become a "service agency," with a relation to the Department similar to that of the Family Welfare Association of America and the Child Welfare League to the departments of the Foundation from which they developed. With this in view, much of the advice on publicity techniques by Mr. and Mrs. Routzahn was given in the name of the Committee.

In 1929 the Committee organized more formally under the name of Social Work Publicity Council. The following year, on request of Russell Sage Foundation, it began to plan to release a large part of Mrs. Routzahn's time as secretary and editor of the News Bulletin. Increased revenue from dues was matched by an appropriation of $1,000 from the Department. Income for 1930–1931 reached about $5,000. At the end of the year there were about a thousand members, and 16 affiliated local councils. Complete independence in the near future seemed assured.

HEALTH MUSEUMS

Mr. and Mrs. Routzahn's original interest in graphic methods of presenting facts about health and social problems continued as an element in these larger developments. In the summer of 1930 they attended the International Hygiene Exposition in Dresden, visiting also the Dresden Museum of Health, the Deutsches Museum at Munich, and smaller health and safety museums in Berlin and London. The visit to Dresden was the beginning of relations with Dr. Bruno Gebhard, then on the staff of the Dresden Museum, who later became a leader in this country in developing exhibits as an important tool for health education.

ART IN RELATION TO SOCIAL WORK

"To bring into the field of social work a greater appreciation of the vital relation of art and beauty to life" was a primary interest of Allen Eaton when he was added to the staff of the Department of Surveys and Exhibits in June, 1920. He believed social work could be strengthened and enriched by a wider recognition of the power of the arts, in a broad sense, and that the arts could gain if there were a clearer conception of their social function. The problem was to find out how the arts could be practically applied in social work.

The number of people engaged in the handicrafts, especially in the rural areas, is very large—larger than in any other branch of the visual arts. It has therefore been the values inherent in the practice of handicrafts which the Foundation has sought to bring out and strengthen in its studies. Although fully conscious of the importance of the economic or indirect returns to many who are engaged in handicrafts, the Foundation has been mainly concerned with the importance of the direct values, those which bring personal satisfaction to the craftsmen. These values the Department has designated as educational, social, aesthetic, and therapeutic. Often one of these values stands out more conspicuously than another, but usually the craftsman experiences them all in some degree; and it is especially to be noted that one value does not exclude the others. Often one who practices a handicraft for its economic return will experience all the other values or benefits. What the work means to and does for the producers concerns this department most.

Another benefit is "a growing appreciation of beauty in the things of everyday life. The effort to make a useful object pleasing to the eye or touch gives the craftsman an understanding of the age-long struggle to bestow on objects of daily use that quality that renders their ownership one of life's little events. And recognizing beauty in things that he had not noticed before, or looking at had regarded as commonplace, he feels himself a joint possessor with those who have designed them and with all others who enjoy them."[1] We need "to find beauty, not only in the

[1] Handicrafts of the Southern Highlands, by Allen Eaton, Preface.

things we make and use but in the relations we sustain one to another."[1]

Twelve years' experience in conducting a book and art store in Eugene, Oregon, after graduation from the university, added greatly to Mr. Eaton's understanding of what the arts in their broad sense meant to many people. The World's Fairs held in Portland (1905), Seattle (1909), and San Francisco (1915) gave him his introduction to the fine arts. While a member of the state legislature he persuaded the Commission in charge of the Oregon Building at the Panama-Pacific Exposition at San Francisco to make the Art Room an expression of the culture of the people of the state. When the Commission was unable to find anyone to carry out the idea Mr. Eaton felt constrained to take the responsibility himself. Everything used in the structure, furnishing, and decoration of the room, except the glass in the windows, was material native to the state and was fashioned by Oregon artists, craftsmen, or manufacturers. Many of the articles were designed by Mr. and Mrs. Eaton, including a completely equipped doll's house and a large Noah's Ark, which they had made for their own children. The emphasis in the Oregon Room was on the possibility of enjoying beauty in objects of everyday use as well as on the beauty latent in the native products of the state. A catalogue describing the room and its contents was printed on paper made from the fiber of native trees.

Mr. de Forest, then president of the American Federation of Arts and of the Metropolitan Museum of Art in New York City had become acquainted with Mr. Eaton in 1916, through correspondence about a loan exhibition of paintings that Mr. Eaton had persuaded the Federation to send to Eugene, Oregon, while he was living there. The acquaintance led to Mr. Eaton's appointment in June, 1919, as the first field secretary of the American Federation of Arts. In this position during the next year he assembled at the Museum the first exhibition in the United States of inexpensive color prints for home decoration; later he arranged for the first large color reproductions from paintings in the Museum; and thus for the beginning of an extensive program

[1] *Ibid.*

370

of color reproductions by the Museum, which stimulated similar "extension activity" by other museums. He also planned a series of exhibitions of Arts and Crafts of the Homelands of Europe as an experiment in Americanization, to be held under the joint auspices of the Federation and the New York State Department of Education. Within the year he directed the first two of this series, at Buffalo and at Albany, and initiated plans for others.

The value of these exhibitions in promoting "Americanization" by displaying and publicly acknowledging the cultural contributions of our immigrants to American life, and the applicability of the idea in many communities, made it seem to the Foundation that there should be a record of them. It was obvious also that in other ways Mr. Eaton's interests and experience would be useful in the Department of Surveys and Exhibits. After joining the staff of the Foundation he continued for many years to give part of his time to the American Federation of Arts.

One of the specific purposes for which the Federation kept a claim on part of Mr. Eaton's time was that he might continue to conduct the annual exhibitions of color prints for home and school decoration. This he did until 1930. Each fall his selection of inexpensive good prints suitable for these purposes was exhibited for two weeks in the Foundation halls. Occasionally the original painting was hung alongside the print to show how faithful the print was to its original. During the time they were on view visits by groups of teachers, students, women's clubs, and parents' associations were arranged, at which special addresses were given and discussions were held. In 1925 the Association of Practical Housekeeping Centers selected 50 of the prints, with Mr. Eaton's advice, framed them in appropriate but inexpensive moldings, and hung them, properly placed, on the walls of four of the 70 model flats installed in the public schools for teaching purposes under the auspices of the Department of Homemaking. Among the color print exhibitions assembled and shown first in East and South Halls at the Foundation, and later circulated by the American Federation of Arts, was one of Country Scenes and Rural Work which was asked for and shown many times, sometimes repeatedly in the same community.

371

Mr. Eaton soon had in manuscript a pamphlet describing the Buffalo and Albany exhibitions. Before it could be published other events similar in purpose had taken place or were in prospect, and it seemed desirable to include a record of them. As the scope of the pamphlet widened, the time Mr. Eaton could spend on it was reduced by other demands.[1] When Immigrant Gifts to American Life was published by the Foundation in 1932 the pamphlet had grown to a book. It was subtitled "Some experiments in appreciation of the contributions of our foreign-born citizens to American culture" and was dedicated to the memory of Robert W. de Forest, "who did so much to bring beauty into the lives of his fellowmen and whose staunch support made possible the pioneer undertakings recorded here."

The book included descriptions not only of the pioneer exhibitions in New York cities but also of festivals and exhibits under various auspices elsewhere in the United States and in Canada. Many of these Mr. Eaton attended and some of them he helped to plan and arrange. Among the features of the book were a chapter of advice on organizing and arranging an exhibit of handicrafts, and a selected list of foreign-born artists and craftsmen who had become American citizens and were working in America.

America's Making Exposition and Festival,[2] held in New York City in the fall of 1921, had a twofold origin: as one of the Arts and Crafts of the Homelands exhibitions and also as a project of an independent committee in New York City, which wished to depict the contributions of all kinds made by immigrants to the building of the nation. Mr. Eaton had been a member of the executive committee of this enterprise before coming to the Foundation and continued to share in its plans. A series of crises in management and finances as the date for opening approached threw the major responsibility on him. By contributing his undivided attention for a number of weeks, the Foundation not only helped greatly to insure the success of the two weeks' pro-

---

[1] For example, by work on A Bibliography of Social Surveys and the compilation for the Welfare Council (see pp. 354, 355).

[2] Described in Immigrant Gifts to American Life, pp. 87–91.

gram but enabled the committee to return a respectable cash balance to the underwriters of the celebration. The research material collected by the committee was offered to the Foundation, which put it into usable shape under Mr. Eaton's supervision and through the Library made it available for study and reference.

Somewhat similarly, it fell to Mr. Eaton in the spring of 1923 to take charge of the exhibits of the New York and Brooklyn Chapters of the American Institute of Architects at the City Jubilee Celebration, commemorating the twenty-fifth anniversary of the consolidation of Greater New York. Again it turned out that much more responsibility and much more work were involved than had been foreseen. With the help of a number of persons, chief among them Charles J. Storey, Mr. Eaton was able to make the exhibit of the architects a success.

From the early years of Mr. Eaton's connection with the Foundation he had opportunities to help on projects within his field that were under way by others. In the spring of 1924 he was asked for suggestions on a study of art in American life contemplated by Carnegie Corporation and became a member of the advisory committee. At Mr. Keppel's request he prepared memoranda later in the year on four topics he had suggested for inclusion in the study. In this he had generous help from the staff of the Foundation's Library.

Within the Foundation his taste was called into service in connection with the decorative panels for the building and changes in the style of the Foundation's publications. One of the first books issued in the revised style was selected by the American Institute of Graphic Arts for its list of "Fifty Books of 1925." Mr. Eaton served on the Institute's committee to select the list for 1926 and again for 1927. For a number of years he either designed or passed upon the title pages of all the Foundation's publications, and his advice on printing was sought by the Regional Plan Committee and other organizations in the city.[1]

---

[1] Mr. Eaton dates his interest in printing as an art from the gift by the librarian of the University of Oregon, in his student days, of the first number of Printing Art, a magazine for promoting better printing that came to the library.

In 1926 Mrs. John C. Campbell asked Mr. Eaton to take part in the Conference of Southern Mountain Workers. For the first time the subject of handicrafts had a place on the Conference program. Besides Mr. Eaton's addresses, there was a small display of products from several leading handicraft centers of the Highlands and several informal conferences were held to discuss markets and other common problems. For Mr. Eaton this was the introduction to work that occupied a large part of his time in succeeding years. Requests came in 1928 for a comprehensive study of handicrafts throughout the Southern Highlands; and from the Women's Educational and Industrial Union of Boston and the Sandwich Home Industries of New Hampshire for a similar study in New England. Neither study could be undertaken at the time because of other work on hand.[1] The invitations from Boston and New Hampshire led to acquaintance with some of the work in handicrafts in New England, and also with the co-operative efforts of official and voluntary agencies in Canada to preserve the traditional arts of the Provinces and of the "New Canadians," and to develop a program throughout the Dominion.

The impetus given handicrafts by the discussions at the Conference of Southern Mountain Workers in 1926 led to a small gathering at Penland, North Carolina, in December, 1928, to consider the advisability (suggested by Mr. Eaton) of forming an organization of persons interested in promoting arts and crafts in the homes and schools of the region. A recommendation favoring such an organization and formally requesting Russell Sage Foundation for advice in the preliminary stages of launching it and for a comprehensive study of the situation as a basis for its work was adopted for presentation to the Conference. At the Conference in April, 1929, the report was adopted and a committee was appointed to carry forward the recommendations. As a result, the Southern Highland Handicraft Guild was organized in December, 1929.

Mr. Eaton participated in all the meetings preliminary to the organization of the Guild and until it was firmly established. He undertook to arrange the exhibit to be held in connection with

[1] Both requests were repeated later, and eventually both studies were made.

374

the Conference of 1930 at Knoxville. Thirty-two groups of craftsmen sent material. "With a good supply of lumber and beaverboard and volunteer carpenters" the Sunday-school rooms of a church were converted into an art gallery, where the articles were displayed to good advantage. The variety was a revelation even to members of the Guild. This was the first comprehensive and representative exhibition of the handicrafts of the region. It began a series that helped make the Southern Highland handicrafts and the Guild known throughout the country.

Throughout the years while he was working on Immigrant Gifts to American Life Mr. Eaton not only kept his connections with the American Federation of Arts and the Art Alliance of America but was drawn into association with agencies interested primarily in immigrants. He served on committees of the Foreign Language Information Service and the Council on Adult Education for the Foreign-Born, and presented a paper entitled "Some Immigrant Contributions to American Culture" in the section on immigrants of the National Conference of Social Work at Minneapolis in 1931.

In the later years of the decade he became more and more occupied with study of the native arts and crafts of America and the contributions they could make to enriching rural life. In addition to numerous connections with the Southern Highlands and a growing acquaintance in New England and Canada, he visited many exhibitions, folk festivals, and state and county fairs, in various parts of the country, and was consulted by many persons who wished to bring more beauty into the life of the average citizen and who had ideas, or wanted ideas, as to how that could be done. In 1930 he became a member of the committee on rural cultural arts of the American Country Life Association. About the same time he was chosen as an adviser to the New Hampshire Commission on Arts and Crafts appointed by Governor John G. Winant to study the possibilities of statewide co-operation for promoting handicrafts—the first state commission for the purpose in America.

As his major original assignments progressed toward completion, he formulated, at Mr. Glenn's request, his ideas of a

375

program whereby the Foundation might contribute to bringing about a closer relation between art and social work in order "to bring a larger measure of beauty, either created or enjoyed, into the lives of all people." By the fall of 1931 the deepening depression was underscoring the importance of doing everything possible to promote wholesome use of leisure time. The Trustees of the Foundation decided that the time had come to extend what it was doing in this field through the Department of Recreation, "in a small experimental way in a new direction" by providing "leadership and assistance in stimulating a wider and more satisfactory participation of people of all ages in cultural arts and handicrafts." Accordingly they appointed Mr. Eaton "consultant with reference to cultural arts and handicrafts."[1]

[1] In the organizational structure of the Foundation, Mr. Eaton's work, like that of Mr. and Mrs. Routzahn, was still, in 1931, part of the Department of Surveys and Exhibits.

Architectural detail from the east façade,
Russell Sage Foundation Building

XXVII

INDUSTRIAL STUDIES: 1918-1931

DURING the period of reduced activity caused by demands of the war on Miss van Kleeck and members of her staff the Division of Industrial Studies, with Mr. Harrison as acting director, carried forward work under way, bringing some of it to completion.

STUDIES BEGUN BEFORE THE WAR

The study of conditions among Italian working women in New York City, begun in 1911 and interrupted in 1913, was completed and published.[1] This was the fifth and last of the series on women's work in New York City. It was not merely a description of conditions affecting a relatively small group of Italian women in a limited area of the city. It was also a contribution to an understanding of the significance of those conditions for standards of family life. It was eloquent, too, of the immigrants' need for help in adjusting themselves to American life, and suggestive of the kinds of help that would be useful. In dramatic contrast with the situation at the time the study was undertaken, when the book was published the number of immigrants entering the United States was about matched by the number of aliens leaving. There were still, however, hundreds of thousands of foreigners in the population who were not yet "adjusted" or "assimilated." The reduced influx presented a particularly favorable opportunity for hastening the process.

In January, 1918, J. Bradley Buell, who as a student had taken part in the preliminary field work of the study on collective bargaining in the cigar industry, was added to the staff to go on with it in Mr. Selekman's absence. Mr. Buell was drafted in August for service in the Army. On his return in February, 1919, he was

[1] Italian Women in Industry, by Louise C. Odencrantz, 1919.

377

assigned to work on the new study of public employment offices directed by Mr. Harrison. By that time changes had taken place in the cigar industry that diminished the outlook for a profitable study on the scale originally planned. It was not completed for publication, but what had been done gave useful background for later studies of industrial relations. Similarly a full report of the study of sickness among wage-earners was prepared for office use. Work was completed on an occupational census of college women, made by a committee of the Association of Collegiate Alumnae of which Miss van Kleeck was chairman, and the report was published by the Association.[1]

Postwar Program

At the close of the war the entire field of industry was reviewed as a basis for deciding what the Foundation could do that would be most useful. There was much industrial unrest in the United States, due in part to the rising cost of living but in part also to mounting dissatisfaction of workers with the slight share they had in determining their working conditions. The great need seemed to be for a plan of organization that would give them a voice in determining the conditions of their employment while at the same time placing upon them more responsibility for the quality and quantity of their output. Experiments of various types were under way. It was the consensus of employers, labor representatives, social workers, investigators, and government officials who were consulted that a record of these experiments, including analysis of procedures and evaluation of results, would be extremely useful. The Foundation was in an exceptionally favorable position to carry on unbiased studies from a disinterested point of view.

For such reasons the Division[2] of Industrial Studies in the summer of 1919[3] embarked on a series of investigations of new experiments in the organization of relations between employers

[1] "A Census of College Women," by Mary van Kleeck, in Journal of Association of Collegiate Alumnae, May, 1918.

[2] "Department" from January, 1920.

[3] See p. 357.

378

and employes. "Wage-earners' participation in management" was the general title used for the project. This was the primary occupation of the Department for more than ten years. Six books resulted; many new acquaintances were made; and a large amount of valuable material was accumulated.[1]

Secondary, but prominent and continuing, interests of the Department throughout this period were the official statistics of employment in the United States, irregularity of employment in coal mining, methods of research, administration of labor laws, and special problems of women in industry. Acquaintance with social workers and industrial investigators in Europe widened, and was cultivated, in the belief that "we cannot fully understand conditions in the United States without some knowledge of the economic forces and experience in human relations in foreign lands, since conditions and practices in each country affect every other country that has developed a similar type of modern industry." Miss van Kleeck participated, on the program and as an officer, in the principal international conferences in her field held during this period.

INDUSTRIAL RELATIONS SERIES

The first experiment selected for study in the new series was the so-called "Rockefeller Plan" of "industrial representation" in the coal mines and the steel works of the Colorado Fuel and Iron Company. It had been devised at the request of John D. Rockefeller, Jr., the largest stockholder of the Company. During the prolonged strike of coal miners in Colorado in 1913 he asked W. L. Mackenzie King of Canada to suggest a plan that would

[1] Throughout the period information was collected about as many experiments as possible, and many were followed for a time until it could be determined whether a case study would be profitable and feasible. One of these was the Works Council in the Rock Island Arsenal. A study was made by Edwin S. Smith of the department staff in the spring of 1920, before work at the Arsenal was curtailed and while the Council was in full operation. Publication of the report was delayed. The Works Council was abandoned. Miss van Kleeck planned to make a brief supplementary study to discover the reasons for the failure of the Council and to contrast conditions when it was no longer in existence with those found in 1920. More pressing work interfered, and this account of "an unusual works council," indicating "certain problems of industrial relations in a government-owned and -operated shop," was not published.

prevent the recurrence of such a disaster. Both Mr. Rockefeller and Mr. King believed that the lack of personal relations between management and employes was at the bottom of labor troubles in modern industry. The essence of the new plan was an application to industry of the principle of representation familiar in political life. Personal relationships were to be restored through representatives chosen by officials and by workers. It was the forerunner of the shop committees and works councils that multiplied during the war and after its close, and was probably the best-known example of employes' representation. Established in the mines of the Company in October, 1915, and in its steel works the following spring, it had been in operation long enough to offer data for a study of methods and results.

Mr. Selekman, who had been a member of the staff of the Department for three years, spent five months in Colorado in the winter of 1919–1920. He visited the steel works in Pueblo and all the mining camps, talked with workers, foremen, superintendents, and higher officials of the Company, with state officials and disinterested citizens, and read a vast amount of minutes and other documentary material generously placed at his disposal. Copies of the preliminary draft of a report were submitted to Mr. Rockefeller, to the president of the Company, and to the secretary-treasurer of the United Mine Workers of America, with requests for criticism. Company representatives questioned the accuracy of some of the statements and disagreed as to the interpretation of many of the facts. Miss van Kleeck then went to Colorado to discuss points of difference with the officers of the Company and to get an independent impression of the views of the workers. Mr. Selekman also returned to review some of his evidence.

After thorough revision of the manuscript, including reexamination of evidence on every disputed "fact," it was again submitted to representatives of the United Mine Workers, who approved it as a whole, and to the officers of the Company and Mr. Rockefeller, who still had objections. Full consideration was given to all their objections, but there remained many differences of opinion as to interpretation and conclusions.

Separate reports were published simultaneously[1] on the operation of the Industrial Representation Plans in the Coal Mines and in the Steel Works. In both cases the aim was "to set forth events, conditions, statistics, purposes, methods and opinions fully enough to enable readers to weigh the evidence and to draw their own conclusions."

In the opinion of the authors definite improvements had followed the introduction of the Plan both in the coal mines and in the steel works, but in neither case had it yet established true "participation in management." It had brought about further improvements in living conditions and provisions for health and safety, in which the Company had long been a pioneer, and it had provided for discussion of grievances. Responsibility for decisions, however, remained with company officials. There had been three strikes in the coal mines since the Plan was established. Reciprocal antagonism between the Rockefeller Plan and trade unionism was the crucial feature of the situation. The title of the closing chapter of the book is "An Incomplete Experiment."

While in the Company's steel mills also the scope of the Rockefeller Plan was found to be "seriously limited," it marked "a distinct step in advance" in "an industry so devoid of any tradition concerning the representation of the workers as the steel industry" was at that time. Under the Plan the men of the steel works obtained "such important gains as the actual eight-hour day, an opportunity to participate in revising wage-scales, a method of presenting and discussing grievances, and a greater degree of security in their jobs through enjoying the right to appeal to higher officials against the decision of foremen and superintendents." By contrast with the general attitude in the steel industry against dealing with workers either individually or collectively, the Colorado Fuel and Iron Company stood out as a pioneer in the improvement of human relations when it introduced a representation plan in a steel plant.

A true example of "participation" was found in the third experiment chosen for investigation, the Partnership Plan of the

[1] Employes' Representation in Coal Mines, by Ben M. Selekman and Mary van Kleeck; Employes' Representation in Steel Works, by Ben M. Selekman, 1925.

Dutchess Bleachery at Wappingers Falls, New York. This study, too, was made by Mr. Selekman. He spent several weeks continuously in the village in 1921, talking with workmen, managers, and townsmen, reading minutes, and attending meetings. This report[1] was the first of the series to be published.

Nearly a century old, the Bleachery was the principal industry of the village. The Partnership Plan had been introduced in 1918 on the initiative of new owners, who thought of it as a "spiritual" undertaking. They wished to correct some of the conspicuous defects common in modern industry. The Plan created a Board of Operatives, elected from among the employes by secret ballot, which was responsible for conditions in the company houses, supervised a recreational and educational program for the entire community, and presented grievances to the management; a Board of Management, equally representative of employes and stockholders, who decided all important questions relating to the conduct of the plant; and a Board of Directors, elected by the stockholders but consisting of representatives of the operatives, of the community, and of the stockholders, who formulated financial policies. Books were thrown open and the workers were kept fully informed about the facts of the business. Profits, above a dividend of 6 per cent and provisions for sinking funds, were divided equally between stockholders and workers. There was no interference with the one local union in the plant.

At the end of three years the company houses had been put in good condition, the appearance of the village was transformed, and a varied program of leisure-time activities was in operation. The attitude of the operatives toward production had been revolutionized. Efficiency increased. Business was good, earnings comparatively high, even in the depression of 1920–1921. The low level of wages throughout the industry and the fact that continuation of the Plan was dependent on the will of the stockholders were two elements of weakness. Regardless of limitations, however, the conclusion was reached that the Partnership Plan of the Dutchess Bleachery, Inc., was "one of the most advanced, most sincere, and most comprehensive schemes of

[1] Sharing Management with the Workers, by Ben M. Selekman, 1925.

industrial relations introduced into industry on the initiative of the employers."

The fourth volume[1] in the Industrial Relations Series reported a study in one of the best-known retail stores in the country, and one of the first firms of any kind to experiment with employes' participation in management. Just conditions of work had always been a matter of consideration with the founder, William Filene. He recognized that success in a retail store depended largely on the employes. When in 1901 he turned the business over to his sons, Edward A. and A. Lincoln Filene, they formulated their principles for the business: permanency, profit, and service to consumers. They would have chosen to be poets or scholars or engineers. Their lot was to be "shopkeepers," but they saw in that occupation plenty of scope for ideals. A number of years later—after this study was made but before it was printed—they both published books setting forth their philosophy. How that philosophy was applied, and with what results, is described in the Foundation's volume.

Miss LaDame had had considerable experience in the problems of retail selling before coming to the Foundation to participate in the study of public employment bureaus. Edwin S. Smith, who helped her on the original investigation, had taken part in other projects of the Department of Industrial Studies and after finishing his part of this study he accepted the position of employment manager in the Filene Store. Most of the field work in the store was done between August, 1921, and August, 1922. Miss LaDame was there again for two months in the fall of 1926. The manuscript was read in whole or in part by 16 representatives of the management and the employes. On the basis of their criticism and supplementary material the account was brought down to January 31, 1927.

By this time changes in the financial organization of the business were bringing changes in managerial policies that seemed to mark the end of the period that began in 1901. The book describes the store and its organization throughout that period—the first quarter of the twentieth century, while net sales grew

[1] The Filene Store, by Mary LaDame, 1930.

from $500,000 to $26,000,000 a year—and analyzes in detail the evolution and significance of the twofold personnel program: the Personnel Division (Employment and Training departments) of the Store Management; and the Filene Co-operative Association, the organization of employes, tentatively created in 1898 and formally established with a constitution in 1903.

A case study of the administration of labor agreements in the bituminous coal mines of Illinois was the fifth volume[1] in the Industrial Relations Series. This was an outgrowth from the study of the industrial representation plan of the Colorado Fuel and Iron Company. In that connection it was necessary to collect some general information about the coal-mining industry and also about the methods of the United Mine Workers, who carried on a constant agitation in Colorado to organize the miners of the Company. A special investigator, Louis Bloch, was engaged in December, 1919, to collect this material.[2]

Thus it happened that when a nationwide strike of coal miners was declared in April, 1922, the Department had on hand data about the overdevelopment of the bituminous coal industry of the country and the consequent irregularity of employment and income for the miner. Within two weeks a pamphlet was issued[3] that gave the public in compact form some of the background for understanding the situation. It showed that in the thirty-two years from 1890 through 1921 the number of days of operation in the bituminous coal mines of the United States had averaged only 214, hardly more than two-thirds of the working days of the year, while the number of new mines opened had steadily increased. Without undertaking to suggest how it should be done, the report pointed out that what was needed was "such thorough-going reorganization of the entire industry as will stabilize production and make employment regular." The facts were widely used by the press throughout the country. Secretary Hoover

[1] Labor Agreements in Coal Mines, by Louis Bloch, 1931.

[2] A mining engineer, Hugh Archbald, was added to the staff for four months early in 1920 to analyze the causes of unrest in the mines arising out of methods of management as disclosed both in the Colorado study and in the investigation of the United Mine Workers. His report was intended for office use, and was not published.

[3] The Coal Miners' Insecurity, by Louis Bloch, 1922.

asked the Foundation to make a similar analysis of employment in the principal coal-producing countries of Europe, and for a number of years statistics were collected as opportunity presented.

Mr. Bloch's study of the methods of the United Mine Workers for purposes of the Colorado investigation led to the decision to develop it into one of the Industrial Relations Series. The state of Illinois, "District 12" of the national union, was chosen as the area for special study. In Illinois collective bargaining had been longest in operation, ample records were available from 1909 on, and the state was the third largest producer of soft coal. The groundwork of the study was an analysis of recorded decisions in disputes over many years. The influence of the trade union agreement upon the daily relations between the miners and their employers, as thus revealed, is the main subject of the book: "how disputes are settled in the industry, how the provisions of the written contract are interpreted in daily practice, how the contract and its interpretations are enforced, and what the effect is upon the functioning of the industry."

Work on this study was interrupted in July, 1922, when Mr. Bloch left the Foundation to be statistician of the Department of Industrial Relations of California. In 1925 he brought his material down to date. Four years later, after the operators' associations in Illinois had been consolidated and a new agreement had been made, Miss van Kleeck attended the biennial convention of the miners' union of the state and in conferences with operators and miners revised the manuscript to conform with the current situation. At the time the book was published it happened there were coal miners' strikes in progress in many states, and this record of the working of plans for joint settlement of disputes in a district of strong union agreements received wide comment in the press, particularly in the coal-mining regions.

From 1919 on labor relations and other events in the coal-mining industry were followed by the Department systematically and its material was used in many ways. Another major study in this industry, constituting the sixth in the Industrial Relations Series, was made after the close of this period.[1]

[1] See p. 549.

CANADIAN EXPERIENCE IN CONTROLLING STRIKES

In September, 1919, Mr. Selekman attended the National Industrial Conference of Canada, called for the purpose of working out fundamental standards which might help prevent industrial unrest. A year later he went to Canada again, for the annual convention of the Trades and Labor Congress. These visits gave him an opportunity to renew and extend his acquaintance with officials, labor leaders, employers, and other persons conversant with the operations of the Industrial Disputes Investigation Act. Since his study in 1916 the attitude of labor in Canada had changed from opposition to cordial support. By 1920 opinion generally was heartily in favor of the Act as an experiment in conciliation. For the lessons it might have for the United States, it seemed desirable to follow the Canadian experience into its later history.

This Mr. Selekman did. He carried the study not only through 1920, but thereafter, year by year as records became available, to the spring of 1925, covering the entire eighteen years that the Act had been on the statute books of the Dominion.[1] The Canadian experience was useful to the United States in showing the futility of attempting to prohibit the right to strike and at the same time demonstrating the value of a definite machinery for mediation under governmental auspices in averting strikes in public utilities.

HOLLYWOOD

In the summer of 1924 the Department was asked by Will H. Hays, president of the Motion Picture Producers and Distributors of America, Inc., to make a study of employment conditions in the motion picture industry in Hollywood. Miss van Kleeck spent a week there in September, to analyze the problems that should be included in a thorough investigation. It did not seem feasible to undertake a comprehensive study, but the quick survey enabled her to make certain definite recommendations in

[1] Postponing Strikes, by Ben M. Selekman, 1927. (This study was submitted by Mr. Selekman as his thesis for the degree of Ph.D. at Columbia University. He resigned from the Foundation in November, 1927, to study in Europe.)

which Mr. Hanmer[1] concurred. One was that the association should establish a free casting bureau for "extras," maintained at the expense of its members, to do away with the abusive fees charged by commercial agencies. Within a short time this was done.

EMPLOYMENT BUREAUS FOR THE HANDICAPPED

Not long after the publication of Public Employment Offices a committee representing placement agencies for the handicapped in New York City asked the Department to make a study looking toward better co-ordination of their work. This was made by Miss Mary LaDame, who had taken part in the general study. Her report was published by the Welfare Council at the expense of the Foundation in March, 1927. There was more demand for the pamphlet than had been anticipated. An immediate practical result was the consolidation of four of the leading bureaus in New York City in the interest of economy and better service, under the name Employment Center for the Handicapped.

EMPLOYMENT AND UNEMPLOYMENT

Next to relations between workers and management, the questions to which the Department gave most attention during this period were probably those affecting irregularity of employment. The studies of conditions in the soft coal mines made clear the extent and the consequences of irregular employment in an important industry. The depression of 1920–1921 brought special responsibilities and opportunities to it and to other Foundation departments.

Miss van Kleeck was a member of the President's Conference on Unemployment, held in September, 1921, under the chairmanship of Secretary Hoover—the first national government conference on the subject in the United States. She served on several important committees of the Conference, including those on mining, statistics of unemployment, and business cycles. Before adjourning, the Conference recommended that provision be

[1] See p. 324.

made for a thorough study of the causes underlying recurrent business depressions and of the more promising proposals for reducing the consequent unemployment. To make this inquiry, Mr. Hoover appointed a Committee on Unemployment and Business Cycles. Miss van Kleeck was one of its members.

This committee asked the National Bureau of Economic Research to conduct its investigation, and included employment statistics as one of the subjects to be covered. Mr. Hoover asked Russell Sage Foundation to make this section of the study, in co-operation with the National Bureau. The Foundation supplied funds by making an addition to the budget of the Department of Industrial Studies and designated Miss van Kleeck to conduct the inquiry. By way of co-operation, the American Statistical Association in February, 1922, appointed a Committee on Measurement of Employment, with Miss van Kleeck as chairman.[1] Mr. Hurlin was a member from the beginning and soon became secretary. Most of the other members were practicing government statisticians. This committee continued the inquiry undertaken by Russell Sage Foundation, and the Foundation's appropriation was used to meet its expenses.

The function of the Committee was to develop a plan for the collection and publication of adequate[2] employment statistics for the United States. Because of the composition of the Committee, its work could be done by the members themselves. They could agree on basic forms and procedures, put them into operation in their own work, watch for weak spots, and try out improvements. Expenses were small, consisting chiefly in the cost of bringing together the widely scattered members for frequent conferences. Through the influence of the Committee, the coverage of current statistics, both geographically and by occupations, gradually was

[1] During the depression of 1914–1915 Miss van Kleeck had taken part in inaugurating a system for regular current collection of employment statistics by the New York State Department of Labor. See p. 164.

[2] The data available at the time, their inadequacy, and an outline of "next steps" under consideration by the Committee of the American Statistical Association, were discussed by Miss van Kleeck in the chapter she contributed to the general report of the Committee on Unemployment and Business Cycles: Chapter XIX, "Charting the Course of Employment," in Business Cycles and Unemployment, McGraw-Hill Book Co., Inc., 1923. (Mr. Harrison contributed Chapter XVI, "Public Employment Offices and Unemployment.")

extended and their usefulness increased in other ways as well. In 1926 the results of its work were published by the Foundation[1] in a volume presenting a plan for collection on a national scale, to which Miss van Kleeck contributed a chapter on "The Uses of Employment Statistics." By this time statistics collected by the federal Bureau of Labor Statistics and ten or a dozen state bureaus made it possible to measure trends in employment and earnings in manufacturing and to some extent in other occupations.

At the end of its first year, the name of the Committee was changed to Committee on Governmental Labor Statistics and its authorized scope was correspondingly enlarged. After the publication of Employment Statistics the Committee began to give special attention to statistics of wages. Requests for information and advice multiplied.[2] To supply a minimum office staff Bryce M. Stewart was appointed executive secretary from June 1, 1928, on part time, with a full-time assistant. Office space was provided by the Department of Industrial Studies and expenses continued to be met through the Department's budget.

A survey of employment indexes published in the United States and Canada was made in 1928. At the instigation of the Welfare Council of New York City, a system for measuring fluctuations in employment and earnings on public works in the city was worked out. Through 1929 recommendations were developed for a census of unemployment as part of the federal census of 1930. After the census was taken the methods employed were analyzed and its weaknesses were discussed. The Committee contributed sections on the United States and Canada to the studies of fluctuations in employment from 1910 to 1930 in representative countries prepared for the World Social Economic Congress held in Amsterdam in August, 1931.

[1] See Chapter XXVIII.

[2] One of these was from Senator Robert F. Wagner of New York in 1928, asking suggestions for federal legislation to provide for collection of more adequate employment statistics by the federal Bureau of Labor Statistics. He used the memorandum that was sent him verbatim in a bill carrying with it an increased appropriation for the Bureau as well as specifying a plan for collection. In the spring and summer of 1929 many uneasy inquiries were received by the Committee as to whether there was any abnormal amount of unemployment.

Early in 1930 the Committee began a study of statistical procedure of public employment offices in Europe. It was carried on in co-operation with the International Labour Office of the League of Nations. The field work was started under the direction of Mr. Stewart, and when he had to return to America was carried through by his assistant, Mrs. Stewart. She spent the rest of 1930 in Europe and on her return studied procedures in Canada and the United States. An interim report, indicating the general direction of the recommendations, was made by Mr. Stewart at the meeting of the International Association of Public Employment Services in September, 1931. The book,[1] which was published by the Foundation later, was an analysis of statistical procedures of public employment offices in Great Britain, Switzerland, Sweden, Germany, France, Canada, and the United States, together with a suggested plan for use in the United States. The proposed plan had immediate pertinence when a law was passed in May, 1933, creating a joint federal-state employment service.

Early in the great depression Miss van Kleeck served as consultant for the National Commission on Law Observance and Enforcement on a study of the influence of unemployment on crime. This was a preliminary inquiry, designed to develop a method of investigation for the subject. The Commission provided funds for four investigators; the Foundation contributed office space, as well as Miss van Kleeck's time. There were two parts to the study: a statistical analysis of trends in crime and in employment in Massachusetts from 1889 and in New York from 1878; and a case study, from data on file in Sing Sing Prison, of 300 men admitted in the year ended February 28, 1930. It was useful not only as a tryout of method but also as indicating the importance of the factor of employment in the prevention of crime and the treatment of criminals. The manuscript was submitted to the Commission in the summer of 1930.[2]

[1] Statistical Procedure of Public Employment Offices, by Annabel M. Stewart and Bryce M. Stewart, 1933.

[2] Under the title Work and Law Observance: A Study of the Influence of Unemployment upon Crime it was published in the second volume of the Commission's reports, issued in the summer of 1932.

Continuing Interests

Questions relating to women in industry continued to come to Miss van Kleeck. She kept in close touch with the development of the federal Women's Bureau, which she had organized, advising on studies and speaking at women's industrial conferences. On recommendation of a conference held in January, 1926, the Bureau undertook a study of the effect of labor laws on women's opportunities in industry. Miss van Kleeck was appointed chairman of the technical advisory committee and wrote an introduction for the extensive and valuable report, completed in 1928. In 1925, acting for a committee of various social science organizations, she prepared briefs for presentation to the Personnel Classification Board that resulted in its reclassifying the positions of director and assistant director of the Women's Bureau as "professional," instead of "clerical or administrative."

Through service on boards and committees, help in conferences and special projects, addresses, articles, and advice on plans, connections were kept up with many of the organizations that had co-operated in the studies of the first decade. Among these were the Consumers League of New York, the National Women's Trade Union League, the National Board and local associations of the Young Women's Christian Associations. Relations with the American Association for Labor Legislation continued unbroken.

When in 1924 and 1925 a proposal was under discussion for an "Equal Rights" amendment[1] to the federal constitution, friends of the hard-won legislation protecting women in industry were apprehensive. Even though there was little likelihood of success for the proposal, the agitation might make improvement and enforcement of existing laws more difficult. Facts bearing on the question from the Foundation's studies were presented in a hearing before the Senate Judiciary Committee and at various meetings. With M. Carey Thomas, president of Bryn Mawr College, who favored the amendment, Miss van Kleeck prepared a study-outline for the American Association of University Women. The

[1] Designed to prohibit special protective legislation for women.

committee of two issued three statements in the Journal of the Association and made a report at its convention in the spring of 1925.

Methods of industrial research, the relation of research to labor legislation, and administration of labor laws, were basic subjects underlying the Department's studies in this period as in earlier years, and determining the director's participation in many conferences and committees. Sometimes they became subjects of special projects themselves.

In the fall of 1922 Gifford Pinchot, governor-elect of Pennsylvania, asked advice in planning the administration of his Department of Labor and Industry. Miss van Kleeck suggested a conference of experts on various phases of the work. Mr. Pinchot asked her to plan and direct the conference and preside as chairman. It was held at Mr. Pinchot's home in Milford, Pennsylvania, in early December. Representatives of federal and state labor bureaus, industrial commissions, and special committees attended. Mr. Harrison, Miss LaDame, and Mr. Selekman, from the Foundation, as well as Miss van Kleeck, presented papers. At the close of the conference a formal request was sent to the Foundation that the transcript of proceedings be used as the basis for a thorough study of good practices and standards in the administration of labor laws, and that the results be made generally available.

Methods of research had necessarily been a primary subject of consideration in all the Foundation's pioneering studies of industrial conditions. In 1925 the Personnel Research Federation, of which Miss van Kleeck had been an active member, made the subject its special interest. Miss van Kleeck served as a committee member, and contributed a description of the procedure followed in the study of the Industrial Representation Plan of the Colorado Fuel and Iron Company as the opening paper of a series. About the same time she began a systematic critical examination of the methods that had been used in the Department's studies and others in the same field, believing that such a record would be suggestive in developing techniques and formulating general principles. A paper for the Taylor Society in

December, 1926, on "The Interview as a Method of Research" was a by-product.

In 1922 the National Research Council appointed a committee to study the scientific aspects of human migration. The Foundation made a grant for the exploratory work of the committee and Miss van Kleeck served as a member until the social aspects of its problem were taken over in 1925 by the Social Science Research Council. By that time the two studies she had helped to plan—an inquiry into the feasibility of an international survey of movements of population and an analysis of the relation between immigration into the United States and business cycles —had been completed by the National Bureau of Economic Research. She had found her association in this "effort to unite psychologists, anthropologists, biologists, and social scientists in a common approach to a human problem demanding scientific study" an "enlightening experience."

Miss van Kleeck took part in the week's conference of the Social Science Research Council at Hanover, New Hampshire, in the summer of 1926, at which methods of research in the social sciences were thoroughly discussed. She became a member of the Council's Committee on Methods of Research and for a time acted as its secretary.

SUNDRY SPECIAL ACTIVITIES

Throughout the twenties Miss van Kleeck was active in promoting the general progress of social work in various ways. She took part in the organization of the American Association of Social Workers and on a number of its committees later. In the National Conference of Social Work she was vice-chairman of the Industrial and Economic Division in 1923, chairman in 1924. Through the Smith College School of Social Work she kept in touch with developments in the training of social workers, first as chairman of a committee of the Alumnae Association and later, during her tenure of office as a member of the Board of Trustees of the College, as chairman of the Board's committee on the School. She served on the Social Service Commission of the Protestant Episcopal Church of the Diocese of New York. In

September, 1922, in Portland, Oregon, she addressed a mass meeting of the Department of Social Service at the Triennial General Convention of the Protestant Episcopal Church, and during the Convention led an industrial conference of clergy and lay members of the Convention which held ten meetings. There resulted a recommendation, subsequently adopted by the Department of Social Service, urging study and conference on ethical problems of industrial relations by laymen throughout the church.

When in 1924 a committee was formed to consider plans for an Encyclopaedia of the Social Sciences, Miss van Kleeck represented the American Statistical Association. On the executive committee that was appointed, under the chairmanship of E. R. A. Seligman, to draw up a tentative outline of contents, she was made responsible for proposing the articles on social work and on statistics. As a member of the board of directors, after the enterprise was incorporated, and a continuing member of the joint committee of the seven co-operating organizations, her special work was to advise about articles on social work and labor problems. The treatment of social work in the Encyclopaedia was strengthened by the addition in 1929, at her suggestion, of Porter R. Lee to the advisory editorial committee and the appointment of Mrs. Alice Campbell Klein to the staff.

One of the important special activities in which Miss van Kleeck engaged during this second period of the Foundation's history was the National Interracial Conference held in Washington in December, 1928. The first interracial conference of national scope had been held in Cincinnati in March, 1925, under the joint auspices of the Commission on the Church and Race Relations of the Federal Council of Churches and the Commission on Interracial Co-operation. Mr. Glenn attended it. Mr. Routzahn and Miss van Kleeck worked on committees, both during the Conference and in preparing a report that was published by the Federal Council. In the fall of 1926 representatives of 16 national organizations, including the two that had sponsored the Cincinnati Conference, determined to find some way to assemble and make known facts about the life of Negroes in the

United States and their relations with their white fellow-citizens. They formed a Central Executive Committee, of which Miss van Kleeck was chairman, and decided to hold a more inclusive conference, making it the occasion for a long preparatory period of study. The theme would be "Negro Race Problems in the Light of Social Research."

Charles S. Johnson of Fisk University was appointed research secretary. In the collection of material generous contributions of time and thought were given by the sponsoring organizations and many individuals. Financial help was given by the Social Science Research Council and a smaller amount by the Foundation. As chairman of the Conference, Miss van Kleeck gave a great deal of time for several months to the investigations and administrative arrangements; presided at the meetings as chairman of discussion; and took an active part in preparing the studies and proceedings for publication.[1] Mr. Glenn was one of the speakers at the closing session.

The three-day conference brought together an exceptional assembly of persons working for improved conditions for the Negroes in America. The discussions and the record of investigations gave them and others much useful material for thought and action in the future.

INTERNATIONAL RELATIONS

In the summer of 1923 Miss van Kleeck, accompanied by Miss LaDame, spent several weeks in Europe, visiting the Scandinavian countries, northern Germany, The Netherlands, Paris, Switzerland, and England. They had conferences with many government officials engaged in administering labor laws, including employment exchanges, and other leaders in the field of their interests. From this time on the Department's work was increasingly enriched by contact with colleagues in European countries.

The following year Miss van Kleeck was appointed a member of the American Advisory Committee of the International Labour

[1] Published by Henry Holt and Co., 1930, under the title The Negro in American Civilization, by Charles S. Johnson, with forewords by Mary van Kleeck to both parts of the book.

Organization and also participated in preliminary planning for the proposed International Conference of Social Work. She served as a member of the American Committee for the Conference, a member of the executive board, and vice-chairman of the Section on the Family and Industry, and attended the Conference in Paris in July, 1928. In 1925 she was asked to be one of the two representatives[1] of the United States on the council of the International Welfare Congress, which was in process of reorganization as the International Association for the Study and Improvement of Human Relations and Conditions in Industry, a title later simplified to International Industrial Relations Association.[2] Visitors from abroad were coming to the office in increasing numbers. That year they included representatives from China, Japan, and eight countries of Europe. Miss Mary L. Fleddérus, director of the International Industrial Relations Association, visited America in 1927, and frequently thereafter.

In two international conferences held in the summer of 1928 Miss van Kleeck had an active part. The International Industrial Relations Association held its first triennial congress at Cambridge, England. She had been chairman of the committee on program. At Cambridge she presided at one meeting, gave the summary of the proceedings on the last evening, and was elected vice-president for a three-year term. At the International Conference of Social Work, in Paris, she presided over one meeting and presented a paper at the plenary session on social research in industry. At the request of the United States Department of Labor she was named by the Secretary of State as one of the representatives of the United States at the series of conferences in Paris called The International Social Work Fortnight. During this trip conferences in Geneva strengthened co-operative relations already existing with the International Labour Organization and the closely related International Management Institute. In Berlin useful contacts were established with government departments and voluntary agencies, and information was obtained

[1] The other was Sam A. Lewisohn, president of the American Management Association.
[2] Later changed to International Industrial Relations Institute.

bearing on several studies of the Department of Industrial Studies.

At the meeting of the executive board of the International Conference of Social Work in 1929, held in Prague on invitation of President Masaryk and his daughter, Miss Alice Masaryk, Miss van Kleeck was elected vice-president of the board. In that capacity she had considerable responsibility in the following years for working out plans for the Second International Conference, to be held in 1932 at Frankfurt am Main.

Her responsibilities in the International Industrial Relations Association increased. Representing a committee of the Association, she presented a report on "Human Relations in the Scientific Organization of Work" at the Fourth International Congress on Scientific Management in Paris in June, 1929. She worked with Miss Fleddérus on the program for the discussions held in the summer of 1929 in Bavaria on "Methods of Promoting Satisfactory Human Relations in a Scientifically Organized Industry," and served as chairman of discussion throughout the conference. She was chairman of the program committee for the second congress of the Association, the World Social Economic Congress held in Amsterdam in August, 1931. At the closing session she summarized the proceedings as she had done at the Cambridge Congress in 1928. Through the Foundation a preparatory report was made available for the Congress on fluctuations in employment from 1910 through 1930 in several European countries, the United States, Canada, and Australia.[1] For the Department of Industrial Studies the comparative analysis was significant because of its emphasis on the international aspects of unemployment in the United States and the light it threw on our own depression.

[1] Published later by the Association, under the title International Unemployment, together with the proceedings of the Congress under the title World Social Economic Planning.

XXVIII

STATISTICS: 1919-1931

WHEN Colonel Ayres returned from government service in
October, 1919, the Division of Statistics resumed work
after two and a half years of inactivity. Ralph G. Hurlin, who
had been with Colonel Ayres in the Statistics Branch of the
General Staff in Washington, as chief of the reports section with
the rank of major, was engaged as statistician. In January, 1920,
the Division was designated "Department." On the resignation
of Colonel Ayres from the Foundation, at the end of 1920, Mr.
Hurlin was appointed director of the Department.

Its primary function continued to be supervision of the statistical work done in the Foundation. As time allowed, assistance
was given to persons outside the Foundation who asked help on
statistical problems. The Department also, from the first year of
the postwar period, carried on some investigations of its own. A
period of expansion in studies initiated by the Department began
in 1926.

In 1919–1920 the staff consisted of Mr. Hurlin and one stenographer. By 1929 two research associates and two statistical assistants had been added. From 1921 to 1927 Miss Frances Brooks
served as assistant statistician. Miss Margaret H. Hogg, in-
structor in economics at Smith College during the two preceding
years, and previously a member of the staff of the London School
of Economics, joined the Department as statistician in June, 1927.
In the following year Miss Anne E. Geddes was engaged as a
research associate, to assist in the development of statistics of
relief-giving in American cities.

SERVICES WITHIN THE FOUNDATION

As a statistical service bureau for the Foundation, the Department reviewed reports prepared for publication and gave assist-

ance to the staff in other ways on a variety of statistical problems. This was the purpose for which it was established, and these services had first claim on its time. The amount of time they required varied from year to year, depending on the number of reports submitted to it for review and the amount of statistical assistance sought by other departments in the course of their studies. Relatively the amount of time given to this work decreased as the Department's own research and assistance to other organizations increased.

Work on the Foundation reports was not limited to checking and correcting the statistics for mathematical accuracy. The interpretation and the conclusions drawn from the statistical material were examined also. Criticisms were discussed in memoranda, often of considerable length, as well as in conferences with authors. Not infrequently sections were rewritten, suggestions were made for reorganization, and new material was contributed. For several major studies statistical portions were originally prepared in the Department. Reconstruction of tables, either to make them conform to the Foundation's standards of presentation or to increase their contribution to the study, was a common service. Diagrams were designed and drawn in large numbers and great variety.

Several of the studies under way in the Foundation during the twenties were based largely on statistics. Nearly all had some statistical content. More than 40 major reports, including a few that originated outside the Foundation, were critically examined by the Department between 1919 and 1931. In subject matter they ranged over the special fields of all the Foundation's departments and included also an occasional topic outside these special fields though within the general interests of the Foundation. In amount of work required they varied greatly. A few needed only verification of calculations, and in exceptional cases manuscript, galleys, and page proof were reviewed within a few weeks. A larger number required much work in the Department and their progress to publication was slower.

Members of the Foundation staff increasingly asked the Department for advice or help, not only on matters related to their major studies, but also on statistical problems incidental to other aspects of their work or brought to them by outsiders. In general this involved the same kind of service as was given on the major studies, but on a smaller scale. Information was supplied or sources were suggested; magazine articles, committee reports, and conference papers were reviewed and illustrations for them were drawn. From time to time also statistical material was prepared for discussions of administrative policies and procedures within the Foundation.

HELP TO OTHER ORGANIZATIONS

Requests for similar assistance came from persons outside the Foundation. The nature of these requests and the amount of work required to comply with them had a wide range.[1] Some could be answered by sending a reprint, a copy of a table on hand, a reference to a published report, or by explaining a point of method in a single interview. Others involved work of a kind and an amount given to the editing of a Foundation book. For example, a large amount of assistance was given, in the early twenties, to the Women's Bureau of the Department of Labor in connection with studies of employment of women during the war and of differences in employment trends for men and women in the important industries employing women. Some of the work growing out of such requests developed into research projects of the Department. Its contributions to the Regional Survey were technically services to an "outside" agency.

A number of social work organizations in New York with purposes closely akin to those of the Foundation became in effect "clients" of the Department, bringing their research problems for advice at frequent intervals. Among these were organizations that received help from the Foundation through grants or office space, or through service from other departments, including the American Association of Social Workers, the American Association for Organizing Family Social Work, the Child Welfare League of America, the national Committee on Publicity Meth-

[1] After the Department of Education was ended, correspondence relating to its studies was handled by the Department of Statistics.

ods, and, after its organization in 1925, the Welfare Council of New York City.

Examples of smaller pieces of work done for persons outside the Foundation in the early twenties were the examination, for the Secretary of War, of a proposed statistical basis for apportioning Army chaplains among religious denominations; a memorandum on a point of technique in graphic presentation, for the United States Bureau of Education; detailed instructions for taking a religious census in Nashville; suggestion for a procedure, devised at the request of the International Office of the Young Men's Christian Associations, for adjusting the salaries of its representatives in European countries to allow for the extreme variations in the value of American money in those countries.

One significant contribution had to do with federal statistics of prisoners. This began with a request within the Foundation. At the instance of Dr. Hart, a study was made in 1922 of the Census Bureau's statistics of prisoners collected in 1910, to test the popular assumption that persons of foreign birth or parentage had contributed more than proportionally to the population of prisons. Further study of these statistics was made the following year, and both Mr. Hurlin and Miss Brooks attended conferences arranged by officials of the Census Bureau to discuss plans for the 1923 census of prison population. Meanwhile Sam B. Warner, director of research for the committee on criminal records and statistics of the American Institute of Criminal Law and Criminology, submitted to the Department for critical examination his report concerning statistics that should be published by state penal institutions, as well as a questionnaire proposed for use by the federal Bureau of the Census. A scheme of classification of prisoners by race, color, and country of birth was prepared by Miss Brooks for use by Mr. Warner in his report.

When the Bureau's report, Prisoners: 1923, was in galley proof, the Bureau, at the suggestion of Dr. Hart, invited the Department to criticize it. The entire report was examined carefully, and a memorandum was submitted to the Bureau, pointing out certain inaccuracies and portions of both tables and text that were open to misinterpretation. Dr. Hart joined in objecting to the method of racial comparisons that had been used. On the basis of the suggestions offered, the Census Bureau made material revisions before publishing the report.

One of the agencies intimately associated with the Foundation was the Committee on Publicity Methods.[1] In November, 1924, it asked help of the Department in assembling comparable statistics on the cost and effectiveness of raising money by circular letters. A form for recording the cost and evaluating the results of appeal letters was prepared, submitted to a number of agencies for criticism, revised, printed, and distributed for trial use. Results of an analysis of records collected from some 30 organizations were reported at the annual meeting of the Committee in June, 1925.[2] The Committee continued to study "mail appeals," consulting Mr. Hurlin frequently in the following years on this and other statistical problems.

Services to organizations outside the Foundation and to social work in general, whether in response to requests or the product of research projects initiated by the Department, increased as the years went by. Some of them from the beginning, most of them after 1925 or 1926, were accomplished under the sponsorship of committees of which Mr. Hurlin was a member, frequently chairman or secretary. Committees of the American Statistical Association and the American Association of Social Workers appeared earliest and most frequently during this period. When the Welfare Council of New York City was established Mr. Hurlin, at the request of the director,[3] drafted suggestions for its proposed Research Bureau. Thereafter, as a member of the Council's advisory committee on research, he not only participated in developing the program of the Bureau but also gave assistance in many of the individual studies. The American Association for Organizing Family Social Work and the North Atlantic District of the American Association of Hospital Social Workers appointed committees to further the Department's projects for collecting uni-

[1] See p. 362.

[2] The form, published for distribution by the Foundation, is still in use in 1946. It was described in an article, "A New Form for Mail Appeal Records," in Better Times, April, 1925.

[3] William Hodson, who had been for several years on the staff of the Foundation.

form statistics in their respective fields. From 1927 on Mr. Hurlin was appointed to various committees of the Social Science Research Council. At intervals he served as a member of, or consultant to, temporary committees in charge of special projects of permanent organizations or committees of such temporary organizations as the White House Conference on Child Health and Protection (1929–1931) and the President's Committee on Statistics of Employment (1931). Mr. Hurlin's connection with a committee was rarely limited to attendance at meetings. It often involved assistance in planning, supervising, or conducting research, or in drafting or revising committee reports.

Trends of Wages and Prices

The Department's first investigation began as an incident to the study of trends in school expenditures that was under way in the Department of Education in 1919–1920. In searching for a basis for evaluating salaries and other expenditures at different periods, official records were found that made it possible to determine the major movements of wages and prices in the United States over the preceding century. By combining the data of several earlier studies index numbers for laborers' wages and wholesale prices were carried back to 1790, and for several series of artisans' wages and certain retail prices back to 1820. In part the results of this investigation were used for comparisons with teachers' salaries and building costs in the report of the study of school expenditures. They were also used in magazine articles discussing the trend of prices and the influence of war on prices. A related brief study at this time was concerned with the increase between 1913 and 1920 in salaries paid to college teachers and a comparison with the increase during the same period in the earnings of public school teachers and other workers.

The original intention to publish a comprehensive report on changes in wages and prices in the United States over the period of a century was not carried out, partly because more intensive studies of the subject were being made in other places. Much of the material developed was supplied to other investigators. Copies of tables and information about sources and methods were given to many inquirers.[1]

PUBLIC EXPENDITURES FOR HEALTH

Some time was spent during 1921 in investigating comparative statistics of public health expenditures, a topic in which other departments of the Foundation had been interested in earlier years.[2] Expenditures of state governments for health purposes were gathered for certain years back to 1880, and current expenditures by cities of over 30,000 population for health work in schools as reported by the Census Bureau were studied briefly. The latter study was reported in a magazine article.[3] It gave evidence that interest in "school health" had spread widely since the Foundation's studies and publications on the subject in 1908–1913, but that many cities nominally giving attention to this work were making only casual and inadequate provision for it. Incidentally, it pointed to the desirability of improvements in the census figures.

STATISTICS OF EMPLOYMENT

Because of current interest in unemployment, the Department, at the time of the President's conference on unemployment in 1921, made a systematic search for records that would yield a reliable index of fluctuations in employment over a long period. Such records were discovered in the long series of annual reports on manufacturing industries of the Massachusetts Department of Labor and Industries. For each year back to 1889 these reports contained monthly statistics, compiled from payroll records, of employment in most of the manufacturing establishments of the state. From these data a continuous monthly index of employ-

[1] Published articles by Mr. Hurlin utilizing these data were: "The Course of United States Wholesale Prices for 100 Years" and "The Long Time Trend of Prices in the United States," in The Annalist, April 11 and July 4, 1921, respectively; "Changes in Agricultural Prices," in World Agriculture, October, 1921; "Salaries of College Teachers in 1920," in School and Society, October, 1920.

[2] See Chapters VII, XV.

[3] "Costs of School Health," by Ralph G. Hurlin, in School Board Journal, November, 1921.

ment fluctuation was constructed for the years 1899 to 1921. Similar records for New Jersey from 1893 to 1917 were found, which resembled the index for Massachusetts. These findings by Mr. Hurlin were published promptly.[1] Covering as they did four previous periods of business depression, they were of great interest at the time.

From this index of employment and other data estimates were made for Mr. Hoover's office of the loss of wages in four recent depressions. After the depression of 1920–1921 was over, Mr. Hurlin published an article on the patterns of recovery in different industries as shown by current statistics of employment.[2]

For the use of Philip Klein in his study for the Foundation of relief measures of cities during the depression, an analysis was made, from statistics collected and currently published by the Cleveland Chamber of Commerce, of the relationships, during the decline of business from the high point of prosperity in 1920, between employment, hours of work, wage rates, earnings, and cost of living. The Cleveland data were used later as the basis of an article by Mr. Hurlin discussing employment adjustments of large employers during the course of the depression.[3]

From the creation in February, 1922, of the Committee on Measurement of Employment (later renamed Committee on Governmental Labor Statistics) of the American Statistical Association[4] Mr. Hurlin was involved in its work, and after he was elected secretary his responsibilities increased. In this connection he made or participated in numerous studies that contributed to the main purpose of the Committee, which was to devise a practicable plan for continuous collection and current publication of adequate statistics of employment in the United States. Two of these interim studies by the Department described statistics of

[1] "Three Decades of Employment Fluctuation," in The Annalist, October 24, 1921.
[2] "The Business Revival in Individual Industries," in The Annalist, March 13, 1922.
[3] "A Record of Industrial Adjustment to the Last Depression," in Journal of the American Statistical Association, March, 1923.
[4] See Chapter XXVII.

employment then currently collected by official bureaus in the United States and Canada.[1]

As secretary of the Committee on Governmental Labor Statistics Mr. Hurlin carried on correspondence with its members and many other persons about its work, shared with the chairman the planning of meetings and the preparation of periodical reports for the Statistical Association, and had the main responsibility for assembling material for consideration by the Committee[2] and preparing its report on employment statistics. He continued as secretary until, with the publication of this report, the original purpose of the Committee had been fulfilled. He himself wrote much of the text; the collection of forms and the preparation of tables and diagrams were made in his office; and he served with William A. Berridge as the editorial subcommittee for the volume, which was published by the Foundation in 1926.[3]

The book presented a plan for comprehensive collection of employment statistics for the United States and discussed in detail methods of collecting, tabulating, analyzing, and publishing them currently. The material, in the words of the Editorial Note, was drawn "from the experience of the members of the committee, from the records of its discussions, and from reports by sub-committees appointed to investigate . . . special problems." A chapter on the uses of employment statistics was contributed by the chairman of the Committee, Miss Mary van Kleeck. The volume was intended primarily as a handbook for government bureaus and other offices dealing with statistics of employment. Portions of the book discussing the sources and current status of employment statistics were reprinted by the United States Bureau of Labor Statistics in its Handbook of Labor Statistics in 1927.

[1] "Employment Statistics of the United States Employment Service" and "Canadian Employment Statistics," by Ralph G. Hurlin, in Journal of the American Statistical Association, December, 1922, and March, 1923, respectively.

[2] Special work was done in the Department on a standard form for collecting these statistics and, in co-operation with Professor Berridge, on a standard classification of industries.

[3] Employment Statistics for the United States, edited by Ralph G. Hurlin and William A. Berridge.

SYMBOLS FOR SURVEY MAPS

As a result of a request by the Department of Surveys and Exhibits for a review of methods of graphic representation on maps used in connection with social surveys, the Department undertook in 1923 to prepare a standard series of symbols for showing on survey maps the location of various social institutions and facilities. There was great diversity in current practice. A wide search was made for the different symbols that had already had significant use and the experience users had had with them. A tentative scheme of 101 symbols was prepared by Miss Brooks. It was submitted to a number of persons for criticism and trial, and revised until it met the approval of the Department of Surveys and Exhibits. The first use of the symbols for study purposes was in an investigation of neighborhood recreation facilities in New York City by Charles J. Storey in connection with the work of the Department of Recreation for the Regional Survey.

At this point a particularly favorable opportunity for testing the usefulness of the symbols presented itself. A citywide survey of recreation facilities in Chicago was in progress by the Department of Sociology of the University of Chicago. At the request of the director of this survey, Professor Ernest W. Burgess, a supply of the symbols he would need was printed. In the light of his use of them and of other experiments the entire series was printed in quantity in 1926 and put on sale through the Publication Department of the Foundation.

SALARIES IN SOCIAL WORK

As the purchasing power of the dollar declined during and after the war, and as social workers became increasingly concerned about their standing among other occupational groups, questions relating to salary arose frequently in social work agencies. But there was little information available as to standards of compensation and other working conditions in this relatively new professional occupation. As a step toward meeting the lack, the American Association of Social Workers in 1922 collected a considerable body of data by sending a questionnaire to its members. At the request of the Association, the Department in 1924 made a full analysis of these data. Although they did not relate to a typical sample of the social work vocation, they yielded useful information concerning the variation of salaries in different fields and different types of position and also concerning the relation of salaries to such factors as sex, education, experience, geographical location, and size of city. The results were used by the Association for various purposes,[1] as well as by other organizations in connection with current salary problems. Their important use by the Department was in planning other studies of social work salaries.

Further investigation of salaries in social work was made by the Department in the summer of 1925, when data were collected from 132 organizations for the purpose of tracing the changes that had occurred in the compensation of social workers during and since the war. This analysis disclosed that, while salaries of social workers in the rank and file had increased gradually in the course of the twelve years since 1913, they were still "surprisingly low"—18 per cent below salaries of elementary school teachers; and that in purchasing power they had been far below the level of 1913 during most of the period and were barely above it in 1925. These facts were of great interest to social workers generally. They were presented at local meetings, in magazine articles, and in a paper at the National Conference of Social Work in June, 1926;[2] and were the subject of much correspondence.

This was a subject it was not easy to drop. The earlier studies had convinced the Department that data for a particular field of social work, if unquestionably representative, would be of greater value than data of uncertain representativeness relating to social work in general. In 1927 a study was made for a committee of

[1] They formed the basis of a paper concerning the professional status of social work presented at the National Conference of Social Work in 1925 by the incoming president of the Association, Miss Neva R. Deardorff.

[2] "Social Work Salaries," in The Survey, February 15, 1926; reprinted as a department bulletin, May, 1926. "Social Work Salaries," in The Compass, May, 1926. "Salaries," in Child Welfare Bulletin, May, 1926. "Measuring the Demand for Social Workers," in Proceedings of the National Conference of Social Work for 1926; reprinted as a pamphlet.

the American Association for Organizing Family Social Work[1] of salaries in the Association's 230 member organizations. The results of this inquiry were issued in mimeographed form and were reproduced in a report on family social work in the Job Analysis Series of the American Association of Social Workers. At the request of the Association, this study was repeated in 1929, with some increase of subject matter. On this occasion, through the co-operation of the Bureau of Jewish Social Research, comparable information was obtained from most of the Jewish family welfare agencies of the country. Altogether the inquiry yielded facts about the salaries in May, 1929, in more than 3,500 positions, professional and clerical, in 260 family welfare agencies— the most substantial body of data on the subject yet assembled. Results of the analysis were published in articles in The Family, and in The Survey, and were then brought together in a pamphlet published by the Foundation.[2] This study has been followed by a long succession of related studies of segments of social work personnel, which have had the purpose of disclosing current tendencies of the salaries of social workers. Several of them, like the one of 1929, have been designed for comparison with preceding studies.

ENUMERATION AND CLASSIFICATION OF SOCIAL WORKERS

Salaries were not the only aspect of social work on which knowledge was lacking. There was no standard classification of positions in professional social work, nor even any reliable information as to the number of such positions.

In 1926 Mr. Hurlin undertook to estimate the number of social work positions in the United States and presented the results, in his paper already referred to, at the National Conference of Social Work that year. On the basis of either actual counts or estimates obtained from community chests and councils of social agencies in about 30 important cities in the United States, and sundry supplementary data, he reached the conclusion that there were probably about 25,000 positions for pro-

[1] Family Welfare Association of America, 1930–1946; Family Service Association of America from 1946.

[2] Salaries and Vacations in Family Case Work in 1929, by Ralph G. Hurlin, 1930.

fessional social workers in the country at that time. The number was increasing, both by growth in the size of agencies and by multiplication of agencies. The demand, he concluded, was far ahead of the supply and the rate of turnover was high. He suggested that the unfavorable salary scale prevailing in social work, as compared with other occupations of similar requirements, might be an explanation for both the inadequate supply and the instability of tenure.

Such questions as these were the appropriate concern of the American Association of Social Workers, organized in 1921. It had undertaken the early study of salaries mentioned on page 407. This study made clear the need for an accepted classification of positions, with an accurate description of the duties attached to each position. This need was keenly realized by the Vocational Bureau of the Association. A committee was appointed to work out a plan for the necessary study. Mr. Hurlin prepared its report outlining a Job Analysis Study. Russell Sage Foundation made a grant to meet expenses, and work was begun in May, 1926. Mr. Hurlin served actively on the advisory committee for this study, which continued over several years and resulted in analytical descriptions of the duties, requirements, and compensation of workers in the frequently occurring positions in the quantitatively most important divisions of social work. The products of these studies were published in several volumes comprising the Job Analysis Series of the American Association of Social Workers.

Following Mr. Hurlin's estimate in 1926 of the number of professional social workers in the United States, the American Association of Social Workers appointed a committee under his chairmanship to draw up a plan for conducting a comprehensive census.[1] The New York Chapter of the Association later undertook, through a committee of which Mr. Hurlin was a member, to use the plan in making a census for its area, New York City and Westchester County. Mr. Hurlin directed the work of the committee and prepared its final report, which was published by

[1] Published in The Compass, October, 1927, under the title "Census of Social Workers."

the Chapter.[1] Nearly a thousand agencies were enumerated, employing full-time paid social workers in 4,502 positions.

When plans for the federal census of 1930 were in preparation, the Association was able to convince the Census Bureau of the practicability of recognizing social workers as a distinct occupational group and to contribute materially to the value of the census enumeration. Using the schedules collected in the New York Chapter study, a list was prepared of types of social work organizations and types of social-work positions in those organizations. From this list the Census Bureau selected 76 titles of social work positions for inclusion in its Index of Occupations used in classifying the gainful workers found by the enumerators in the Fifteenth Census of the United States. The Association, furthermore, conducted an educational campaign among social workers throughout the country to encourage the furnishing of accurate information to the enumerators. The Census Bureau's category "social and welfare workers" did not include all the occupations commonly regarded as in the field of social work. Adding certain groups from other categories Mr. Hurlin estimated the total number of social workers in 1930 as between 40,000 and 42,500, exclusive of 15,000 or more public health nurses.[2]

STATISTICS OF SOCIAL CASEWORK

In the winter of 1925–1926, when the book on employment statistics was ready for the printer, Mr. Hurlin inaugurated the most ambitious project the Department had yet undertaken. The lack of comparable statistics of social work—comparable as between agencies and from year to year—had long been deplored.[3]

[1] An Approximate Count of Social Work Positions in New York City and Westchester County, 1929.

[2] "The Number and Distribution of Social Workers in the United States," in Proceedings of the National Conference of Social Work, 1933. Reprinted as a department pamphlet.

[3] This same winter the American Statistical Association was considering the establishment of a Committee on Social Statistics. It was appointed in April, 1926, with Mr. Hurlin as chairman. Its chief objects were to consider the problem of a dependency index, to study statistics of social work, and to keep informed on statistical work in progress in that field. It held an open meeting on "Measurement of Dependency" in March, 1927. Its program at the Association's annual meeting in December, 1927, was on "Statistical Evaluation of the Results of Social Experiments." After resigning as chairman in December, 1928, Mr. Hurlin continued as an active member.

Mr. Hurlin had felt the need of them in his own studies.[1] To supply this lack in one field he undertook to organize a system for family casework.

Invitations were sent in February, 1926, to 40 prominent family welfare agencies, asking them to co-operate by making regular monthly reports on a uniform schedule. A tentative form, with definition of terms, was supplied for reporting statistics for the two preceding months. In response, data were sent by 29 of the agencies. By April all but three of the 40 had begun to report. Early in the following year the number reporting had increased to 42.

The information provided by each agency included counts of cases served, expenditure for relief, visits, office interviews, and staff, with subdivisions of most of these items. The data for each month were tabulated on receipt, significant ratios were added, and the results were reported currently to the co-operating organizations. An annual summary was prepared at the end of the year, and from time to time comparative studies were made on special topics. The schedule and the definitions of terms were modified as desirability of change became apparent. After a year or two the report form was printed by the Foundation and sold through the Publication Department.

A group of five persons in New York City acted as an informal advisory committee at the beginning and was the nucleus of a committee on statistics soon appointed by the American Association for Organizing Family Social Work, which made the promotion of this project its primary concern. Mr. Hurlin conducted a discussion on family casework statistics at the National Conference of Social Work in June, 1926; presented a paper on "Measurement of Family Case Work" at the New York State Conference of Charities and Correction in November, 1926;[2] and explained the plan to various audiences in New York City and elsewhere. At the request of the Detroit Department of Public Welfare he examined its statistical system in March, 1928, and

---

[1] In connection, for example, with his studies of fluctuations in employment and Mr. Klein's study of emergency measures in the depression of 1921.

[2] Printed in Proceedings of the Conference and reprinted as a pamphlet.

recommended a plan, later adopted, that would serve administrative purposes and at the same time yield statistics for comparison with other family welfare agencies.

After the experiment had been in operation two full years, Mr. Hurlin described it and reported preliminary results to the National Conference of Social Work in May, 1928.[1] By this time its value had been so generally recognized by the family welfare agencies that it was no longer an experiment.

Meanwhile the plan had been extended to other casework fields, as had been in mind from the beginning, and a statewide laboratory had been provided when Mr. Hurlin agreed to conduct a study for the Public Charities Association of Pennsylvania of the welfare statistics in that state, on condition that the primary objective should be the same as that of the Department's studies: to promote compilation of standardized monthly statistics describing current operations, and from these statistics to discover characteristics of the work of the various groups of agencies and record fluctuations in their operations. The Pennsylvania study, beginning in January, 1928, continued during eighteen months.

Hospital social work was the second field to become interested. After conferences in 1927 with a Committee on Records of the North Atlantic District of the American Association of Hospital Social Workers, regular collection and exchange of monthly statistics was begun in January, 1928, for a group of about 35 hospital social work departments in and near New York City. A similar collection was begun at the same time in Pennsylvania. In May, 1928, Mr. Hurlin spoke on "Comparative Statistics of Hospital Social Work" at the annual meeting of the American Association of Hospital Social Workers.

In February, 1928, collection of statistics of mothers' aid was begun. The Department's national study of these statistics began with reports from 18 large cities scattered through the country. It was discontinued at the end of 1929, partly because

---

[1] "Some Results of Two Years' Study of Family Case Work Statistics," by Ralph G. Hurlin, in Proceedings of the Conference, 1928; reprinted as a pamphlet. At the same conference Mr. Hurlin conducted a round-table discussion on "Evaluation of Results of Social Work."

413

by that time a similar collection was being made by the Committee on Registration of Social Statistics.[1] In February, 1928, also collection of child welfare statistics was begun in Pennsylvania from a sample group of 40 institutions and placing-out agencies. No effort was made to develop this project on a national scale, but previously, at the request of the New York State Conference on Social Work, Mr. Hurlin had made a study from official reports of trends in the care of children outside their own homes in that state.[2]

The Pennsylvania study initiated a system of regular collection and publication by the Public Charities Association of statistics in the four fields: family casework, mothers' aid, child care, medical social work. In addition, several special studies were made for state agencies, including a complete accounting of children under care of child-care agencies and institutions in the state, designed to establish procedures for succeeding annual censuses.[3] Because of the expense involved, the Public Charities Association did not continue its statistical collections after Mr. Hurlin's service ended.

By 1931, the closing year of this period of the Foundation's history, results of the Department's quiet crusade for the improvement of casework statistics begun in 1926 were manifest in various directions. The Department itself, in its two continuing projects, was regularly collecting, analyzing, and reporting month by month on the work of 59 family welfare agencies in all parts of the country and the social work departments of about 50 hospitals in the New York City region.[4] The accumulating material was used increasingly by individual agencies and several comparative studies had been made by the Department.[5]

[1] See p. 415.

[2] "Trends in Loads and Costs in Child Welfare in New York State," in Proceedings of New York State Conference, 1927; reprinted as a pamphlet.

[3] Children Under Supervision of Pennsylvania Child Caring Organizations, by Ralph G. Hurlin. Bulletin 35, Pennsylvania Department of Welfare, Harrisburg, 1928.

[4] The collection of hospital social work statistics was discontinued in June, 1932, but was resumed with a revised plan in 1942.

[5] For example, following an exploratory study for the Jewish Social Service Association of New York City, a comparative study was made by Miss Hogg of the relief giving of that agency, the Charity Organization Society of New York, and the

Methods, form, and definitions worked out by the Department were made available to other agencies experimenting with the collection of similar statistics, including the Committee on Registration of Social Statistics,[1] the Bureau of Jewish Social Research, and the Children's Bureau. The Department was consulted by national associations wishing to standardize statistics of their local branches, by the New York and other state departments of social welfare on problems of statistical reporting, and by numerous other organizations.

On the basis of his experience in Pennsylvania, Mr. Hurlin in 1931, as a member of the Committee on Social Statistics of the Social Science Research Council, proposed a "Demonstration Project in the Development of Statewide Social Statistics in a Selected State." With funds obtained through the Council, a three-year demonstration along the lines suggested was undertaken by the Department of Social Welfare of New York State, which had recently created a bureau of research. The demonstration was put under the supervision of an advisory committee, of which Mr. Hurlin was chairman. Among its results was a series of four handbooks for use in preparing statistics by different groups of agencies and institutions, which were prepared and published by the New York Department.

INDEX OF RELIEF EXPENDITURES

From the beginning of the Department's interest in the improvement of statistics of social work, the development of a trust-

---

Brooklyn Bureau of Charities. At the National Conference of Jewish Charities in June, 1930, Mr. Hurlin presented a paper on "Differences Between Jewish and Non-Jewish Family Case Work Agencies," published in the Jewish Social Service Quarterly, December, 1930. He contributed an article to the Quarterly of June, 1931, on "The Quality of Current Family Case Work Statistics." At the Pennsylvania Conference of Social Work in February, 1931, he spoke on "Comparison of Volume of Work in Medical and Family Case Work," and the paper was published in Hospital Social Service, September, 1931.

[1] A joint committee of the Association of Community Chests and Councils and the University of Chicago, which in 1928 launched a comprehensive plan for collecting monthly statistics of 24 types of social work in selected cities. The project grew out of a study of the volume and cost of social work in 19 cities in 1924 by Raymond Clapp for the American Association for Community Organization. It was taken over by the federal Children's Bureau in 1930.

worthy index of variations and trends in expenditures for relief to families in their homes ("outdoor relief," it was still called) had been one of the hoped-for products. In 1926, at the request of a joint committee of the American Association for Community Organization and the American Association for Organizing Family Social Work, Mr. Hurlin made a brief exploratory study of relief expenditures in 36 cities over the previous ten years.[1] He found a decided upward trend, both in number of families receiving relief and in amounts received per family, which was continuing through the prosperous twenties.[2] A trial index was compiled regularly from the monthly data reported by the family welfare agencies, and during 1928 a simple scheme was devised to get the essential information for a comprehensive index of relief expenditures in American cities.

In January, 1929, the important relief-giving agencies, public and private, in the 80 cities of over 115,000 population in the United States and Canada were invited to contribute to it. Two items each month, and only two, were asked for: the amount of financial aid given to families in their own homes during the month and the number of families to whom it was given. The report form was an addressed postcard. Tables summarizing results for the preceding month were mailed to the agencies toward the end of each month, with a card for the report for the current month.

By September, 1929, reports were coming from 285 agencies in 71 of the 80 cities. A year later the number had been increased to 380 agencies in 79 cities. Many agencies, it was found, did not have the basic data necessary for participation. Some had not previously kept any record of the number of cases assisted and others no monthly records of either cases or amounts disbursed. Another year brought the number reporting to some 450 agencies in 81 large cities, 76 in the United States and 5 in Canada. In most of the cities all the important relief agencies were co-operating, including emergency organizations. For the first time

[1] He had spoken on "The Trend of Relief" at the National Conference of Social Work in June.

[2] "The Monthly Bill for Relief," in The Survey, November 15, 1926.

a comprehensive system of regular monthly reporting, compilation, and analysis of relief to families in their own homes in the larger American cities was in operation.

This material could hardly have become available at a more opportune time. Beginning as it did in January, 1929, the series supplied a record of the volume of relief and dependency in the prosperous months before the stock-market crash as well as in the period of deepening depression. By 1931 its usefulness was widely recognized. The unpretentious monthly bulletins[1] were welcomed by economists and others for the indications they contained inferentially as to the course of the depression. They were studied in connection with the planning of emergency measures by all kinds of agencies, from the President's Emergency Committee for Employment and national welfare agencies to local community councils, local emergency committees for relief of the unemployed, and individual agencies.

Mr. Hurlin and Miss Geddes were in demand for articles and addresses, for consultation on use of the material, and to supply information for special studies. At the National Conference of Social Work in June, 1931, they presented the record to date.[2] The wall charts shown with this paper were lent for use later in the summer and fall at the Institute of Public Affairs of the University of Virginia, the National Conference of Catholic Charities, and the annual convention of the International City Managers' Association. Miss Geddes discussed the data at a

[1] Issued in a small edition of 500 at first, 1,000 by 1931, to co-operating agencies and a selected list of other interested persons.

[2] "Public and Private Relief During the Current Depression," by Anne E. Geddes and Ralph G Hurlin, in the Conference Proceedings; reprinted as a pamphlet. Mr. Hurlin had described the project when it was new in a general discussion of "Statistics of Dependency" at the annual meeting of the American Statistical Association in December, 1929. The paper appeared with others presented at the meeting in Statistics in Social Studies, edited by Stuart A. Rice, published in 1930 by the University of Pennsylvania Press. At a local meeting of the American Statistical Association in May, 1931, Mr. Hurlin presented a "Summary of Trends in Relief During Depression," which was used in part in an article by Meredith B. Givens in the Journal of the American Statistical Association, September, 1931. At the annual meeting of the Association in December, 1931, he contributed "Relief Trends in American Cities, 1929 to 1931." In June, 1930, Miss Geddes presented a paper at the annual meeting of the Family Welfare Association of America on "The Emergency Relief Situation in 79 Family Societies During the Winter of 1929–1930," based on a canvass made in the spring, at the request of the Association.

meeting of field representatives of the Association of Community Chests and Councils at the beginning of its Relief Mobilization Campaign in September, 1931.

Special presentations of the material were made during 1931 and 1932 at the request of such agencies as the President's Emergency Committee for Employment, the President's Organization on Unemployment Relief,[1] the National Committee on Mobilization of Relief Resources, the subcommittee concerned with unemployment relief of the United States Senate Committee on Manufactures,[2] and the New York State Legislative Committee on Unemployment, as well as emergency committees and individual agencies in many cities.

In February, 1932, this project was transferred to the federal Children's Bureau. The Bureau had begun collecting similar data in December, 1930. It had received the Department's more extensive material regularly and had combined the two sets of data. The transfer was made at the request of the Bureau, and on assurance that the collection and publication of the statistics would be continued as one of its permanent activities. To facilitate the transfer a six months' leave of absence was granted to Miss Geddes to accept appointment with the Bureau as director of the project. At the National Conference of Social Work in June Miss Geddes described the new arrangement and the material it would make available.[3]

[1] The Department assisted the Bureau of the Census in its inquiry into the increase of relief expenditures, made for the President's Organization in the latter half of 1931, by supplying data for agencies in the 76 United States cities represented in its index: Relief Expenditures by Governmental and Private Organizations, 1929 and 1931, Government Printing Office, Washington, 1932.

[2] This was the most important use made of the material. Mr. Hurlin's testimony, diagrams, and tables appear in Unemployment Relief: Hearings Before a Subcommittee of the Committee on Manufactures, U. S. Senate, 72nd Congress, 1st Session, on S. 174 and S. 262, pp. 158–177.

[3] "The Relief Statistics of the Children's Bureau," by Anne E. Geddes, in Proceedings of the Conference, 1932. Later the project was transferred to the Bureau of Public Assistance of the Social Security Board. In 1942 a study under the direction of Miss Geddes, then director of statistical research of the Bureau of Public Assistance, presented the full series of data through 1940: Public and Private Aid in 116 Urban Areas, 1929–38, with Supplement for 1939 and 1940, by Enid Baird with collaboration of John M. Lynch, Social Security Board, 1942.

Statistics of Unemployment

The depression roused fresh demands for statistics of unemployment. Records of relief might show how many persons or families were receiving help and how much they were receiving, but they gave no indication as to how many more there were who also were in need of assistance. Notwithstanding the difficulties involved in making a count of "the unemployed" a number of communities tried to do it and the Bureau of the Census undertook an enumeration in connection with the population census of 1930.

A plan was recommended to the federal Bureau in 1929 by the Committee on Governmental Labor Statistics, after expert consideration by a subcommittee appointed for the purpose. Through another subcommittee it made recommendations to the New York State Department of Labor for extension of its employment statistics. Mr. Hurlin was a member of both these subcommittees.

A comparison of the methods used in several local studies and of those recommended to and those used by the Census Bureau in the federal enumeration was made by Miss Hogg,[1] after which, with the co-operation of the Yale University Institute of Human Relations, she made an experimental study in New Haven. The employment status of all persons in a purely random sample, comprising 5 per cent of the households of the city, was obtained between May 18 and June 30, 1931. Preliminary results, showing the rate of unemployment in New Haven at that time, were announced on July 13. A full report was published by the Foundation the following year.[2] This was primarily a study of method. In addition to revealing the volume and incidence of work shortage in New Haven in the early summer of 1931 it dealt with the relative desirability, for the purpose of such studies, of strictly random samples as compared with samples chosen judicially.

[1] "Sources of Error and Incomparability in Employment-Unemployment Surveys," in Journal of the American Statistical Association, September, 1930.

[2] The Incidence of Work Shortage, by Margaret H. Hogg, 1932.

The Twelve Years

During this twelve-year period the Department of Statistics contributed anonymously to most of the studies under way in the Foundation—some 40 books and an uncounted number of smaller items—through its editorial services on their statistical aspects. It gave similar assistance to organizations and individuals outside the Foundation on a large number and variety of studies —also uncounted. In addition to these services of criticism and counsel, it initiated and carried through investigations on its own account, which added to the material and tools at the disposal of students of social conditions and social work.

In its original work, the Department was concerned mainly with two types of studies: construction of long-term indexes that supplied historical background for economic conditions; and establishment of systems of recording and reporting of operations of social work agencies on a sound basis, which supplied useful information immediately and the means of accurately determining changes with the passage of time.

Contributions to the statistics of social work began with the collection of information about social workers: their salaries, their number, their duties. In 1926 the Department began its work for the promotion of comparable statistics of work done by social workers, a practical step toward realizing an end long desired and frequently discussed. The system developed in the field of family casework became firmly established as an instrument [for better understanding of the field as a whole and for studying differences in the programs and methods of work of individual agencies. The index of relief operations begun in January, 1929, was the only record available as the depression deepened of the response of different localities and different types of agencies to the needs resulting from rising unemployment.

In the closing year of the period under review Mr. Hurlin was engaged in analyzing, for the President's Committee on Recent Social Trends, the shifts and trends in occupations of the people of the United States since 1870.[1] Miss Hogg in this year began a study of the cost-of-living statistics of the federal Bureau of Labor Statistics, which contributed to the Bureau's subsequent revision of its cost-of-living index.[2] The demonstration in developing a statewide system of statistics of social work, proposed by Mr. Hurlin through a committee of the Social Science Research Council, was just getting under way in the New York State Department of Social Welfare.

A new committee of which Mr. Hurlin was a member, formed in 1930, was one that might be expected to take a great deal of attention over a long time. This was a Committee on Statistics of the Blind, representing jointly the American Foundation for the Blind and the National Society for Prevention of Blindness. It had already carried out a plan proposed by the Department for testing, through a survey of two districts in Connecticut, the adequacy both of a state register of the blind and of the federal census statistics of blind persons. It was at work on a standard form for reporting diagnoses of blindness and methods of classifying causes and severity of blindness.

[1] The results were incorporated in a chapter by Mr. Hurlin and Meredith B. Givens in the Committee's report, Recent Social Trends, published in 1932. Two assistants for this piece of work, Miss Esther Lucile Brown and Miss Dorothy S. Davis, were supplied by the President's Committee. Work begun for the Committee by Miss Brown became later a department project.

[2] One of the immediate results was the discovery of a logical fault in the method used in constructing the index, which was reported in the Journal of the American Statistical Association, March, 1931.

XXIX

LIBRARY: 1918-1931

CONTINUING development of resources, clientele, and
usefulness, by means of policies and procedures established
in earlier years, characterized the course of the Library between
the war and the great depression. Until the last two years of the
period growth was steady and sure rather than spectacular.

STAFF

Mr. Jenkins returned from government service in January,
1919. Early in the twenties he contracted an illness from which he
never recovered. After a period of increasingly limited activity,
he definitely retired in the fall of 1929.[1]

Fortunately, when Mr. Jenkins became incapacitated he had
a staff of assistants who not only were proficient in their respective
duties but also were alert to the special needs of the Foundation's
Library and had been working together harmoniously for years.
Each addition had been carefully made with those ends in view.
Mr. Jenkins' four professional assistants had been on the staff for
periods ranging from nine to fourteen years; the two clerical
workers for seven and eight years respectively. All but one of the
six remained on the staff throughout this period of the Foundation's history and for many years beyond 1931.

Mrs. Bertha Hulseman, who had joined the staff in 1914 and
had been in charge of the Library during the absence of Mr.
Jenkins in 1918, became acting librarian in fact early in his
illness and by title in 1927. In November, 1929, she was appointed librarian. There was no increase in size of staff during
the period 1918–1931, notwithstanding a great increase in
volume of work.

---

[1] He died at his home in Mount Vernon, New York, on April 12, 1940.

GROWTH OF THE COLLECTION

Between 1917 and 1931 the number of bound volumes in the Library doubled, increasing from 15,695 to 31,568, and the collection of unbound items tripled, reaching a total of 105,772. Special attention continued to be given to filling gaps: finding desired books that were out of print and missing numbers in series of reports and other periodical publications. The emphasis on serial publications was justified not only by their unique value to students of social problems and social work but also by the fact that few libraries undertook to keep complete files, except of some of the better known magazines. Mounting evidence of the usefulness of the Library's "check list" led to the decision to prepare it for publication. The resulting source book[1] contained a list of the serial publications of 4,000 agencies; also a selected list of periodicals of value to social workers and librarians arranged alphabetically and by subject.

Exchange of material with other libraries continued to be mutually profitable. Welcome additions frequently came in this way, particularly after a "want list" was published about 1922. Other libraries filed "want lists" with the Foundation, to be kept on hand for reference whenever duplicates were received. With the growth of the collection miscellaneous gifts from regular and occasional donors decreased in importance as a direct source of accessions, though they still supplied material for exchange. Items not needed by the Library were not discarded until thorough search had been made for a place where they would be appreciated. Sooner or later most of them were so placed. Some notable acquisitions, moreover, were made by the Library in the twenties through gift. After the death of Zebulon R. Brockway his library of criminological literature was presented to the Foundation by his daughter. Valuable material on the feeble-minded came from the library of W. P. Letchworth; and the State Charities Aid Association contributed reports of the United States Sanitary Commission, in which Mrs. Rice had been active as a young

---

[1] Social Workers' Guide to the Serial Publications of Representative Social Agencies, by Elsie M. Rushmore, 1921.

woman. When the Foundation's Department of Education was discontinued in 1921, and later, as other departments were closed or finished special projects, their accumulations of reports and other material were sent to the Library for disposition or custody.

As early as 1922 the shelving that in 1913 had been thought ample for an indefinite future was becoming crowded, and additional stacks for reports were installed on the "third" floor of the Library (the ninth floor of the building). By 1929 increasing congestion again demanded relief, which was provided temporarily by placing additional small stacks on each floor, adding shelves in the Periodical Room, and storing in the basement some of the material needed only infrequently.

Growth of Clientele

Increase in the number of persons using the Library went on also, but at a slower rate than increase in material until the depression set in at the end of the period, and far behind the ambitions of the librarians. Circulation of books, to be sure, more than doubled, rising from 10,524 in 1916–1917 to 23,917 in 1930–1931, but 40 per cent of the increase came in the last two years. The number of visitors increased from 18,378 to 29,483, and a large part of the increase—more than 50 per cent—took place in the last two years. By 1931 the seating capacity of the reading rooms was often severely taxed.

How to make the Library more useful to persons interested in social problems, especially the social workers of New York City, and how to reach more of them, was constantly in the thoughts of the staff. To increase its usefulness to readers, thought was given continuously to the myriad unseen details of library technique and routine, to improving arrangement and indexing of the material, to expediting service by these and other means. To extend the circle of users, "satisfied customers" were the chief reliance, though other means also were adopted to bring the Library and its resources to the attention of its natural clientele.

Six bibliographies on topics of general interest to students of social problems were printed every year as Library bulletins, continuing the series begun in 1911. The selected list of books on social subjects published during the preceding year, which was an annual feature, was used by many libraries as a guide for their buying in this field. From time to time bibliographies in greatest demand, such as the list of American Foundations (first issued in 1915) and the list of Directories of Social Agencies (August, 1925), were brought up to date and reissued. As the number of topics covered by the printed bibliographies lengthened, a larger proportion of inquiries could be met by sending one or more of the Bulletins. Each year, however, many special lists were compiled in response to individual requests for help. Frequently the actual information wanted, sometimes involving a substantial amount of research, was sent to a correspondent, instead of mere references to the volumes where it could be found. Both the printed bibliographies and the special lists reflected current interests. In 1930–1931, for example, one of the Bulletins was on Unemployment, and references on old-age pensions, unemployment insurance, and homeless men were in demand from correspondents.

As a means of stimulating greater use of the Library, monthly distribution of a short list of recent accessions was begun in 1924 and became an established feature of the Library's service. In 1929, as an experiment, a list of German material in the Library was sent to the Deutsches Haus and the social science department of Columbia University. To keep on hand a general description of the Library and an account of its origin, the Handbook prepared by Mr. Jenkins in 1917 was revised by him and reissued in 1925. From 1928 on the Library was regularly represented[1] at the National Conference of Social Work by the librarian and when feasible by other members of the staff. They assisted at the Foundation's publication booth, made new acquaintances and renewed old ones, and gave advice to inquirers on bibliographies and selection of books.

PROFESSIONAL RELATIONS

During this period the cordial relations already established with other libraries were strengthened and extended. Systematic

[1] As it had been occasionally in earlier years.

exchange of duplicate material with libraries all over the country continued, as did inter-library loans of books wanted temporarily for special purposes. For several years the Foundation lent a collection, reaching 100 volumes in 1930, to New York University for a summer course in sociology. Small collections were sent farther away: to several summer camps in 1930, and to an institute in public health held at Hyannis, Massachusetts, by the State Department of Public Health; to the Fletcher Memorial Library in Ludlow, Vermont, in 1931.

On the development of special libraries, which was going on rapidly after the war, the Foundation had considerable influence. Mr. Jenkins lectured for several years at the Library School conducted by the New York Public Library. Classes from several training schools came each year to see the equipment and study the methods of the Russell Sage Foundation Library. Some students elected to do their field work here. The Library's special classification, which is a modification of the Dewey Decimal Classification, was adopted by several libraries containing similar collections. Visitors came from all parts of the country and from foreign lands. Japanese studying American methods of relief and rehabilitation began to be conspicuous after the Tokyo earthquake of 1923, and delegates from abroad to the celebration in 1926 of the fiftieth anniversary of the American Library Association[1] visited the Library on their way through New York.

Members of the staff participated as fully as possible in the American Library Association, the Special Libraries Association and its New York Chapter, and the New York Library Club. They attended annual conferences and other meetings within reach, served on committees, and held office, particularly in the Special Libraries Association and its local chapter.[2] In 1927 the

[1] At which Mrs. Mabel A. Badcock and Miss Constance Beal represented the Foundation.

[2] Mrs. Hulseman served on the publication committee of the Special Libraries Association (national). Miss Beal was made secretary of its Civic-Social Group when that group was organized in 1928–1929 and was a member of its committee on Classification and Indexing as well as of the Regional Catalogue Group of New York and its Environs affiliated with the American Library Association. She was also secretary-treasurer of the New York Chapter of the Special Libraries Association for two years (1929–1931), and Mrs. Badcock was chairman of its Civic-Social Group in 1930–1931.

British Library Association celebrated its fiftieth anniversary, in Edinburgh. Mrs. Badcock, who was visiting in England, represented the Foundation.

Conditions in 1931

At the end of this period of the Foundation's history the Library was contending for the first time with serious problems of congestion—on its shelves, in its files, and at the tables in reading rooms—and with consequent pressure on the staff. Since the beginning of the period the number of bound volumes had doubled and the number of unbound items had tripled. Notwithstanding the expedients adopted to provide for the expanding collection, available space was overtaxed. The increase in circulation of books and in attendance, which had proceeded moderately until 1929, was now, in the second year of the depression, going on at an unprecedented rate. There were times during the winter when every seat in the reading rooms was occupied. The depression brought leisure to some persons for reading they had been wanting to do; it sent others out in hunt for a comfortable place to spend the day; and it greatly increased enrollment at the New York School of Social Work, with correspondingly increased demands on space and service in the Library.

Ever since the Library was established, one of the most cherished objects of its director and staff had been to enlarge its circle of usefulness. Now that they were seeing the attainment of this hope, they found it gratifying, in spite of the personal difficulties it involved. Results were still, however, short of their expectations. Mrs. Hulseman closed her report for 1930–1931 on the familiar note: "Serious consideration should be given to means and methods of acquainting a larger number of social workers of the city with the Library and its resources."

XXX

PUBLICATIONS: 1918-1931

IN THE fourteen years of this second period the Foundation published 37 clothbound books compared with 47 in the first decade. Pamphlets were fewer than in the earlier years, but a number of them were the equivalent of books, though issued in paper covers.[1] The twelve volumes reporting the Regional Survey and Plan of New York and Its Environs, initiated and entirely financed by Russell Sage Foundation, were issued between 1927 and 1931, at the expense of the Foundation but not under its imprint.

BOOKS PRODUCED BY DEPARTMENTS

All but two of the 37 books published in this period were written by members of the staff, permanent or temporary, in comparison with only 16 of the 47 in the first decade. Of the five departments represented in the prewar output,[2] two (Education and Recreation) contributed no books to the list in the years 1918–1931, though they published some noteworthy pamphlets and the Department of Recreation supplied important sections of the report on the Regional Survey. The other three (Child-Helping, Industrial Studies, and Charity Organization) added respectively three, seven, and eleven volumes to the seven, five, and two, respectively, published before 1918. The Department of Surveys and Exhibits entered the list in 1918, contributing a total of eight books by 1931. Other departments appeared in the following order, each with a single volume: Library, Southern Highlands, Delinquency and Penology, Statistics, and Remedial Loans. Finally, in the fall of 1930, appeared the first issue of the Social Work Year Book, for the year 1929. It was not a product of any of the existing departments but itself constituted a new department.

[1] Both pamphlets and books produced by the departments in this period are described in the accounts of the departments, Chapters XXI–XXIX. All books and the more important pamphlets are included in the list of publications in Appendix C. [2] See p. 219.

Social Work Year Book

In a class by itself among the Foundation's publications is the encyclopedic "year book." The idea originated with Fred S. Hall, associate director of the Charity Organization Department. In January, 1928, Mr. Hall proposed that the Foundation undertake the publication of a Social Work Annual and Who's Who. Unlike many other professions and occupations, social work had no comprehensive year book recording developments in its various branches, no consolidated list of its practitioners; nor was the subject treated at all adequately in the general encyclopedias.

Mr. Hall proposed an annual volume, which would include topical articles on the various fields of organized social work; brief entries about national agencies, public and private; and a list of the leading social workers of the country, selected by objective criteria, with such biographical information about each one as ordinarily is given in a condensed Who's Who. The proposal was approved in October, 1928, and Mr. Hall was appointed editor. Public announcement was made in The Survey of January 15, 1929. From the beginning the new project had the status of a distinct department of the Foundation's general work. An advisory committee[1] under the chairmanship of David H. Holbrook was appointed early in 1929, to assist the editor in deciding the many questions that inevitably would arise.

Modifications, naturally, were made in the original plan as the work got under way. The Who's Who idea was abandoned at an early stage. The topical articles, which were intended to be primarily a record of developments in the year 1929, with a brief historical introduction and a general description of the field of work, turned out to be largely general description. In assembling information for these articles, co-operation was sought from the American Association of Social Workers and was generously given by its chapters in 42 cities.

The first issue of the Year Book, for the year 1929, appeared late in 1930. It was welcomed as an indispensable book of

---

[1] The only other department that had an advisory committee was Surveys and Exhibits in its early years.

reference for social workers and students, and also as giving the public for the first time a general view of social work in a single volume. The first edition of 2,605 copies was nearly exhausted by the following spring and a second printing, of a thousand copies, was ordered in March. A year after publication only 390 copies of the 3,605 were still on hand.

At the time the first Year Book appeared, biennial issues were contemplated. This was announced in the Preface. Plans were promptly begun for a volume to cover the calendar years 1930 and 1931, on the same general lines as the volume for 1929—"improved, however, in the light of experience and criticisms received." In September, 1931, at the close of the Foundation's fiscal year, publication early in 1932 was anticipated.

Two Special Studies

The two books not prepared under the auspices of one or another of the Foundation's departments were on subjects that did not fall within the scope of any department. They were written, as were a larger number in the first decade, by specially qualified persons who were immediately responsible to the general director. One of them[1] supplemented the Handbook of Settlements, prepared for the Foundation by the same authors and published in 1911. The other[2] was undertaken by the Foundation because of a new situation created by the World War; and its author had not previously been on the Foundation's list.

When the Handbook of Settlements was published Mr. Woods realized that in the material he had gathered he had the nucleus for a volume on the history and significance of the settlement movement. The Foundation made an additional appropriation to further the preparation of such a book. In the same year the National Federation of Settlements was incorporated, and Mr. Woods and Mr. Kennedy were made its joint secretaries. This connection both facilitated their study and delayed its completion. Year by year their store of knowledge about the back-

---

[1] The Settlement Horizon, by Robert A. Woods and Albert J. Kennedy, 1922.
[2] Education and Training for Social Work, by James H. Tufts, 1923.

grounds, spirit, activities, and influence of the 500 or more settlements in the United States grew, adding to the task of analysis and synthesis. When at length the results were published, the book was described as the first authoritative history and philosophical interpretation of the settlement movement and a practical guide for individual settlements in shaping their policies and development.

The great and sudden expansion of social work during the World War, and the consequent urgent demand for social workers in unprecedented numbers and variety, not only affected the existing schools for the training of social workers but also led to the establishment of new centers that undertook to give a quick preparation for certain positions and to the multiplication of courses in practical social work in the social science departments of colleges and universities. There was much diversity in the instruction offered and the qualifications required for admission, with resulting confusion. The older schools and some of the leading agencies became apprehensive that lowered standards in social work would follow. It seemed an opportune time for an authoritative study that would clarify views on methods of preparing for social work and lead to improvement.

In June of 1920 the Association of Training Schools for Professional Social Work, organized the preceding year, asked Russell Sage Foundation to provide for such an inquiry. The Foundation agreed to do so. An appropriation was made in the fall, and James H. Tufts, professor of philosophy in the University of Chicago, who was spending the academic year in New York, was engaged to make the study. In his work, which continued to the close of the year 1921, he talked or corresponded with officers and teachers of the institutions that offered preparation for social work, visited many of them, and conferred with leaders in various lines of social work. His report did not describe and evaluate individual programs of training. Rather, as might be expected of a philosopher, it discussed principles, leaving to the individual institutions to make their own applications. Part I (88 pages) examined the field of social work. Part II (124 pages) analyzed current problems of education and training for that field.

431

Publication Department

When the Foundation in 1917 took over from Survey Associates, Inc. the handling of its own publications, it established a new department for the purpose and appointed F. W. Jenkins, who was also the librarian, as director. Mr. Jenkins had visions of a large potential market. He enthusiastically set about increasing sales. "How can we reach more buyers?" was the question constantly in his mind, as in the Library he was constantly trying to enlarge its circle of readers.

To bring the Foundation's publications to the notice of possible buyers Mr. Jenkins made use of circulars about new books and about groups of books, news releases, a small amount of paid advertising in selected media, a liberal policy of supplying copies for review, and circulation of a comprehensive catalogue. He urged publicity about the work of the Foundation as a whole through general reports and magazine articles, because he thought that would stimulate interest in its publications, and also because frequent requests for information as to what the Foundation did came to the Department.

He equipped a "book room" in the department offices, where prospective purchasers could examine publications of the Foundation at their leisure, but this was discontinued after a year's trial, as it had no perceptible effect on sales. In January, 1920, the first number of a house organ called The Record was issued, designed to introduce the Foundation's books and pamphlets, new and old, to possible customers. It was planned as a monthly, but second-class mailing privileges were denied, and accordingly it was discontinued after the issue of two numbers.

Beginning in 1917 a separate display[1] of all the Russell Sage Foundation publications in print was taken to the National Conference of Social Work every year. One or more members of the Department's staff were in attendance to answer questions, take orders, and advise about choice of books. In 1920 and usually thereafter they were assisted by one or more representatives of the Library. From the first year the table at the National Conference

[1] Before 1917 they were included in the display of Survey Associates, Inc.

432

brought good returns, both in sales on the spot and in extending acquaintance. At Atlantic City in 1919, where attendance was exceptionally large, 707 copies of the Foundation's publications were sold.

As an experiment in 1925 a professional publicity agent was engaged to bring several new books to the attention of general readers. Excellent publicity resulted—about 24,000 press stories —but it had little effect in increasing sales. Apparently readers assumed that the books were free. Many who wrote for copies returned them on finding they were expected to pay for them.

Of all Mr. Jenkins' devices for increasing sales, the "Standing Order List," which he instituted soon after taking charge of the Department, was the most effective. The list was made up of persons who indicated a wish to receive a copy of each publication of a general nature when it was issued, with the privilege of returning it if they did not care to buy it and a liberal discount from the regular price if they did. By September, 1920, there were 330 names on the list. Three years later the number was 480, remaining from a total of 700 that had been on the list at one time or another.

Libraries were "fairly permanent," but even they were affected by fluctuations in their budgets. Among individuals there was a high rate of turnover. They were constantly dropping out because of changing interests or fortunes, or because they received a book presenting facts they did not like to see in print. Some had to be dropped because they failed to return books they did not want to keep or did not pay their bills. It was "a constant struggle" to find replacements. After Mr. Jenkins fell ill no special effort was made to enlarge or even to keep up the list. At the end of September, 1928, it had declined from the high point of 480 in 1923 to 380. All but 51 of the 380 were libraries.

After Mr. Jenkins became incapacitated in 1926, the work of the Department was carried on for two years under the direction of Henry A. Taylor, who had been his assistant since 1919. In the summer of 1928 Mr. Taylor resigned. In November F. Emerson Andrews, who had just resigned from a position with the Macmillan Company in order to do free-lance writing, was

433

engaged by the Foundation to study the methods of the Publication Department, "with a view to increasing sales." In December he was appointed director of the Department, on a half-time basis.

Mr. Andrews saw great possibilities in the Standing Order List and began an aggressive campaign to build it up, setting an eventual goal of 1,200. As one feature of the campaign he distributed widely a booklet called Your Share in $15,000,000.

By September, 1930, the goal was nearly reached. There were 1,180 names on the list, compared with 380 two years before. The number of libraries had increased only moderately, from 329 to 373. The bulk of the gain was in individuals, the more variable element of the list. The deepening depression brought about a net loss of 176 names in 1930–1931, leaving the list at 1,004 at the close of the fiscal year.

SALES: 1918–1931

Volume of sales depended not only on the scope and general character of the Foundation's publications, but on their reputation for reliability, the expanding market for such books, and success in bringing them to the notice of persons likely to be interested. The number and variety of titles on sale was also a factor. For old customers, already familiar with the list, who had bought previous volumes they wanted, it was the new titles that were of interest.

At the beginning of this second period of the Foundation's history (October 1, 1917) 40 of the 47 books published in the first decade were on the active list. Before the end of the period (September 30, 1931) all but nine of these had gone out of print; also some of the 37 titles added during these fourteen years. Additions did not quite keep up with subtractions and removals. The net result was 39 on the active list at the end of the period, compared with 40 at the beginning. From year to year the number offered to purchasers fluctuated between 47 in 1919[1] and 35 in 1928 and 1930.

[1] Throughout this section the years are fiscal years ending September 30, not calendar years.

The number of books sold during this period averaged about 6,800 per year, and ranged from 3,580 in 1927 to 9,964 in 1931. Low figures were recorded in three successive years: 1926, 1927, and 1928. In 1926 no new book was published; in 1927, one; in 1928, two. A high mark of 8,339 in 1919 is related to the appearance of nine new books in that year and the one preceding. The high figures at the close of the period reflect the publication of nine new volumes in 1929, 1930, and 1931, including in 1931 the first Social Work Year Book, which accounted for more than a quarter of the sales that year.

Sales of pamphlets were high in the early years of this period. After Mr. Jenkins took charge of publications he gradually standardized and improved the appearance of the Foundation's pamphlets, which previously had been printed and distributed by the departments individually, without any central supervision. He used his influence also to increase sales and diminish the amount of free distribution. In general, too, the pamphlets were becoming more substantial in size. Some of them were equivalent to small books. Leaflets had almost disappeared. In the six years 1918–1923 the number of pamphlets sold annually averaged about 22,500. In 1924 there was a sharp drop in sales, and in the eight years 1924–1931 the annual average was about 6,500.

These figures do not include sales of the Library Bulletin, a regular bi-monthly medium primarily for the publication of bibliographies. Through most of this period it had a regular mailing list of 700 to 800. The nominal subscription fee met the cost of printing an edition large enough to provide a reserve supply to use in replying to requests for references on the subjects covered by the bibliographies.

Sales in foreign countries were never large. Canada and Great Britain were the best customers. In 1922 a consignment of books was placed with a firm in Shanghai, but sales in China were small. There were none in 1926 or in 1927. In 1928 the stock was recalled. For several years after the great Tokyo earthquake, which sent visitors to America to study our methods of rehabilitation after disasters, a number of orders came from Japan, amounting in one year to $200 in value. They fell off toward the end of the twenties but rose again to a total of 101 books and 50 pamphlets in 1931.

Less conventional forms of publication than books and pamphlets were the scales of the Department of Education for testing proficiency in writing, spelling, and silent reading; the record forms prepared by the Charity Organization Department and the Department of Statistics; and the symbols devised by the Department of Statistics for use on maps to show the location of various types of social agencies.

Scales had their highest demand in the early twenties, after the picture-tests for measuring ability to read were published. Not only were these new, but each copy could be used only once, for one child, while the writing and spelling scales were used over and over by teachers for an entire class at a time. In 1922 over a million copies of the scales of all kinds were sold. The average per year for 1921 through 1927 was above 560,000. After 1927 the number diminished each year to 111,000 in 1931.

Forms for the use of charity organization societies had an average sale of about 160,000 per year—above the average in the depression years at the beginning of the twenties; rising to 272,000 at the end of the period, when the great depression was in its second year, and to nearly 450,000 the following year. Statistical forms for collecting data on casework of family welfare societies for the project inaugurated by the Department of Statistics in 1926 were put on sale in 1927. In 1931 about 27,000 were sold. Symbols for use on maps were first sold in 1926. Demand fluctuated with activity in map-making for social surveys.

Gross receipts from sales of publications of all kinds fluctuated between $13,634 in 1918 and $33,312 in 1931. This by no means represented a gradual increase. The amount in 1922 was not far below the maximum. Nor did fluctuations in receipts correspond closely with fluctuations in volume of sales. Price per unit was also a factor. There was no change in the Foundation's policy of setting prices with a view to recovering barely the cost of manufacture—a very small percentage of the total cost of production. But during the war and the period of inflation that followed, prices of labor and of all the materials used in printing increased greatly. Prices set on new publications in the twenties, therefore, were on a somewhat higher level than in the prewar years.

DEVELOPMENT OF PROMOTION POLICIES

At the beginning of this period the Foundation had only recently established its own department to handle the production and distribution of its publications. Development of the Publication Department was interrupted by the war but was resumed in 1919 and carried on vigorously until Mr. Jenkins became ill a few years later. During this initial period the new Department not only assumed the responsibilities previously delegated to Survey Associates, Inc., but also relieved the departments of the work of printing and distributing their pamphlets, incidentally standardizing and greatly improving the general appearance of the Foundation's small publications. A number of expedients were tried with a view to enlarging the market for the publications. Two of them became trusted producers: the annual display at the National Conference of Social Work, begun in 1917; and the Standing Order List, started not later than 1919.

Again at the end of the period, after several quiet years, the Department under its new director, Mr. Andrews, became active. Special attention was given to building up the Standing Order List and to circulars, the two methods that had been found most productive in bringing in orders. Representation at the National Conference of Social Work, and, by arrangement with The Survey and the Family Welfare Association of America, at state conferences of social work and other meetings not attended by a member of the department staff, was continued. The amount of paid advertising in selected periodicals was expanded. More general publicity was sought through personal correspondence and news releases, and by stimulating independent articles by feature writers and news services on phases of the Foundation's work. In 1931, as the depression deepened, circulars were distributed calling attention to all the Foundation's publications that had a bearing on problems of unemployment.

XXXI

REGIONAL SURVEY AND PLAN:
1921-1931

FROM its earliest years the Foundation had shown its interest in housing and city planning by making grants to educational agencies in those fields and for experiments in reducing the cost of construction of small houses. It had supplied the capital for planning and building a model suburban community on Long Island. In 1921 it undertook to survey the entire New York metropolitan region and prepare a plan for its physical development that would serve for years to come as a guide in making it "a better place to live in and a better place to work in."[1] It was the most ambitious single enterprise sponsored by the Foundation.

ORIGIN OF THE PROJECT

The vision and compelling enthusiasm for its inception came from Charles Dyer Norton, who had been a trustee since November, 1918. Mr. Norton had been an initiator and chairman of the Committee on Plan of Chicago. After coming to New York he was made chairman of the advisory committee of the short-lived Committee on City Plan created by the Board of Estimate and Apportionment in 1914 at the suggestion of George McAneny, then president of the Borough of Manhattan. It was then that Mr. Norton drafted a memorandum that embodied his conception of the kind of plan that was needed. "No plan of New York will command recognition," he said, "unless it includes all the area in which New Yorkers earn their livelihood and make their homes." His ideal was a comprehensive plan for the entire area, based on long and patient study of its varied needs and possibilities, and prepared with imagination—such "a plan as the young people would adopt in their hearts and carry out as they grew up." He had no illusions as to the labor that would be

[1] Mr. de Forest's formulation of the Foundation's interest in the project.

438

involved. "City planning requires imagination. It requires vision. It requires a long continuing effort and it costs a great sum of money." Mr. Norton was fond of quoting Daniel H. Burnham, who directed the Plan of Chicago, as follows:

> Make no little plans; they have no magic to stir men's blood and probably themselves will not be realized. Make big plans; aim high in hope and work, remembering that a noble, logical diagram once recorded will never die, but long after we are gone will be a living thing, asserting itself with growing intensity.

After joining the Board of Trustees of the Foundation Mr. Norton talked about the idea informally with some of the members and continued to discuss it with other persons who were interested. In February, 1919, at the request of Mr. de Forest, he wrote a memorandum for the Trustees outlining the need and possibilities of such a plan and suggesting a grant of $300,000 to be spent for its preparation under the direction of a special committee of five to be appointed by the president. This was discussed at several conferences with Mr. de Forest, Mr. White, and Mr. Glenn. At the last of these conferences, in December, 1920, Nelson P. Lewis, formerly chief engineer of the Board of Estimate and Apportionment of New York, was present. It was then agreed that Mr. Norton's memorandum should be submitted to the Trustees with a favorable recommendation, and that Mr. Lewis should be asked to become adviser on the physical aspects of the plan and to make a preliminary survey of its possibilities.

These proposals were submitted to the Trustees on February 4, 1921. They authorized the appointment of a committee[1] with power to devise and formulate plans and methods by which a plan of New York and its environs, as recommended by Mr. Norton's memorandum, might be created. They recognized that over three or four years "as much as $300,000" might be expended by this committee, and made an appropriation of $50,000 for immediate use. The engagement of Nelson P. Lewis was also authorized.

[1] Mr. Norton, chairman; Mr. de Forest, Mr. Delano, Mr. Glenn, and Mr. Morrow. Mr. White had died a few days before this meeting.

On February 11, 1921, Mr. Norton invited a few men who were interested in city planning to dine with him at his home. Those present were Edward M. Bassett, Robert W. de Forest, John M. Glenn, Ernest P. Goodrich, Shelby M. Harrison, Nelson P. Lewis, George McAneny, Frederick Law Olmsted, Frederic B. Pratt, Lawson Purdy, and Lawrence Veiller. They all agreed that Mr. Norton's plan could be carried out successfully and that it was desirable to launch it as soon as possible.

Mr. Norton's conception was a bold plan, which would "visualize the commercial, the industrial, the social, and the artistic values and possibilities of our glorious harbor and all of its broad and varied environs." The Committee would "seek to record what New York may reasonably aspire to become in the far future." It would propose no great increase of public expenditures. A plan generally accepted by public opinion would tend to direct public expenditure into projects of permanent value, each one taking its place in a coherent scheme. It could "become a reality by the expenditure of the very funds which will be expended in any event."

Preliminary Work

For the next fifteen months the Committee worked quietly, getting advice from many competent sources, formulating scope and plans, and making a start on some of the basic studies. Mr. Lewis was installed in offices in the Foundation's building and began work on topographic maps. Shelby M. Harrison prepared several comprehensive memoranda on the social studies that should be undertaken. Edward M. Bassett, leading authority on zoning, was engaged to study the legal problems that would be involved, with Frank B. Williams, an authority on the law relating to city planning, as his assistant. Frederick P. Keppel was engaged as executive secretary, to begin work as soon as he could leave Paris, where he was secretary of the International Chamber of Commerce. Flavel Shurtleff, who had been secretary of the National Conference on City Planning since 1909, and was co-author of Carrying Out the City Plan,[1] was engaged as his

[1] Published by the Foundation in 1914.

assistant. He was later made director of public relations. Henry James was also engaged to assist the executive secretary and as consultant on special studies. Mr. Keppel took charge of the work in September, 1922. East Hall and other rooms in the building were assigned for the Committee's use until a tenth story to the building, to provide offices and drafting rooms for the staff, was completed in August, 1923.

Public announcement of the project was made on May 10, 1922. At this meeting Mr. de Forest, Mr. Norton, Herbert Hoover, Elihu Root, John C. Carty, Miss Lillian D. Wald, Charles Dana Gibson, and Mrs. August Belmont spoke of various aspects of the proposed plan and of its great importance for the Region. By fall further progress had been made in selecting staff and organizing advisory groups, in establishing relations with city-planning specialists in America and in Europe and with local organizations within the Region whose activities had a bearing on a plan, and in deciding on specific problems for study within the four main divisions of inquiry—Physical, Economic and Industrial, Social, and Legal. A number of special studies had already been made. Others were under way. During the summer Mr. Norton and Mr. Keppel had visited planning projects in France, England, Belgium, and Holland. They met a number of the specialists in those countries. Raymond Unwin of London came to New York in the fall at the invitation of the Committee for further conference. Jacques Lambert of Paris came in 1923 to study gardens and parks of Manhattan.

In November, 1922, the Trustees approved an additional appropriation of $500,000, payable in amounts of not more than $100,000 in any one fiscal year.

ORGANIZATION

In its organic relation to the Foundation the Regional Survey and Plan was unique. It began as "direct work"—a "special study" under the direction of a committee of the Trustees. Before long, however, the Foundation decided that it might be easier to win public interest and support for the project if it were not identified with any existing agency. Later on John H. Finley,

Henry James, George McAneny, Frank L. Polk, Frederic B. Pratt, and Lawson Purdy were added to the Committee and it was given the status of an independent organization, not subject to supervision by the Board of Trustees or the general director. Throughout its existence, however, a majority of its members were trustees of the Foundation. The Foundation met the entire cost of the Committee's work at a total expenditure of over $1,000,000.[1] It supplied offices and workrooms free of charge. In addition much time and thought were contributed by several members of the staff of the Foundation. Results of the studies made for the Committee did not appear under the Foundation's imprint. They were published by Regional Plan of New York and Its Environs and copyrighted by the Committee.

Mr. Norton died in March, 1923. He was succeeded as chairman by Frederic A. Delano, who with Mr. Norton had been one of the initiators of the Chicago City Plan. Mr. Keppel served as the executive secretary only until September, 1923, when he resigned to accept the position of president of Carnegie Corporation. After resigning he continued to act as a consulting member of the Committee. Nelson P. Lewis, who organized the engineering studies and got them well started, died in March, 1924. In 1923 Thomas Adams was chosen to head the staff as general director of plans and surveys,[2] and held that position through 1929.

Mr. Adams was born in Scotland. He had had a large experience as a city planner in England. He had been a founder and secretary of the Garden City Association, which in 1900 established Letchworth, the first garden city in England. He was also the initiator and first president of the Town Planning Institute of Great Britain in 1904. From 1914 to 1921 he was adviser on town planning to the Canadian government. He had taken a prominent part in early conferences on city planning in the United

---

[1] Technically the amounts provided by the Foundation were grants. They are mentioned in Chapter XXXII and listed in Appendix D, but because of the special character of this project, and the unique relation of the Foundation to it, it has seemed best to give an account of it in this separate chapter.

[2] The full staff, including consultants, the personnel of advisory committees of architects, engineers, lawyers, and city planners, and other information about the organization of the work, may be found in the first volume of the Plan, pp. 12–14.

States in 1911 and later. In 1921 he returned to England and established a town planning firm of which he was the senior member. His firm made plans for several towns in Great Britain and was engaged as consultant for others. From 1921 to 1938 he was a visiting lecturer on town planning at the Massachusetts Institute of Technology. In 1922 his advice was sought as to the organization of the Regional Plan of New York and Its Environs. In 1923 the Regional Plan Committee engaged six prominent city planners to make a preliminary study of the Region, each of the six being allotted a special section. Mr. Adams was the chairman of the group, and had the special direction of the Westchester section. The following quotation from his Introduction to his book, Outline of Town and City Planning,[1] expresses his conception of city planning:

> City and town planning is a science, an art, and a movement of policy concerned with the shaping and guiding of the physical growth and arrangement of towns in harmony with their social and economic needs. We pursue it as a science to obtain knowledge of urban structure and services and the relation of its constituent parts and processes of circulation; as an art to determine the layout of the ground, the arrangement of land uses and ways of communication and the design of the buildings on principles that will secure order, health, and efficiency in development; and as a movement of policy to give effect to our principles.

> What matters is not whether we plan but whether we plan intelligently. This means, first, that we must have sound social and economic objectives; second, we must strive to achieve these by design based on knowledge and by methods that will lead to results; and, third, we must not overemphasize the value of the administrative processes by which plans are carried out as compared with the technical processes by which plans are made.

> A plan is only a means to an end, and that end is a stable and well-balanced physical structure so designed as to secure health, safety, amenity, order and convenience, and, generally, to promote human welfare.

[1] Russell Sage Foundation, 1935.

443

Scope of the Study

As the work on the preliminary surveys of the four main fields of the project proceeded, its magnitude and complexity were more clearly realized. The quantity and variety of the detail that seemed necessary, said Mr. Delano in presenting the Plan to the public in 1929, were "almost terrifying." The "Region"[1] contained 5,528 square miles and a population of 10,000,000, ranging in density from 45 to 104,000 persons per square mile. Daily travel of 2,870,000 people into and out of lower Manhattan (below Fifty-ninth Street) made the mere study of its circulation system an "enormous task." It had 1,800 miles of waterfront and 60,000 manufacturing plants. Taxable land was valued at $9,000,000,000, ranging from $57 to $460,000 per acre. Topography was exceedingly varied, presenting both advantages and difficulties. The area lay in three states and embraced 436 local governmental authorities. Financial problems were "staggering."

Besides the mere number of elements that had to be studied, there was the necessity of studying relations "between comparatively static physical conditions, and dynamic and evolutionary economic and social conditions affecting millions of associated beings."[2] In its functional scope, in the attention given to economic, industrial, and human interests, as well as in its geographic scope, the New York Survey was "an advance in comprehensiveness" over any that had been attempted before.[3] In its temporal scope it limited the period for which it would undertake to plan to forty years, ending about 1965.

Co-ordination, Interpretation, Presentation

It was recognized as essential not only that the Survey and Plan should be directed by one individual, but "in an even

[1] Briefly, the commuting area around New York City, with certain modifications suggested by observation and general knowledge. Its boundaries included the large outlying recreational areas within easy reach of the metropolitan center; they followed the boundaries of cities and counties at the periphery; and they had regard to significant physical characteristics. The whole of Long Island was included, for example. Looking back from 1931, the Committee said it would not change its definition of the "Region" if it were doing its work over.

[2] Mr. Adams, in his Preface to the first volume of the Survey, p. x.

[3] Ibid.

444

greater degree . . . that the complete analysis of the innumerable related problems, the sifting of essentials and non-essentials, the logical sequence of their presentation in the text of the reports, and the determination of the grouping and co-ordination of all the elements of the Plan in a single concept, should be done by one person." This involved, on the part of Mr. Adams, "the initiation of many ideas and projects in addition to the supervision and co-ordination of proposals and designs of collaborators; the development of a new philosophic conception of city planning under modern conditions in a democratic country; and the study of every fact and every line of text in the reports leading up to the whole ten volumes of the Survey and Plan."[1]

Major reports were published as monographs as soon as they were ready, and the public was kept informed of progress through the newspapers and magazines and by addresses at public meetings. Close relations were maintained with the public authorities and private agencies of the Region that had, or should have, an interest in a comprehensive plan. A Regional Council of 150 members was formed in April, 1925, which held several meetings in 1926 and 1927. Mr. Shurtleff and other members of the staff aided in creating local planning agencies throughout the Region, in stimulating interest through public discussion, and here and there in promoting local planning projects in harmony with the main plan. In 1923 there were only ten planning commissions in the Region. By 1927, largely through the efforts of the staff, 32 new commissions had been appointed in various political units. By 1931 there were 87. When Mayor Walker in 1926 appointed a City Committee on Plan and Survey, which had neither powers nor funds, the staff co-operated with it in carrying on its studies and preparing the report it submitted in 1928. Its principal recommendation was that a permanent City Planning Board be established.

For a permanent record the Committee published between

[1] Mr. Delano in his Foreword to the second volume of the Plan, p. 3. Mr. Adams wrote this volume and numerous interpretative introductions and entire sections in the other volumes of the Survey and Plan. He was also, said Mr. Delano, "more or less responsible for a great deal that he has not signed."

1927 and 1931 twelve[1] quarto volumes, aggregating nearly 3,700 pages, illustrated with hundreds of maps, photographs, diagrams, and drawings. Ten of them present the Survey—"the essence and results of the principal studies carried on as a basis for planning," many of which had been issued previously as monographs. The other two present the Plan that had been developed on the basis of the Survey. Volume 1, The Graphic Regional Plan, contains an atlas in 96 sections, depicting a regional system of communication facilities and land uses,[2] together with text discussing the underlying principles and describing the 470 proposals included in the Plan. In volume 2, The Building of the City, Mr. Adams sets forth "a conception of the spirit that enters into the making of cities, an outline of the principles and standards that must be followed in guiding the building of cities in the New York region, and a series of illustrations of special opportunities for development in the Region."[3]

Contributions by Foundation Staff

Substantial contributions were made to the Survey by the staff of Russell Sage Foundation. The Foundation departments most deeply involved were Surveys and Exhibits, and Recreation.

[1] The titles with dates of publication of the Survey and Plan volumes are:

Survey Volumes

1. Major Economic Factors in Metropolitan Growth and Arrangement. 1928
1A. Chemical, Metal, Wood, Tobacco and Printing Industries. 1928
1B. Food, Clothing and Textile Industries, Wholesale Markets and Retail Shopping and Financial Districts. 1928
2. Population, Land Values and Government. 1929
3. Highway Traffic. 1927
4. Transit and Transportation. 1928
5. Public Recreation. 1928
6. Buildings: Their Uses and the Spaces About Them. 1931
7. Neighborhood and Community Planning. 1929
8. Physical Conditions and Public Services. 1929

Plan Volumes

1. The Graphic Regional Plan (Atlas and Description). 1929
2. The Building of the City. 1931

[2] "Circulation by all forms of conveyance into, out of, and within the Region, and the location of industry, commerce, business, residence and recreation—these are fundamental elements upon the treatment of which the soundness of the physical development of a city or metropolitan region depends." (Letter of Presentation, p. 7.)

[3] Mr. Delano, in his Foreword to the volume, pp. 3-4.

446

The Departments of Industrial Studies and of Statistics, the consultant in delinquency and penology, and the editorial staff also helped in various ways.

Mr. Harrison was consulted in the initial stages of the project, and as director of the Social Division, one of the four main divisions of the Committee's staff, he participated in conferences on general plans throughout the ten years. His division included the studies in population, recreation, housing, neighborhood units, and the location of schools, correctional institutions, and hospitals. He promoted the general interests of the Committee by speaking and writing and by organizing meetings, notably a Round Table of seven sessions on Regional Planning at the Third National Conference on the Science of Politics, held in New York in September, 1925. His associates in the Department of Surveys and Exhibits were called on for help in their special fields.

Miss van Kleeck advised on preliminary plans for the Economic and Industrial Survey[1] and also at later stages, as the plans were carried out. Ben M. Selekman, a member of her staff, and Miss Henriette R. Walter, a former member, made two of the unit studies of leading industries in the Region that were basic material for the Survey: the men's wear industry and the women's garment industry respectively.[2]

Mr. Hanmer was in charge of the Recreation Section of the Social Division. He had the chief responsibility for volume 5[3] of the Survey series. This volume considered how much and what types of recreation space were needed for the Region, how it should be distributed, the gaps between existing provisions and needs, the opportunities, at the time, for acquiring additional areas to fill the gaps, and the legal questions involved in doing so. As in the other volumes of the Survey, the aim was to present conditions, standards, and needs, in a way that would be useful in framing a general plan for the Region. Specific proposals would have been out of place.

[1] Directed by Robert Murray Haig in collaboration with Roswell C. McCrea, both of Columbia University, and reported in volume I of the Survey.

[2] Published as monographs in 1924 and 1925, and included in volume IB of the Survey.

[3] Public Recreation, published in 1928.

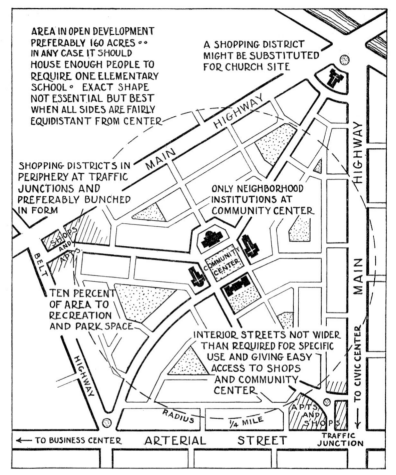

NEIGHBORHOOD UNIT PRINCIPLES
Reproduced from New York Regional Survey, Volume 7

The survey of existing provisions represented 14 separate studies made for the Committee at different times by Mr. Hanmer with the assistance of Charles J. Storey, a member of the Committee's staff who was assigned to Mr. Hanmer for this purpose for four years beginning October, 1922, and who then was kept on the staff of the Foundation for four years more to help in meeting requests that came to the Department of Recreation in consequence of its work on the Survey.

Mr. Perry's distinctive contribution was his plan for The Neighborhood Unit, which he first formulated in January, 1924, and later developed in a monograph.[1] His idea was that as arterial highways were built the population of the city would spread out and tend to divide into neighborhoods bounded by these arteries, and that these natural neighborhoods should be planned so as to provide not merely for good, well-placed buildings, but also for more favorable conditions for sound family life and community intercourse than are usually found in large cities or in most suburbs.

One of Mr. Perry's main interests while a member of the staff of the Foundation had been the study of the possibilities of community centers and the education of school authorities and others as to their importance, and as to how to maintain and operate them. He had also lived for many years at Forest Hills Gardens. These experiences gave him a stimulus and a foundation for devising the Neighborhood Unit. His formula for its physical plan requires, first, that it should include an area large enough to provide a self-contained community to the extent that all its residents "will be within convenient access to an elementary school, adequate common play spaces, and retail shopping districts";[2] and, second, that the Unit must be surrounded "by arterial streets sufficiently wide to facilitate its by-passing, instead of penetration by through traffic"; further, its internal streets should be planned to meet its special needs and to discourage through traffic. "The essence of Mr. Perry's report is a scheme or principle of arrangement for the physical elements of a residential district . . . which brings into harmonious relation the various conditions that have been observed to favor a safe and satisfying community life."[3]

Mr. Hurlin's contributions were in connection with the Economic and Industrial Survey and the preliminary studies in population. He gave statistical help to the staff investigating selected industries, recommended a standard form of tables for

[1] Regional Survey, vol. 7, pp. 20-140.
[2] Housing for the Machine Age, by Clarence A. Perry, 1939, p. 50.
[3] Shelby M. Harrison in Introduction to Mr. Perry's Monograph, p. 24.

their use, and put at their disposal throughout the summer of
1923 all the mechanical equipment of his office. At the request of
Mr. Harrison he suggested a list of special studies in population
that would be useful in the Committee's work. For the use of the
Committee he prepared a memorandum on various estimates of
the future population of the city that had been made in the past.
At his suggestion the American Statistical Association sponsored
a meeting in New York on October 30, 1925, for which he arranged the program, to discuss methods of forecasting changes in
population, with special reference to New York City.

Dr. Hart, who for several years beginning in 1924 was studying
the prisons of the city and making recommendations for improvement at the request of the Department of Correction
and various private organizations, supplied the chapter on
"The Present and Future Prison System of New York City" for
volume 8 of the Survey. His discussion in this place was limited
to questions pertinent to a city plan: the location and adequacy
of existing institutions, and the principles that should govern
their distribution and arrangement. Geographically it was
limited to Greater New York, but it called attention to the
general inadequacy of provisions in the other portions of the
Region.

With the publication of the second volume of the Plan in 1931
the task the Committee had undertaken ten years before was
finished. A contemporary London editorial[1] spoke of the New
York Plan as "the envy of the world." The work of the Committee, however, was only a beginning, a foundation on which
others might build. Its report was addressed to "the public." It
had supplied "an analysis of the physical needs of the New York
Region and a conception of a way to meet them."[2] What the
Plan would achieve, said Mr. Adams,[3] "is what the people will
it to achieve."

[1] The Listener, July 15, 1931.
[2] Letter of Presentation, vol. 1, p. 7.
[3] The Plan, vol. 2, p. 576.

The Plan Entrusted to the Public

On May 27, 1929, at a large meeting held in New York and attended by municipal officials and other prominent citizens representing various phases of community activity, the Regional Plan, as portrayed in volume one of the Plan, was submitted as a gift from the Foundation to the people of the Region with the expression of the hope that it would be used freely by public authorities for the benefit of the public.

At the same time there was launched the Regional Plan Association, a voluntary organization of citizens of the Region, under the presidency of George McAneny, to carry on the educational work and guide the development of the Plan and of the Region in harmony with it.[1] The Foundation made a grant of $25,000 to the Association "to enable it to get a proper start and secure contributions from other sources." Other substantial contributions were obtained and the Association has given effective aid to all parts of the Region in developing sound plans, as will be seen later.

[1] See p. 464.

XXXII

GRANTS: 1918-1931

ABOUT $4,000,000 was given in grants to 62 organizations in the fourteen years of this second period of the Foundation's history, compared with nearly $1,800,000 to 47 organizations in its first ten and one-half years. Nine of the 62 had received grants before October 1, 1917, including the three that accounted for about half of the total disbursement to other agencies in the opening period. Fifty-three were added to the list between October 1, 1917, and September 30, 1931. Although none of these 53 had previously received grants of money, a few had been helped materially with free office space and free services from members of the departmental staff.

Again early in this period, as on several occasions in the first years of the Foundation, the general director expressed his conviction that "on the whole, in the long run, we shall get surer and larger results from spending money on work which is under the control of the Foundation, than we can get from grants to outside agencies." On the other hand, he continued, "there arise, from time to time, new opportunities for social work which cannot be taken advantage of unless a considerable sum of money can be made available for their maintenance until they have had a chance to demonstrate their usefulness and secure sufficient support to establish them permanently." In his opinion the Foundation should make grants only in such cases, "and preferably for fostering work which is fundamental and helpful to social work as a whole."

For a few years after the war expenditures for grants were less than expenditures for the Foundation's departments and special studies, but from 1923 on, and for the period as a whole, as for the first period, they were considerably higher. Consideration of new requests and requests for increases, which had been practically suspended since 1912, was resumed when knowledge of the terms of Mrs. Sage's will brought prospects of larger income. Disbursements on account of grants rose from the low figure of less than $83,000 in 1917–1918 to more than $300,000 in 1922–1923, when expenditure for the Committee on Regional Plan was at its highest point. After that, as it had become apparent that requirements for the Regional Survey and Plan and for several of the other new grantees would continue longer and would be larger than had been anticipated originally, a second period of caution in assuming new obligations set in. Aggregate annual disbursements for grants, however, remained near or well above $300,000 throughout the period. The highest figure for any year, not merely in this period but in the entire history of the Foundation, was about $440,000 in 1928–1929. This included an exceptional payment of $100,000 on a grant to the New York School of Social Work[1] out of a reserved income fund.

There were shifts in the relative prominence of types of work promoted by grants. By 1918 the anti-tuberculosis movement, which was the leading single object of expenditure in the first decade, had ceased to need grants as it had developed substantial support, notably through the Christmas seal sale, conducted jointly with the American Red Cross. In the second period the ranking position was taken by city and regional planning.

Continuing Grants

Nearly a third of the $4,000,000 entrusted to other agencies in the fourteen years 1918–1931 went to nine grantees carried over from earlier years. Two of the nine received only $1,000 each in the second period. A final payment, in accordance with an understanding reached earlier, was made to the International Children's School Farm League in 1917–1918. In 1926 a contribution was made to the National Tuberculosis Association toward expenses of the meeting of the International Union Against Tuberculosis, held in New York City in September under its auspices.

[1] See p. 459.

Three of the nine continued to receive substantial amounts for several years. The National Committee for the Prevention of Blindness, an outgrowth of early work by the Foundation, was making rapid progress toward self-support. Contributions from the Foundation were discontinued in 1921–1922 in confidence that they were no longer needed. Similarly the New York Probation and Protective Association (later called Girls' Service League), which had been helped by the Foundation with annual grants of money from its beginnings in 1908 and had occupied offices free of rent in the Foundation's building from 1914, was not only expanding its work but was developing its resources at a gratifying rate. A moderate grant of $1,700, in addition to office space, was continued until 1925, when the League was trying to raise a fund of $100,000 for current work and investment in a headquarters building. In terminating the annual grant, the Foundation made a special gift of $5,000, with the request that a room in headquarters be named for Mrs. Sage. In 1929 a contribution of $1,000 was made to the League's Twentieth Anniversary Fund on the recommendation of the general director.

Survey Associates, Inc., to which the Foundation had made annual contributions since 1907, at the end of the war had not only editorial plans for expansion but an encouraging financial outlook. To the Trustees of the Foundation it seemed "desirable and proper" to help them "take advantage of this favorable current to place the organization on a firm and independent footing." Aside from their interest in the success of the journal, they hoped that by giving extra help at this time they would be relieved of further responsibility for its development. In the three fiscal years 1919, 1920, and 1921, accordingly, payments were made amounting to $72,000, an average of $24,000 a year, compared with the $13,400 given in 1917–1918. Grants were then discontinued and were not resumed until 1931.

The other four of the nine grantees carried over from the first period were the State Charities Aid Association of New York, the Charity Organization Society of the City of New York, the Brooklyn Bureau of Charities, and the National Housing Association. These four were among the earliest organizations on the list and were recipients of large amounts. They all received grants for one or more purposes every year to the end of this period and well beyond.

Because of the growing success of the Christmas seal sale, the State Charities Aid Association needed no help from the Foundation after 1919 for its continuing campaign against tuberculosis and its other health work. Its work in behalf of dependent children throughout the state, however, which has been described in Chapter XVIII, was practically financed by the Foundation through a regular grant of $20,000 a year. By 1931 the local committees established through the stimulation of the Association throughout the rural districts and small cities of the state were having an influence of great value in shaping child welfare activities and policies on sound and progressive lines.

In 1920 the state legislature created a commission to revise the laws relating to children. Special grants for several years, totaling $23,500, made it possible for the Association to employ Miss Elsie M. Bond to study the laws and make suggestions for improvement. Many of them were incorporated in the revised laws, and her thorough knowledge of the subject enabled the Association to be influential in preventing the adoption of ill-advised and harmful amendments. When this revision was completed the Association undertook to promote, in co-operation with the State Board of Charities and the State Association of Poor Law Officers, a complete revision of the Poor Law, originally based on the old English statutes, and modified over the years by scores of amendments that merely patched it up and frequently clouded its intention. Toward the expense of this work the Foundation contributed $5,000. Many fundamental improvements were obtained by 1929. Miss Bond, who in the ten years of her work on these laws had come to be recognized at Albany as exceptionally well-informed, able, and impartial in matters with which she was concerned, was continued by the State Charities Aid Association as its legislative representative.

Another special undertaking of the Association to which the Foundation contributed was an educational campaign requested by Governor Alfred E. Smith, to acquaint the people of the state with the need for a $50,000,000 bond issue that was to be submitted to the people in November, 1923.[1] The money was to be used for the construction of state institutions. Overcrowding in hospitals for the insane had become extremely serious, interfering with proper care of the patients and lessening their chances of cure or improvement. There was grave doubt as to what the response of the people might be. They had never before been asked to vote on such a question. The Association organized committees throughout the state to explain conditions in the state hospitals and the need for new buildings. On election day the bond issue was approved by a large majority.

For the anti-tuberculosis work carried on in New York City by committees of the Charity Organization Society and the Brooklyn Bureau of Charities, as for the "upstate" campaign, no grants from the Foundation were needed after 1919. In 1919 the Committee on the Prevention of Tuberculosis of the Charity Organization Society joined other local agencies with allied objects to form the independent New York Tuberculosis Association.[2] Grants to both the Charity Organization Society and the Brooklyn Bureau of Charities for the work of their Tenement House Committees and Committees on Criminal Courts were continued throughout this period.[3]

As in earlier years, the Tenement House Committees followed all legislative proposals and took measures in advocacy or opposition. They carried on a long campaign to rouse public opinion against the city's "conscious or unconscious policy" of "slow starvation" of the Tenement House Department, which resulted in increased appropriations in 1927. They gave much help

---

[1] At the Trustees' meeting Mr. de Forest asked to be recorded as voting in the negative. He was in favor of the bond issue and of the Association's campaign, but he questioned the advisability of the Foundation's making a grant to be used to influence the result of a popular vote.

[2] Later expanded to New York Tuberculosis and Health Association.

[3] In 1918 the Tenement House Committee of the Charity Organization Society was transferred, for administrative purposes, from the Department for the Improvement of Social Conditions to the Department of General Work. Lawrence Veiller, who had been responsible for its creation in 1898 and had guided its development for twenty years, now concentrated his work in the Charity Organization Society on problems of the criminal courts, though as director of the National Housing Association he continued his participation in the housing movement.

to the State Commission to Revise the Tenement House Law, appointed in 1927, both in preparing the new legislation and in promoting its passage. After the Multiple Dwelling Law was signed on April 18, 1929, they co-operated with the special committee that was formed to defend its constitutionality and observe its operation.

For the Committees on Criminal Courts the twenties were a time of great activity. The Charity Organization Society Committee reviewed every bill affecting these courts that came before the legislature and took the lead in initiating and promoting important new measures. In all its work it had the co-operation of the corresponding Committee in the Brooklyn Bureau of Charities, which also constantly studied the work of the inferior courts of Brooklyn and aided in improving their methods.

It was the constant policy of the Charity Organization Society Committee to work co-operatively with public officials, avoiding publicity for itself and seeking no credit. The grants from Russell Sage Foundation made it unnecessary to appeal to the public for funds. Among the accomplishments in this period for which the Committee had a large, frequently the primary or sole, responsibility were a study of the treatment of offenders sixteen to twenty-one years of age in New York City; a thorough study of administration of the criminal law in England; enactment in 1923 of the so-called Wayward Minors' Act, making it possible for parents to enlist aid of the Women's Court in behalf of wayward daughters before they committed any crime; a new Parole Law and a law for "a proper system" of criminal records and statistics, in 1928; successful opposition to a movement in 1929 to abolish the district magistrates' courts and substitute one large centralized court, coupled with a counterproposal to establish a Felony Court in the Magistrates' Court system; preparation, in 1930, and promotion of passage, of a new Family Court Law (in operation October, 1933) which provided, among other things, for a specialized family court, outside the criminal-court system.

In addition to the grants for these co-operative activities of the Charity Organization Society and the Brooklyn Bureau of Charities, each agency received contributions for work not paral-

457

leled in the other. In Brooklyn it was for the training and employment of blind women in a workshop and in their own homes. This work of the Brooklyn Bureau was financed largely by income from an endowment, the Fox Fund. In 1919 reduction of income from its investments created an emergency. The Foundation made a grant of $5,000, on the understanding that it was not to be considered a precedent. The following year, however, renewal was requested by Alfred T. White, president of the Bureau, shortly before his tragic death, because of continued loss of income from securities. Renewal was approved, "in view of the fact that this was Mr. White's last request of the Foundation." Thereafter regular annual contributions were made, but in smaller amounts ($2,500 after 1924). They were used chiefly to pay salaries for teachers of blind women in their homes.

To the Charity Organization Society new grants were made after the war for the School of Social Work,[1] which had received help for its Bureau of Research, but nothing since the Bureau was discontinued in the summer of 1912. The first of the new grants was occasioned by the acute need of competent personnel for expanding social work and by the number of applications for fellowships coming to the School from well-qualified students who without financial help would not be able to attend. This situation led the Foundation to provide fellowships for two exceptionally promising candidates in the academic year 1919–1920 and for another in 1920–1921, and then, beginning in 1921, for ten scholarships in the Summer School each year through 1930. The primary object of the scholarships was to attract men just graduating from college, in the hope that this introduction to social work would lead them to adopt it as their profession and take time for the necessary preparation for it.

Next, in 1921 a combination of circumstances presented a unique opportunity for contributing to the development of education for hospital social service, which was still in its formative stage. A committee of the American Hospital Association had recently completed a survey of hospital social service. One result was the decision by the Association to appoint a committee to

[1] Originally School of Philanthropy, renamed in 1918.

study the problems involved in education for hospital social service in all its complicated aspects—medical, nursing, and administrative, as well as "social." The School's Department of Medical Social Service had been in abeyance for two years, chiefly because of lack of satisfactory arrangements for field work for students, but now the Committee on Dispensary Development, of which Michael M. Davis, Jr., was secretary, was about to begin work, promising better prospects in this direction. Plans were made for Mr. Davis to become director of the School's Department, with Miss M. Antoinette Cannon as assistant. Miss Cannon would also serve as secretary of the committee of the American Hospital Association, which had no funds for its expenses. For seven years the Foundation supplied the money needed, under this arrangement, to meet the expenses of the committee.

By the end of 1924, as attendance continued to increase, the School was finding it increasingly difficult to meet expenses. The Trustees of the Foundation, considering it important that the officers of the School should be free to devote their time to increasing endowment, rather than merely meeting annual deficits, made a grant of $3,000 toward its budget for the year 1924–1925. This became an annual contribution, and was doubled in amount after three or four years.

Not long after making its first contribution to the current expenses of the School, the Foundation gave it an addition to its endowment. This was the only instance in the history of the Foundation of a grant for the purpose of increasing the endowment of a social agency.[1] Early in 1926 Mr. Glenn, "looking ahead several years" to the end of financial obligations for the Regional Plan, suggested to the Trustees the advisability of making other larger grants from time to time as opportunities might arise and funds permit. In January, 1927, he reported that the Income Reserve stood at about $200,000 and that the Regional Plan would need $75,000 less in the following year and still less after that; and proposed a contribution, to be paid out of income, to the endowment of the New York School of Social

---

[1] "One of the best things we ever did," in Mr. Glenn's opinion.

459

Work. After discussion at a later meeting, and then by a small committee of the board, action was taken in November, 1927. A grant of $250,000 was approved: $100,000 to be paid immediately by transfer of securities held for the Income Reserve Account; $150,000 in installments of not less than $30,000 a year. By July, 1931, payments amounted to $205,000.

With annual grants from the Foundation, the National Housing Association continued to collect and distribute information about the progress of the housing movement throughout the United States and in foreign countries, to stimulate interest in it, and to serve as a central bureau of advice. National conferences, which had been regular annual events from 1911 through 1918, were held in 1920, 1923, and 1929. The quarterly bulletin grew in size until in March, 1928, it became the substantial, well-printed quarto magazine Housing, issued four times a year. A numbered series of monographs, chiefly reprints and addresses, had reached No. 62 when it was discontinued in 1930, and a miscellaneous series (unnumbered) contained 10 or 12 items.

Through the proceedings of the conferences and the pages of the magazine a remarkable record was kept of developments in theory and practice in housing reform and related fields. English and continental experience, as well as American, was analyzed and reported. Mr. Veiller took an active part in housing conferences abroad, contributing papers, establishing personal relations with leaders, and collecting material to bring home. All material was systematically classified and filed. Annual bibliographies of 30 to 40 pages listing accessions were published for a number of years. The Association's office became known as the best place to find the text of laws, copies of reports, and other documents, as well as for expert advice.

A report by Mr. Veiller on How England Is Meeting the Housing Shortage, written on his return from the London Conference on Housing in the summer of 1920, attracted much attention. Another notable informative study by him, published in Housing in June, 1931, was a review of the experience of the leading countries of the world in dealing with slum clearance.

In connection with the White House Conference on Child Health and Protection, 1930, Mr. Veiller brought about formulation of proper housing standards for the homes of the children of the country and their adoption by the Conference. As chairman of a committee of the President's Conference on Home Building and Home Ownership, in December, 1931, he prepared an up-to-date statement of standards and objectives of the housing movement, which was presented to the nation by the Conference as "a housing bill of rights."

Aside from the Foundation's grants to the Association, averaging about $12,000 a year, its only appreciable income was dues from members, which reached their maximum of about $5,000 in 1919 and 1920. When the national conference ceased to meet annually, membership dues dwindled. The large amount of work accomplished in the twenties testifies to the devotion and capacity of Lawrence Veiller, who had other exacting obligations throughout the period and at times serious illness, attributed by his physician to overwork.

First New Grants

The first grant to a "new" agency, though not for a new purpose, was made to the National Social Workers' Exchange at the end of 1918. The Exchange had developed from the branch for social workers opened by the Intercollegiate Bureau of Occupations in 1913 with a little financial help from the New York School of Philanthropy and the Foundation and rent-free offices in the Foundation building. Believing that a well-managed placement bureau would be "of fundamental value to social work" in raising the grade of persons employed and the standards of work, and realizing that it was a kind of organization for which it was not easy to raise money, the Foundation gave the independent new Exchange substantial grants in money, as well as free quarters.

When the American Association of Social Workers was organized in the summer of 1921, it took over the Exchange as its central activity. Grants by the Foundation, averaging $10,000 a year, were continued for the vocational bureau of the Association, and in 1925 a new grant of $7,500 was made for an analytic study of requirements in different types of positions. Grants for this purpose were continued until the study was brought to an end. In 1926 the vocational bureau of the American Association of Social Workers and the National Organization for Public Health Nursing were merged to form an independent organization called Joint Vocational Service, which began operations on January 1, 1927, with continued support from the Foundation.

The second new grant, made in January, 1919, was $10,000 to the American Federation of Arts, on the understanding that the Federation would raise $15,000 in addition. This was for a novel purpose, one that Mr. de Forest had much at heart—to bring the beauties of art into the lives of people of small means and in remote communities through traveling exhibits and through inexpensive reproductions of the world's great paintings and photographs of sculpture and architecture, suitable for hanging in homes, schools, and libraries. Allen Eaton was engaged by the Federation to take charge of this extension program and in 1920 he was added to the staff of the Foundation's Department of Surveys and Exhibits. Unlike most of the Foundation's grants when first made, this one from the beginning was expected to be a continuing obligation for some years. It was renewed annually in the same amount through 1932, and then in diminishing amounts for several years longer.

In contrast with these first two new grants, each of which entailed a long series of subsequent expenditures, were two single payments made about the same time. To the New York Committee on Aftercare of Infantile Paralysis Cases, formed to coordinate all the efforts in the city to provide treatment and appliances for children left crippled by the epidemic of 1916, a contribution of $5,000 was made in April, 1919. It was hoped that a permanent federation of agencies for crippled children would be a result of the Committee's work. The other instance was a grant of $1,000 in the summer of 1919 to Robert A. Woods of Boston, to defray the expense of a guide and interpreter for him in Japan and China on a visit he was about to make at the request of the secretary of the Young Men's Christian Associations in China. It was understood that he would "make some investigation of social conditions in those countries and report to the Foundation, in order that it may have some basis for determining whether it can properly do anything to aid in improving social conditions in those countries."

REGIONAL AND CITY PLANNING

Measured by amount of expenditure, regional and city planning was the leading object of grants between the war and the great depression. Grants for various aspects of this and allied purposes[1] amounted to about $1,500,000 in the fourteen years, not including large contributions of free rent and free services. This was about 38 per cent of the total expenditure for grants in the period, compared with approximately 28 per cent for the leading purpose in the first decade, prevention of tuberculosis.

Considerably more than two-thirds of the $1,500,000 was for the survey of New York and its environs and preparation of a plan for future development of the region. Expenditure for this undertaking began in May, 1921.

Two years earlier the first of a series of grants for promoting interest in city planning throughout the country and appreciation of sound principles had been made to the National Conference on City Planning. Assistance had been given to the National Conference between 1910 and 1914, incidental to the preparation of the book by Flavel Shurtleff and Frederick Law Olmsted on Carrying Out the City Plan. Government activity in housing during the war aroused new interest in planning among city engineers, landscape architects, and builders, and new appreciation of the importance of co-operation. In 1919 the time seemed auspicious for a campaign to enlarge the membership of the Conference and make it self-supporting. With the help of grants from the Foundation good progress was made in the next few years.

[1] Including the sums given for continuing work for improvement of housing conditions.

In the fall of 1924 a merger was arranged of the National Conference on City Planning, the American Civic Association, the National Parks Association, the National Conference on State Parks, and the American Park Society, under the title of the Federated Societies on Planning and Parks. The Foundation contributed to the expenses of effecting the amalgamation and of carrying on the new agency during its brief existence, and then, from 1927 and 1928 respectively, made annual grants to the National Conference on City Planning and the American Civic Association. Grants to these two agencies were continued to the end of this period and beyond. Aggregate expenditure for these kindred agencies amounted to about $84,000 for the period ending September 30, 1931.

In addition to the large grants direct to the Committee on Regional Plan, two smaller ones were made to other agencies for purposes that would contribute to its work: $500 in 1924 to the New York State Association, toward the cost of printing and distributing its report on a comprehensive and unified plan of state parks; $2,500 in 1925 to the International Planning Congress toward the expenses of its highly successful conference and exhibit, brought to New York City in April of that year largely through the efforts of Mr. Adams and Mr. Shurtleff; and in 1926 a grant of $10,000 was made to the National Municipal League for a study of the problems of "regional government" in planning that crosses political boundaries.

The Committee on Regional Plan and its friends realized that the Plan would not go into effect automatically after its publication. Accordingly in 1929 the Regional Plan Association was incorporated, with George McAneny as president, for the purpose of promoting adoption of the Committee's recommendations and continuing its work. In the spring of 1929 the Foundation made a grant of $25,000 "to enable the Association to get a proper start and secure contributions from other sources." Prospects for contributions from other sources were soon dimmed by the general financial situation of the country, though as late as October, 1930, it was still hoped that the Association would soon be able to meet its obligations without further support from the

Foundation. If not, the Trustees agreed it would be better to make additional advances, to be repaid if possible, than that the Association should reduce its expenditures to a point where it would cease to be effective.

At the very end of this period, the increasing difficulty in obtaining contributions brought a request for help to the Foundation from the Zoning Committee of New York City. This committee had been organized in 1916 by Frederic B. Pratt, Lawson Purdy, Edward M. Bassett, and Herbert S. Swan, to support the pioneer zoning laws, just passed, and to promote the principle of zoning, then in its infancy, throughout the state and in cities outside the state. In view of the intimate relation of its work to city and regional planning, a small grant was made to meet this emergency.[1]

Housing

Toward the improvement of housing conditions, the Foundation contributed steadily in other ways throughout this period, as has already been told, by its annual grants to the Tenement House Committees of New York and Brooklyn and to the National Housing Association. In the late twenties an occasion was presented for smaller, temporary grants in the same field. A commission to examine and suggest revision of the Tenement House Law of New York was created by the state legislature of 1927. When the commission finished its work, it did not have enough money left out of its appropriation of $25,000 to print its report. The Foundation provided funds for this purpose. The new Multiple Dwelling Law proposed by the commission superseded the old Tenement House Law on April 18, 1929. Foreseeing that the new law would be subject to attack and would stand in need of understanding help through a period of adjustment to the complicated conditions existing in the city, the lay members of the commission constituted themselves a committee to support it, observe its operation, promote improvements, and prevent unde-

---

[1] Assistance was continued year after year through the continuing emergency and until in 1942 the Committee disbanded because it had "successfully accomplished" its major purposes. (See p. 656.)

sirable amendments. The Foundation made a small grant to defray incidental expenses.

NATIONAL ASSOCIATIONS

Another prominent object of grants between the war and the depression, second only to planning in amount of money given, was the development of national associations of agencies and individuals to promote acquaintance and raise standards in their respective fields of social work. To six of these associations the Foundation made grants aggregating not far from half a million dollars in this period. The general object of all these grants was to enable the associations to improve and expand their work and to increase their income from memberships and other sources.

The American Association for Organizing Family Social Work had been formed in 1911 at the instance of the Foundation's Charity Organization Department, to carry on and develop the field work of the Department. Although it had not previously received grants in money from the Foundation, it had received every year the equivalent of substantial financial assistance. It shared the offices of the Department in the United Charities Building and after 1913 in the Foundation's building; Mr. Hall spent large blocks of time on several of its projects; both Miss Richmond and Mr. Hall advised on its problems; and incidental help was given in various ways by other members of the Foundation's staff.

In the spring of 1919 the Association applied for a grant of $20,000 for the coming year in order that it might increase its staff of field workers and launch a monthly magazine, The Family. There was exceptional need, under postwar conditions, of strengthening the charity organization societies already in existence, and exceptional opportunities to organize new societies. Success in stimulating its members to greater activity and in effecting the establishment of new societies brought mounting requests for service to the Association. Its efforts to increase income were moderately successful but were hampered by the depression of 1920–1921 and could not keep up with mounting expenses. The grant of 1919 for a single year was followed by a series of regular annual contributions for its general work. In 1927 the Foundation made an additional grant to enable the Association to wipe out an accumulated deficit and establish a Finance and Extension Service on a firm basis. This also became a continuing annual contribution. A special grant was made toward the expenses of the celebration of the fiftieth anniversary of the founding of the first charity organization society in America, held under the auspices of the Association in Buffalo in the fall of 1927.[1]

Free office space and other contributions "in kind" were continued throughout the period. Money grants to the Association for all purposes to the end of 1930–1931 amounted to over $300,000, about 45 per cent more than was spent during the same time for the Charity Organization Department of the Foundation, of which the Association was an outgrowth.

Another national association that had grown out of the work of the Foundation was the Child Welfare League of America. Originating in 1915 as an informal co-operative association of child-caring agencies for exchange of information and promotion of acquaintance, its work was done for three years in Dr. Hart's office by C. Spencer Richardson, associate director of the Child-Helping Department of the Foundation. When Mr. Richardson went to France in the summer of 1918 other arrangements were made to continue a minimum service. After the war the agencies interested began to make plans for expansion into an organization comparable in its field to the American Association for Organizing Family Social Work. With promise of generous help from the Commonwealth Fund, the Child Welfare League of America was organized in 1920, under C. C. Carstens as director. The Foundation provided free offices from the beginning, and in 1926, when the grant of the Commonwealth Fund was expiring, made a substantial contribution to its budget. Annual contributions were made in the following years.

Beginning in 1922 the Foundation made annual grants, doubled after the first few years, to the American Association of Hospital Social Workers, an association of individuals rather

[1] See p. 317.

than of agencies. It had been organized in 1918, to serve as a center of intercommunication, to improve standards, and to stimulate the introduction and expansion of social service departments in hospitals and dispensaries. Miss Ida M. Cannon, who had written for the Foundation the pioneer book on this subject, was president of the Association. This grant supplemented the one given for several years in the twenties to the New York School of Social Work for its department of medical social service.

The National Association of Legal Aid Organizations was formed in 1923 to promote the organization of new societies, improve standards of work, co-operate with the judiciary and the bar, and study particular problems involved in providing legal services for persons unable to pay for them. By 1927 there were 28 local societies in its membership. Both the national organization and many of its members gave much help to the Foundation's Department of Remedial Loans. When a contribution was asked by the Association toward its budget for the year 1927 it was given, and this began a series of annual grants.

An older national association applied to the Foundation for a grant for the year 1929. The National Association of Travelers Aid Societies had been formed in 1917 for the purpose of developing co-operation among the local societies in different cities, standardizing and improving their methods of work, and of promoting the organization of new societies in cities where they were needed. In the twelve years, with the aid of grants from two foundations, it had made great progress in all three directions. Grants from other foundations had now ceased, and income from the constituent societies and from other contributors, although it was increasing, was not yet adequate. Russell Sage Foundation gave $10,000 for the year 1929, "at least $5,000 of which shall be used for increasing its income from other sources." The grant was renewed annually in the same amount for several years, and then at a diminishing rate.

As national associations of local agencies in various fields multiplied and became conscious of common problems and common interests, an association of associations was a natural development. During the war executives of several of the national associations were thrown together in their work for the Commission on Training Camp Activities. Howard S. Braucher, secretary of the Playground and Recreation Association of America, was so impressed with the advantage of the closer acquaintance thus fostered that after the war was over he took the initiative in arranging an occasional gathering of the group. In September, 1920, twelve of the executives decided to meet regularly once a month at lunch, to talk over matters of common interest. The group had no name, no constitution, no treasury. Mr. Braucher acted as chairman and David H. Holbrook, who had recently come to New York as executive director of the American Association for Organizing Family Social Work, performed such secretarial services as were indispensable. After two years the participants were convinced that a more formal organization would be appropriate and that the full time of an able executive was needed. Organization was effected about a year later, under the name National Social Work Council. The Laura Spelman Rockefeller Memorial pledged $10,000 a year for three years. The Foundation agreed to give $10,000 for the year 1924, to provide for the employment of a competent secretary, "with the expectation that, should the necessity for continued employment of this secretary be demonstrated, the national societies included in the Council will themselves provide the necessary means to carry this work on after the expiration of the year 1924," and on the understanding that the Foundation would not provide more than half the expenses during that year.

Delay in deciding on the "competent secretary," Mr. Holbrook, and further delay while he was completing obligations in his previous position, postponed opening of the Council's office until August 1, 1925. The $10,000 grant of Russell Sage Foundation sufficed to meet half the expenses to the end of the calendar year 1926. In May, 1927, Mr. Glenn recommended that the Foundation make another grant sufficient to cover half the expenditures for the year beginning May 1, 1927, but not to exceed $10,000. The national agencies associated in the Council, he said, were not at the time in position to do anything toward its support as their own financial problems were "extremely difficult." The Council, which was "proving to be something in the nature of a much needed national or central board of strategy and planning for social work," would, it was expected, "help the agencies to solve these difficulties."

From this time forward the Foundation annually or semi-annually renewed its assurance of aid, not to exceed half the Council's expenditures. Until 1929 the other half was supplied from the $30,000 grant of the Spelman Fund. In 1930 a number of the national agencies began to contribute "to the extent and in the manner permitted by their circumstances." Besides grants in money, the Foundation contributed largely to the Council's development through the personal interest and participation of the general director and members of its departmental staff. In acknowledging payments, the secretary regularly referred, in one way or another, to "our even greater dependence on you for the encouragement and assistance you so freely give."

In objects and methods the National Social Work Council was unique among agencies in social work. Its purpose was not to conduct "activities" but to stimulate thinking. Its method was that of the informal association from which it sprang, to provide a meeting ground for free exchange of thought. Temptations to expand staff and premises and to complicate administrative machinery were resisted. Mr. Braucher, who continued as chairman of the Council after its formal organization, never wavered in his belief that limitation of executive staff and office facilities was a protection, a help in keeping to the original basic ideal of the Council as a center for thinking together. Accomplishments of an agency with such methods and such ideals are not spectacular. Until the depression forced the Council to undertake "special projects," its contributions to social welfare were hardly appreciated outside its own membership, and even among its members they were so intangible that they were taken for granted and rarely formulated. "To me," said Linton B. Swift in 1929, "the significance of the National Social Work Council has not been so much in the practical suggestions which have come out of it . . . but rather that basic philosophy which is the mother of invention." In that philosophy he had found many ideas that could be the source of invention in his own "particular job." Its founder and chairman, Mr. Braucher, writing in 1932, said that, while he recognized that the Council was of distinct value to the national movements represented in it, he thought of it primarily as an instrument through which all the national movements could "help in making a contribution to the united thinking of the social work movement as a whole."

SERVICE AGENCIES

In addition to the agencies providing particular services that have already been mentioned a number of others in this category received grants from the Foundation for the first time between the war and the depression. Most of them had not been in existence before the war. Some were national in scope, some local.

One of the new agencies was the National Information Bureau, incorporated in 1917 to supply reliable information to its members about national agencies appealing to the public for support. From 1920 on the Foundation contributed to its expenses: at first by an annual membership fee of $1,000 and in 1923 by a special grant of $3,000 to clear up a deficit in connection with a study of a number of important agencies made by Porter R. Lee and Walter W. Pettit; from 1928 until 1940 by an annual contribution of $2,000 toward its budget.

A new national agency in which the Foundation had a natural interest because of its origin as well as its purpose was the American Country Life Association. It was organized in 1919—on the very day, as it happened, that Theodore Roosevelt died— through the initiative of men who had served on the Roosevelt Commission of 1908. The object of the Association was to promote discussion of rural problems, to further efforts for their solution, to disseminate information calculated to produce better understanding of country life. After holding two annual conferences and effecting the organization of a National Council of Agencies Engaged in Rural Social Work, the Association decided that the time was favorable for expansion. A full-time executive secretary was engaged; a monthly bulletin was started; and a service of advice and information was instituted.

Mr. Hanmer and Mr. Perry were active in the Association from its early days.[1] In the summer of 1923 the Foundation gave $3,000 to meet the cost of printing the proceedings of 1921 and 1922. In December it promised $10,000 for the year 1924 (half of it conditional on the raising of at least $15,000 from other sources), to be used for publications and for establishing a finance and membership bureau, in order to "put the Association on a solid foundation."

For several years receipts from other sources increased encouragingly, but expenses increased faster. The Foundation renewed its grant annually, hoping that with this help the Association would be able to establish "an ampler and sounder financial footing." When the depression made such hopes vain and at the same time reduced the funds available for grants by the Foundation, assistance was continued, but in smaller amounts. Throughout the twenties the Association was a strong educational influence. Each of its annual conferences had a large and enthusiastic attendance and produced a volume of valuable papers. Its monthly bulletin was full of useful information. Such special activities as the conference of farm women, held in the early twenties, and the program on Rural Social Work in connection with the National Conference of Social Work at Des Moines in 1927, were stimulating events. Its central idea, wrote one of its directors in 1929, was "the need for a co-ordinated country-life program in which each of the special-interest groups develops its work with a view to its place in the total program." "The acceptance of this idea," he added, "with its resulting friendly co-ordination of efforts, appears to be gaining steadily."

A local effort for improving economic conditions was the Farmers Federation, Inc., a co-operative association of farmers around Asheville, North Carolina. After several years of marked success in increasing their market and improving methods of production a fund was sought in 1927 for developing co-operation among farmers over a larger area of the Appalachian Mountain

[1] As was Mr. Eaton in the thirties.

region. The Foundation contributed $5,000 to this fund, payable in annual installments of not less than $1,000. This initial appropriation was exhausted in 1930–1931.

Three new grants in this period were to agencies engaged in work for improving the condition of Negroes. Following the exploratory survey of conditions in Harlem by George E. Haynes in the summer of 1921, the Federal Council of the Churches of Christ in America chose Mr. Haynes to be secretary of its new Commission on Church and Race Relations (later called Department of Race Relations). The Commission was created at the request of an Atlanta committee composed of white and Negro citizens, which for two years had been developing better understanding and sympathy between the two races, chiefly by means of frank discussion. It was the purpose of the Commission to promote the formation of similar committees in other cities and to stimulate the interest of the churches in questions of race relations. To these ends it served as a clearinghouse for information; promoted the observance of Race Relations Sunday, when white and Negro ministers exchanged pulpits; protested against mob violence; and sought to further equitable provision for the Negro in education, housing, recreation, and medical care, and fair opportunities of employment.

To this work of the Federal Council the Foundation from the start made annual contributions averaging about $5,000. To the National Urban League, organized in 1910, it began to make a small grant in 1931, when continuation of certain of its activities relating to employment of Negroes was threatened by the depression. Annual grants of $5,000 to the Atlanta School of Social Work, a pioneer enterprise for training Negro social workers, were begun in 1925. This institution, established in 1920, had been developed largely through the efforts of Miss Helen B. Pendleton, supervisor of casework for the American Red Cross in Atlanta, with co-operation from local social agencies and Negro colleges. When the American Red Cross in 1924 decided it could not continue its appropriation for a supervisor, a grant was obtained from the Laura Spelman Rockefeller Memorial for 1924–1925, which was renewed in a smaller amount ($5,000) for

1925–1926. An equal amount for 1925–1926 was promised by the Foundation if it could be matched by contributions from other sources. This grant has been renewed from year to year through 1946.

In behalf of the foreign-born, who like the Negroes were a handicapped element of the population but with somewhat different disadvantages, grants were made to four new agencies. The Foreign Language Information Service, organized in 1918 to assist and assimilate the immigrant and to promote tolerance and better understanding among the people of the United States, had an extensive program by 1922. It was supplying about 800 newspapers printed in foreign languages with translations, ready for them to use, of information about American life and institutions; encouraging adult-education activities by agencies interested in immigrants; providing reliable information on questions related to immigration and naturalization; advising individual immigrants; and in various ways was interpreting the immigrant to America as well as America to the immigrant. It had pledges of $150,000 from two foundations and one individual toward a budget of $200,000. Russell Sage Foundation began annual contributions of $5,000 in 1923, and a few years later made a special gift of $5,000 to be used in increasing its resources.

In New York City an emergency Committee on the Education of Non-English-Speaking Women was developing a new method of teaching foreign-born women English, sending teachers to visit among them, organize small classes of neighbors, and arrange for a convenient meeting place in one of the homes. Initial results were so encouraging that the Committee, which soon changed its name to Education Committee for Non-English-Speaking Women, and in 1927 to Neighborhood Teacher Association, hoped to make a demonstration sufficiently impressive to bring about general adoption of its method. Toward the cost of this demonstration the Foundation made a contribution of $5,000 in 1923, conditional on the obtaining of $25,000 more, and continued to help for a number of years.

The Council on Adult Education for the Foreign-Born, also a New York City agency, received its first grant from the Foundation in September, 1931, the last month of this period. It was a small contribution toward the expense of preparing an exhibit of teaching material to be held in the Foundation halls.

Annual grants to the American Branch of the International Migration Service began in 1925, "in view of the value of this work to families in America and to various American national and local social agencies and to our own federal government, and in view of the difficulty of raising the funds in the early stages of the work." Originating in 1921 as "Migration Service, World's YWCA," the purpose of the Service was to give help to individuals whose problems were a consequence of migration and involved action in more than one country, and to study from an international standpoint the conditions and consequences of migration in their effect on individual, family, and social life.

In the creation and development of the Welfare Council of New York City grants from the Foundation had an important part. Mr. de Forest was chairman of the Committee on Co-ordination of Social Agencies in New York City, appointed in 1924 to elaborate the winning plan in a contest sponsored by the magazine Better Times for plans to promote the effectiveness of the social agencies of the city through closer association among them. The Foundation contributed to the expenses of this committee. When the Council was organized in 1925 in pursuance of the Committee's recommendations, William Hodson, director of the Foundation's Department of Social Legislation, was chosen as its first executive. Annual contributions toward the general expenses of the Council were made by the Foundation, and were supplemented by special grants for special purposes. In the fall of 1930, for example, when the Council created a Co-ordinating Committee on Unemployment Relief, for which there was obvious need, increasing as the depression deepened, annual contributions toward the extra expense were begun, in the same amount as the grants for the general work of the Council.

Temporary help was given during the twenties to several local agencies: to the New York Federation of Agencies for Homeless Men, formed by 13 agencies in the depression of 1920–1921 to help in maintaining a central registration bureau for homeless applicants, which would refer them to the appropriate agencies; to the Caroline Country Club for social workers in 1926, toward cost of repairs and alterations on the clubhouse; to the Citizens Committee on Teachers' Salaries, toward the expense of obtaining action in 1927 on the recommendations made in its report on standardizing salaries in the public schools of New York City; to the Family Welfare Society of Queens, Inc., for several years beginning in 1927, to establish and maintain an extension department for developing interest in the Society and increasing support for it; to the Employment Center for the Handicapped, from its organization in 1928 by the merging of four agencies following a study made by the Foundation for the Welfare Council.[1] An unusual application was received by the Foundation in 1927 from the Nassau Industrial School, established by Mrs. Sage in 1907 near her summer home on Long Island, with an endowment that had yielded sufficient income for operating expenses until the war. Since her death the management had devolved on a group of her personal friends, who were now seeking an addition to the endowment, in order to assure the annual income needed under changed conditions. The Trustees agreed with Mr. de Forest that this represented an obligation to Mrs. Sage's memory and contributed half the $15,000 sought for additional endowment.

STUDIES AND DEMONSTRATIONS

Several studies and demonstrations conducted under other auspices received financial aid from the Foundation, and in some cases participation by members of the staff as well.

In 1919 Dr. Raymond Pearl, of the Johns Hopkins University, began a study on the relation of physical and social environment to tuberculosis. The National Tuberculosis Association provided $10,000 for the investigation. After six months of work a fire destroyed all his records. The National Tuberculosis Association could not duplicate its appropriation. On the request of Dr. William H. Welch, the Foundation contributed $8,000 toward the cost of completing the investigation.

[1] See p. 387.

Soon after the organization of the Federated American Engineering Societies, Herbert Hoover, its first president, appointed in January, 1921, a committee to investigate the causes of labor waste in industry. The Foundation contributed $10,000 toward the cost, estimated at $79,000. With the co-operation of some 80 engineers and their associates the committee within five months completed analyses of the building, textile, and printing trades, and of the manufacture of men's clothing and of boots and shoes. Its report, Waste in Industry, was presented to the American Engineering Council in June, 1921.

To the National Research Council the Foundation made a grant for the exploratory work of its Committee on Human Migration, of which Miss van Kleeck was a member, appointed in 1922 to consider whether scientific studies of the effects of migration were practicable and if so what studies should be made. It was an opportunity to focus on the social problems of immigration and emigration, contributions from biology, anthropology, psychology, economics and other social sciences, and the experience of social workers. The committee mapped an extensive plan for research. In 1925 responsibility for the social aspects was assumed by the Social Science Research Council.[1]

The Committee on the Costs of Medical Care was formed in 1927 to make a five-year survey of the economic aspects of the care and prevention of illness, and to formulate, on the basis of the facts gathered, recommendations that would point the way to the provision of adequate care for all at reasonable cost and at the same time assure adequate income to physicians, nurses, and others concerned. Dr. Ray Lyman Wilbur was chairman of the Committee, and Harry H. Moore of the United States Public Health Service was director of its studies. Toward the administrative budget of the Committee the Foundation made an annual contribution of $5,000 for five years and a smaller final grant in 1932.

A demonstration of the therapeutic and educational value of music in treatment of the insane and of wayward girls, begun during the war, was carried on after the war under the auspices

[1] See p. 479.

of the Committee on Music in Institutions, formed for the purpose, of which Mr. Hanmer was secretary. Grants were made by the Foundation for three years, 1922–1924, to underwrite the salary of Willem van de Wall, who conducted the demonstration. The money represented only a small part of the Foundation's contributions, which extended over many years.[1]

In 1921 the Central Committee of the American Red Cross, in co-operation with the Department of Health of New York City and a number of private health agencies, established the East Harlem Health Center, to demonstrate the advantage of bringing together in one place the various health facilities available for the population of a district of 100,000 inhabitants. The building housed clinics, nursing services, and a "health shop" for lectures, exhibits, classes, and distribution of posters and other educational material. By the end of three years the anticipated advantages were apparent in a greatly increased use of the facilities provided. The Red Cross, considering the demonstration made, withdrew its appropriations, and the co-operating agencies needed outside help to continue the Center. The Foundation made annual grants toward the cost of maintenance from 1924, and a special contribution in 1929 to a campaign for raising a fund for a new building. Early in the depression the Center was incorporated into the city's system of health centers under the Department of Health.

Before the depression was a year old a State Advisory Council on Employment Problems was appointed by Miss Frances Perkins, industrial commissioner of New York. On recommendation of the Advisory Council an "employment bureau demonstration" was undertaken in Rochester, to study qualifications needed in the personnel of a public employment office, formulate specifications for the various positions, and outline a pattern of procedure. Mr. Glenn and Miss van Kleeck, as well as Mr. Harrison, were in close touch with the plans. William Hodson, of the Welfare Council, served as treasurer for the Demonstration. The Foundation contributed $5,000 to the budget of $75,000 for the year 1931, without commitment for later years.

[1] See p. 327.

An event of major importance to everyone interested in the study of social conditions was the organization in 1923 of the Social Science Research Council, on the initiative of the American Political Science Association, the American Sociological Society, and the American Economic Association. Its purpose was the promotion, development, and co-ordination of research in the social sciences and the encouragement of scientific methods and adequate technical training for such work. Mr. Harrison represented the American Sociological Society on the Council and was a member of its Committee on Problems and Policy, serving as secretary of this committee for several years. Miss van Kleeck was a member, and for a time secretary, of its Committee on Methods of Research. Beginning in 1925 the Foundation made annual contributions to the administrative expenses of the Council.

Conferences and Publications

After the Southern Highland Division of the Foundation came to an end in 1919, contributions in relatively small amounts were continued toward the expenses of the Conference of Southern Mountain Workers, which owed its origin to the Division. In the twelve years of this period the amount averaged a little over $1,000 a year.

Toward the expenses of the National Interracial Conference held in Washington in December, 1928, the Foundation gave $1,000. A much larger contribution by the Foundation consisted of several months of Miss van Kleeck's time, who was chairman of the executive committee of the Conference, presided at its discussions, and helped to prepare the studies and the proceedings for publication.

In 1923 the National Conference of Social Work celebrated its fiftieth anniversary in Washington. Toward the extraordinary expenses involved in making this a noteworthy occasion, the Foundation contributed $10,000—an absolute grant of $5,000, and an additional $5,000 conditioned on the obtaining of $30,000 from other sources. Contributions were made also toward the cost of preliminary planning for the first International Conference of Social Work, held in Paris in 1928, and toward the budget of the second, to be held in 1932 at Frankfurt am Main. Miss van Kleeck took part in the program of the Paris meeting, and in 1929 was elected vice-president of the executive board of the International Conference.

Two new periodicals in the field of social work had financial encouragement from the Foundation in getting started during this period. Both were founded by George J. Hecht of New York City. Better Times, a small monthly sheet reporting news of the social agencies of the city, was intended to promote closer relations among the agencies by keeping them informed of their respective activities. For four years, 1922–1925, the Foundation contributed to the cost of publication. After the Welfare Council was established, as a result of a contest conducted by Better Times, the magazine became the organ of the Council.

Mr. Hecht's other publishing venture in this period was eventually a spectacular success financially as well as in its influence. He organized in 1926 a limited-dividend corporation, Parents' Publishing Association, Inc. (later, Parents' Institute, Inc.), to publish a new magazine, Children, A Magazine for Parents. The Foundation subscribed $5,000 for the purchase of capital stock, because there seemed to be "a place and a need" for such a magazine and Mr. Hecht was believed to have the ability to develop it. The subscription was in the nature of a grant, not an investment. It was paid out of income. About ten years later the corporation began paying dividends to stockholders. In 1944 a recapitalization plan was adopted, whereby the stock was replaced by twenty-five-year income bonds. By 1946 the Foundation had already received substantial pecuniary returns and its "grant" had become an income-producing asset. The original publication, now called Parents' Magazine, had a paid circulation of more than 700,000, and the Institute was issuing several specialized publications in its field.

Two other publications useful to social work, different from the periodicals just mentioned and different from each other, were furthered by the Foundation in this period. To the Cities Census Committee of New York, organized to obtain tabulation of the federal census returns for New York City by small tracts and as promptly as possible, grants amounting to $44,000 were made in the years 1924–1932 toward the expense of preparing and publishing the material. The tabulation was of basic value to many local health and social agencies and to the studies of the Committee on Regional Plan.

In January, 1927, plans for an Encyclopaedia of the Social Sciences had been matured by the committee representing the seven learned societies that had initiated the project three years earlier, and funds were being sought to meet the cost of production, estimated at $550,000. Russell Sage Foundation promised $25,000, to be paid in installments over the six years it was expected would be required to complete the work. The last installment on this grant was paid in 1931. The following year, as additional funds were found to be needed, a supplementary grant of $2,500 was made. The Encyclopaedia, for which the need had long been realized, was welcomed as a work of general reference, invaluable to students of social conditions and efforts for their improvement.

PART FIVE
DEPRESSION AND WAR

XXXIII

GENERAL VIEW: 1932-1946

THE FINAL period of this record began in September, 1931, when Shelby M. Harrison became the Foundation's second general director, and extends to October, 1946. It was a period of upheaval, socially and politically. The nation was already in the grip of a depression, the severity and length of which were then unguessed. Only partial recovery had occurred when war broke out in Europe, instituting in America a defense period which shortly gave way to the violent exertions and adjustments of global, all-out war, on a scale without parallel. The period ended in October, 1946, with the United Nations ready to begin sessions at Lake Success, New York, but with the end of hostilities not yet officially declared, and with the peoples of the world facing the tremendous implications, for evil or for good, of the release of atomic energy.

In such a period the program of a foundation devoted to "the improvement of social and living conditions in the United States" had to be tempered to the realities of emergencies, with sometimes the emphasis on prevention of further deterioration rather than "improvement"; but the long goal was not forgotten.

COMPOSITION OF THE BOARD

In September, 1931, the Board of Trustees consisted of nine persons, Johnston de Forest, Frederic A. Delano, John H. Finley, John M. Glenn, Mrs. Frederic S. Lee, Dwight W. Morrow, Lawson Purdy, Mrs. Finley J. Shepard, and Harold T. White.

Only four of these trustees remained on the Board in October, 1946. Mr. Morrow died on October 5, 1931. Mrs. Shepard resigned in February, 1936.[1] As Helen Gould, she had been one of the incorporators with Mrs. Sage; after her resignation Mr.

---

[1] She died December 21, 1938.

Glenn was the only member of the original group still on the Board. The remaining woman member, Mrs. Lee, died on November 5, 1938.

Mr. Delano found his duties on the National Resources Planning Board in Washington increasingly heavy, and declined re-election when his term expired in November, 1939. Mr. Finley died on March 7, 1940; he was serving his twenty-seventh year on the Board, having been nominated by Mrs. Sage in 1913.

In addition to the vacancies created by these five deaths and resignations, three more places were created by the only important amendment to the constitution adopted during this period. The Board had consisted of nine trustees, serving without term. In March, 1934, the number was increased to twelve, with provision for three-year terms, arranged so that each year the terms of four trustees would expire. This new provision did not result in rapid changes in the Board, however; in the twelve succeeding years of this record, all trustees with expiring terms have been re-elected except for the two resignations already noted.

Lindsay Bradford, vice-president of the City Bank—Farmers Trust Company and a member of the executive committee of the Charity Organization Society of New York, was elected trustee in November, 1933, to fill the vacancy created by Mr. Morrow's death.

After the 1934 change in the constitution creating three new vacancies, Joseph P. Chamberlain, professor of public law in Columbia University, was elected in March, 1934, followed in May by Morris Hadley, of the law firm of Milbank, Tweed and Hope. The third vacancy was filled in February, 1936, with the election of Harry Woodburn Chase, chancellor of New York University and already a trustee of the General Education Board and the Phelps-Stokes Fund.

In November, 1939, upon the decision of Mr. Delano not to serve longer, the Trustees elected Arthur H. Ham, vice-president and executive officer of the Provident Loan Society of New York and from 1909 to 1918 director of the Foundation's Division of Remedial Loans.

Two trustees were elected at the 1940 annual meeting, Professor Robert M. MacIver, faculty member at Barnard College and Columbia University, and Dave H. Morris, Jr., vice-president of the Bank of New York. When the war began, Mr. Morris was sent on a mission to the Pacific as a captain in the armed forces, and submitted his resignation as of February, 1942; the Trustees did not accept his resignation, however, asking him to remain on the Board, with attendance excused for the period of the war.

The final election during this period was that of Eli Whitney Debevoise, of the law firm of Debevoise, Stevenson, Plimpton, and Page.

In October, 1946, the Board was at its full strength of twelve. Its members were the eight trustees elected during this period together with four trustees remaining from the earlier Board, Mr. Johnston de Forest, Mr. Glenn, Mr. Purdy, and Mr. White.

Changes in Officers

After Robert W. de Forest died in the spring of 1931, the Trustees did not immediately elect a new president. Mr. Purdy, vice-president since 1926, continued to serve in that office, and as acting president, until November, 1936, when he was elected president. He also served as treasurer until May, 1937. After seven annual re-elections as president, Mr. Purdy expressed his desire to be relieved of the duties of that office, and his resignation was accepted at the May, 1944, meeting of the Trustees. Mr. Hadley was elected president at the November meeting, and remains in office.

Mr. Hadley had succeeded Mr. Purdy in the combined offices of vice-president and treasurer. When he in turn was elevated to the presidency, the offices were separated, and since November, 1944, Professor Chamberlain has been vice-president and Mr. Ham has been treasurer.

Upon his resignation as general director in 1931, Mr. Glenn continued as secretary to the Board, and has remained in that position. He has an office in the Foundation building and has been active in Foundation counsels.

The assistant secretary throughout the fifteen years of this record has been Johnston de Forest.

Mr. Harrison has been general director throughout the period, beginning his term of office on September 1, 1931. In addition to performing the administrative duties of this distressed time, he has served in many other capacities related to the interests of the Foundation. At the beginning of the period, he was completing his work as a member of the President's Research Committee on Social Trends; this and his other activities in the field of surveys are elsewhere noted.[1] He has been a member of the Social Science Research Council since 1925, and chairman of its executive committee for twelve years, from 1933 to 1945. He was president of the National Conference of Social Work in 1942, the first year of World War II, delivering at New Orleans his presidential address, "Attacking on Social Work's Three Fronts." His was the first Conference presidency by a person concurrently active on the Foundation staff.[2] In 1945 he was appointed a member of the allocations committee, United National Clothing Collection for overseas war relief. He was chairman of a committee appointed by the National Council of the Young Men's Christian Associations which has made two studies of YMCA services among Negro youth in urban communities, and a member of the Research Council set up by that body a few years ago. He has been a member, since its establishment, of the General Committee of the Department of Research and Education, Federal Council of the Churches of Christ in America, and, earlier, of the Commission on the Church and Social Service. Both he and Mr. Glenn were appointed delegates to the National Social Welfare Assembly, and assisted in the plans for its organization. Mr. Harrison delivered a number of addresses and has received two honorary degrees, from Northwestern University in 1932 and Boston University in 1942. In the fall of 1946, he announced his plan to retire on July 1, 1947, at the completion of thirty-five years with Russell Sage Foundation.

[1] See p. 566.

[2] Other Conference presidents closely associated with the Foundation, but not at the time of their presidency, were Hastings H. Hart in 1893, John M. Glenn in 1901, Robert W. de Forest in 1903, and William Hodson in 1934.

In September, 1943, the Trustees created the new position of assistant general director, to which Russell H. Kurtz was appointed.

THE GREAT DEPRESSION

The severe depression, which was to last almost ten years, brought heavy problems to a foundation organized "for the improvement of social and living conditions." Reduction in its own income was one of them, but because of the types of investment which had been made, this reduction was gradual, extending over a number of years. The urgent problem was how to plan expenditures and program to meet the public emergency.

There were those on the outside who were sure that they knew. The Foundation should abandon its regular program, they sincerely believed, and help feed the starving.

A meeting of the Trustees was called in November, 1931, for sole consideration of this question. They had memoranda prepared, presenting the arguments for both sides. A telephone call brought to the meeting last-minute word that still another large foundation was curtailing regular program in favor of a substantial contribution to the New York Emergency Unemployment Relief Committee. After extended discussion a resolution was presented and passed:

> *Resolved*, that the policy of the Russell Sage Foundation in the present emergency, as always, is in its permanent contribution to the improvement of living and social conditions by its studies and its wide co-operation with agencies, rather than by contributing directly to relief. Therefore, be it resolved that the Russell Sage Foundation make no contribution to the Emergency Relief Committee.

It was a difficult decision. Soon, however, New York City alone was spending some $18,000,000 a month on relief from public funds. At that rate, the Foundation's income for a whole year would have paid the relief bill in New York City for hardly more than a single day, and its contribution might have done no more than delay for a day the necessary transfer to public auspices.

489

Meanwhile, through the direct work of its departments the Foundation was making substantial contributions toward solving depression problems. The Charity Organization Department abandoned its regular program to prepare material for the President's Emergency Committee for Employment, to conduct studies on work relief, subsistence gardens, cash relief, the expanding state and federal programs, and the Works Progress Administration (WPA). The Recreation Department helped to organize needed recreational outlets for the enforced leisure of the unemployed. The Department of Consumer Credit Studies continued to attack the problems of the needy borrower, which were multiplied by the depression, and conducted a long-range study of the influences of consumer credit upon the business cycle. The Department of Statistics conducted studies of the extent and incidence of unemployment, the composition of the cost-of-living index, and the statistics of relief. Its director was lent for a period to the New York Emergency Relief Bureau to organize and conduct a new statistical service which was vital in planning the expenditure of the $18,000,000 a month previously noticed, toward which the Foundation could have made no such significant contribution in dollars. All other departments made contributions in their own fields toward meeting depression needs; these are presented in some detail in the chapters which follow.

The Financial Picture

In the years just preceding the depression, the Foundation's income was at its highest level, averaging $697,200 a year for the five years ending in 1929, and standing at $737,000 in that year. The portfolio then consisted chiefly of bonds and real estate, and the depression drop was not precipitous, as it was with some other foundations. But as the depression deepened and continued, the income declined with disturbing regularity from $730,000 in 1932 to $501,000 in 1944, with only 1937 showing a partial recovery.

In view of declining income and other considerations, a steady effort was made to reduce the "indirect," or grants, program. A policy of elimination of long-continuing grants was adopted, and recipients of such grants were notified of reductions and the prospect of early termination. But the same influences which made it necessary for the Foundation to try to reduce its grants, created unusual financial emergencies for many of its grantees. Their other contributors fell off; their programs, which Russell Sage Foundation considered important, were in danger of being abandoned entirely. As a result, some grants were increased rather than reduced; but the general trend was downward.[1] From $349,000 in 1932 they dropped, fairly regularly, to $129,000 in 1946. The Regional Plan Association was the heaviest charge for the period, with contributions to this organization amounting to over $500,000 since its creation in 1929.

The declining income made it necessary to curtail some of the activities of the departments, and a desired renewal of activities in such fields as social and community surveys and penology could not be undertaken. A committee composed of staff members made recommendations for savings in office procedures and building operation. Toward the end of the period, when a slight improvement in dollar income occurred, the postwar inflation more than offset this advantage through increased costs of materials and personal service.

Marsh Island

Marsh Island became, unexpectedly, an element in the financial picture. It has already been noted[2] that this tract of about 75,000 acres was transferred to the state of Louisiana under strict covenants concerning its use as a wild life sanctuary, and with certain residual rights on the part of the Foundation Trustees.

In 1937, oil having been discovered on lands close by, suggestions were made that explorations be conducted on the Island, but in view of its character as a bird refuge, they were not then seriously considered. After World War II broke out, pressure was brought both by the Department of the Interior and the state of Louisiana for the right to explore for oil. In the spring of 1944, the

[1] See Chapter XLV.
[2] See p. 270.

Trustees agreed to the requested exploration on condition that it proceed under adequate protection of the Island for the purposes for which it was donated, with minimum disturbance of wild life, and with the further provision that any revenues resulting be divided equally between the Foundation and the state of Louisiana, with the state devoting its revenues to "maintaining, policing, and improving Marsh Island as a wild life refuge." Any surplus beyond amounts needed for that purpose were to be applied to statewide programs of propagation and protection of wild life, and then to health and educational work in Louisiana.

By October, 1946, exploration had not been completed. However, the exploration rights involved an original payment of rent of $503,000, of which half was received by the Foundation and added to its principal account.

Developments Among Departments

The active program of the Foundation throughout this period continued to be conducted chiefly by its departments, in the general pattern of preceding periods. This work is detailed in the chapters that follow, but an outline of the major changes which occurred among these departments is included here.

The Department of Recreation, under Mr. Hanmer, was closed in 1937 after the retirement of both Mr. Hanmer and Mr. Perry. It was felt that the development of the National Recreation Association provided services in this field which the Department had helped initiate, and this phase of Foundation activity could be abandoned.

The Charity Organization Department began the period under its new director, Miss Joanna C. Colcord, and under her leadership conducted an intensive program centering upon depression needs, followed by studies of social security and public welfare reorganization. Toward the close of the period it transferred its program to the special problems of war and international relief, but in 1944 Miss Colcord suffered a disabling illness, and resigned the following year. In 1946 Donald S. Howard was made director of the Department, which changed its name to Department of Social Work Administration, and was embarking on an enlarged program, not yet fully defined, as the record closes.

The Department of Remedial Loans was under direction of Leon Henderson in 1932. When he resigned for service with the National Recovery Administration in 1934, Rolf Nugent was appointed director; in 1938 the name of the Department was changed to Department of Consumer Credit Studies, signifying its broader field of research. The regular work of the Department was largely suspended during the war years when its director was in government service, and came to a full stop upon his death in 1946 in an accident overseas.

The Department of Surveys and Exhibits underwent several major changes. Only two phases of its earlier work continued active in this period, the "exhibits" program, which broadened into studies of interpretation and publicity methods in the field of social work, and the special activities in the arts, emphasizing handicrafts, which Mr. Eaton was developing. Both these fields became separate departments, a Department of Social Work Interpretation under Mrs. Routzahn being created in 1936, and a Department of Arts and Social Work under Mr. Eaton in 1941. However, both these directors had reached retirement age by 1946 and the future of their departments was undecided as the record closes. Survey activities, the third area of the original department, were largely suspended, though a Department of Surveys was in nominal existence with Mr. Harrison remaining as director. The Department had no budget, and Mr. Harrison's responsibilities as general director permitted little more than advisory service on survey planning and personnel.

The Department of Industrial Studies, under the direction of Miss van Kleeck throughout the period, continued its studies of labor problems and of the influence of technological developments on living standards, with increasing emphasis upon industrywide conditions and national and international backgrounds.

The Department of Statistics, likewise, remained under the same director, Mr. Hurlin, continuing its general program of statistical research and special assistance to other departments and agencies. A series of studies of professions which it initiated

493

grew in 1944 into the separate Department of Studies in the Professions, under Miss Esther Lucile Brown. At the close of the period this new department was continuing an active program.

The relatively new Social Work Year Book Department changed directors and broadened its scope. When Mr. Hall retired in 1935, Russell H. Kurtz was appointed to succeed him. The Year Book was published on the biennial basis established by 1933, but the Year Book office added a program for development of other needed social work literature.

The two service departments, the Library and Department of Publications, continued their usual operations, but were starting on programs for substantial expansion by 1946. The Library, which had been under the direction of Mrs. Hulseman until October, 1941, and then under Mrs. Badcock until 1946, invited Raymond W. Holbrook to become director; in September, 1946, he entered upon his duties with a considerable program of expansion in service in prospect. The Department of Publications remained under the direction of Mr. Andrews throughout the period, but in the spring of 1946 it added, on an experimental basis, an information secretary, to enlarge its services in the field of public information and education.

During this fifteen-year period studies by the various departments resulted in publication of 38 full-length books and a number of pamphlets. Four other books, not written by members of the staff, were published by the Foundation. It was a period, however, when the longer-range planned programs were constantly being interrupted by emergency demands, first of the great depression, and then of war. Conditions changed with such rapidity that in some cases longer studies had to be abandoned; they would have been out of date before they were finished. Nearly all departments were flooded with urgent requests for emergency services. Such services, however useful, interfered with research projects.

Toward the end of the period a frequent subject of discussion at the meetings of the department directors was the organizational structure of the Foundation with respect to future program. But since major changes were about to occur through retirement of the general director and several department directors, it seemed wise to attempt no final recommendation.

THE BUILDING

The original building continued to house all of the Foundation's own departments and offices, and in addition gave free office space, which was the equivalent of a grant, to a few organizations in the welfare field. In 1935, with a view to bringing these grants into the accounting records, such agencies were charged rent for their space, but were given offsetting grants which covered all, or nearly all, this rental.

Four organizations received substantial amounts of free space during this period. The American Association of Social Workers had continuous occupancy of most of the second floor. The Child Welfare League of America moved into the tenth floor in 1935, some time after the Committee on Regional Plan transferred its remaining functions to the Regional Plan Association, with independent offices at 400 Madison Avenue. The Family Welfare Association of America[1] was housed on the third floor until 1939, when it moved into the West Wing with an adjusted, and diminishing, rental grant. The National Publicity Council for Health and Welfare Services, which had begun as the Social Work Publicity Council in the offices of the Department of Social Work Interpretation, was promptly housed in the quarters given up by the Family Welfare Association. Smaller units of space were granted to a number of other organizations or special projects, often for limited periods.

The West Wing, with a separate street address as 122 East Twenty-second Street, had been completed just before the opening of this period at a cost, exclusive of land, of about $750,000. The New York School of Social Work was the chief tenant throughout the fifteen-year period; by 1946 the School was occupying not only all of floors one through six in the West Wing, but several offices in the old building.

In October, 1946, the directory boards at 122 and 130 East Twenty-second Street listed, in addition to Russell Sage Founda-

[1] Which became the Family Service Association of America in 1946.

tion and its various departments, 19 separate agencies, many of them national, a few local. With the agencies housed in the United Charities Building a short block away and the nearby Children's and Domestic Relations courts with their associated services, an important focal center of social welfare activity had been established.

The Foundation continued to open its halls—East Hall, South Hall, and Room 200—for public meetings of social agencies, conferences, and committee sessions. In 1935, a typical year, 73 different organizations took advantage of these public rooms for a total of 517 meetings. Attempts at classification are difficult, but the range of activities represented is suggested by the tabulation, for that year, of 147 meetings held by New York City social work organizations, 91 meetings by national social work organizations, 83 by employes' groups, 40 by educational groups, 38 by industrial study groups, 27 for aid of the handicapped, 21 by health groups, 14 for art exhibits, and 56 miscellaneous. As many as 5,000 people visited a single exhibit. The top record for meetings was established in 1938, with an average of nearly two meetings a day scheduled—a total of 714. Refugee physicians attending special classes constituted a part of this total.

Employe Relations

While the number of employes varied from time to time, throughout the fifteen-year period the professional and clerical staff stood in the neighborhood of 85; the building service staff, including the West Wing, about 43. Employes were not laid off during the depression, nor was there a program of wage reduction, though usual increases were suspended for a time.

With the coming of World War II, special provisions were made for supplementing the pay of Foundation personnel in the service, and in 1942 wartime allowances were granted to all staff members in the lower salary brackets. The rate of these allowances was increased in 1944, and early in 1946 they were incorporated in regular salary. The inflation which grew to severe proportions in 1946 resulted in a new system of temporary allowances which went into effect just as this record closes, in October, 1946.

Foundation employes were not eligible for social security insurance as the Social Security Act of 1935 exempted welfare organizations. The Foundation, however, continued its contributory retirement plan for salaried workers under the Teachers Insurance and Annuity Association of America, and instituted another plan, under which the Foundation met the total cost, for wage workers on the building force. In addition, several kinds of voluntary insurances were opened to employes at various times, usually with the Foundation making a contribution toward their cost. A hospital plan was initiated in 1935; group life insurance in 1941; and in 1944 a combined plan was presented which included membership in Group Health Insurance, Inc., offering medical services during hospitalization; Optical Membership Plan; and Associated Hospital Service. The Foundation met more than half the cost of participating staff members.

Relations between the building service employes and the Foundation developed into unionized collective bargaining in 1938. In June of that year the general director received a letter from the Social Service Employees' Union, Local 19, United Office and Professional Workers of America, CIO, stating that a majority of the employes in the building service department had organized a chapter within the Union and desired to enter into collective bargaining with the Foundation's administration. Representatives were appointed for the Union and for the Foundation, and met frequently through that summer and autumn for informal but thoroughgoing discussion of all aspects of employment relations and consideration of ways for improving them. An agreement was drafted; on November 3, 1938, it was signed by the general director and the acting president of the Union. This agreement includes under its subject headings union recognition; classification, wages, and hours; leaves; seniority; dismissals; grievances; medical service; and status of contract. Among details of the 1938 agreement which were in advance of many agreements elsewhere in effect at that time were recognition of ten legal holidays; two weeks' vacation with full pay for all

497

employes in service at least one year, with three weeks after two years' service, and four weeks after fifteen years' service; and liberal sick leave. The section on grievances provides for arbitration if a satisfactory settlement cannot be reached at any of the levels of appeal provided for within the Foundation.

This agreement remains in effect, with minor revisions which from time to time have seemed necessary or desirable. Its provisions are interpreted, and changes are recommended, by a Joint Committee on Building Employment Relations.

World War II

The second World War did not result in suspension of department activities to the extent that occurred in World War I. Services which Foundation personnel had performed—and often themselves developed—on a volunteer basis in World War I were in most cases highly organized and adequately financed by the government itself in World War II. Two of the departments came to a virtual halt because of war-connected absences. All the other departments made contributions, each in its own field, by advisory service and the reorientation of existing work to wartime needs.

Five members of the staff or building force served in the armed forces.[1] As was the case throughout America, nearly every staff member not in the armed forces volunteered for special home-front services as wardens, draft board members, first-aid volunteers, contributors to blood banks, and in some cases took leaves of absence for war work and service with the Red Cross.

Many important contributions to the war effort, and to the problems left in its wake, came out of the special knowledge and training of various members of the staff. Mr. Harrison's presidency of the National Conference of Social Work in the first war year, with its responsibility for leadership in setting before the profession goals related to the emergency, has already been mentioned. In the spring of 1941, when the United States was in the defense period but not yet at war, Mr. Kurtz undertook an

[1] Francis Leo, Walter L. Maers, Frank Queenan, Louis Stefani, and Robert Winchester. C. Benjamin Curley, a captain in World War I, was given leave to serve as plans and training officer for the 15th Regiment, Harlem Unit.

informal survey of conditions in communities near training camps and in some towns and cities inflated by sudden war industry. He used his observations in articles, addresses, government committee service, and as background for the next Social Work Year Book, of which he was editor.

Miss Colcord was granted a leave of absence for a part of 1942 to serve as a consultant to the Office of Defense Health and Welfare Services in Washington, making available to that organization her special knowledge in the fields of family welfare and community organization in the United States. Her department's further services in special studies related to the war, and its major project in preparing material from past experience which would be of value in the administration of relief abroad and in the rehabilitation of liberated territories, are described in some detail in Chapter XXXV.

The material on relief methods was prepared chiefly by Mr. Howard, associate director of the Department. As an outgrowth of this special knowledge his services were requested by the Office of Foreign Relief and Rehabilitation Operations and several other federal agencies; he began work in October, 1943, at first on loan, but soon on leave of absence. He participated as a consultant on welfare matters in the organization meeting of United Nations Relief and Rehabilitation Administration (UNRRA) in Atlantic City in the fall of 1943, and the following year he was chiefly responsible for welfare research and planning and assisted in drafting UNRRA's welfare policies. In late 1944 he flew to England to observe actual emergency relief operations in London, then under the V-bomb barrage, and to help effect closer liaison between welfare activities of the UNRRA London and Washington offices. He later worked with Supreme Headquarters of the Allied Expeditionary Forces in Paris on welfare aspects of the military-UNRRA program for the care of United Nations nationals displaced in Germany. In the summer of 1945 he was transferred to China as UNRRA's chief welfare officer. Soon he was made deputy director of the UNRRA China office, in charge of UNRRA's services for health, welfare, displaced persons, and refugees. He returned to the United States in March, 1946, and shortly thereafter was appointed director of his former department, which at the same time was renamed the Department of Social Work Administration.

Service to his country resulted in the death of Rolf Nugent, director of the Department of Consumer Credit Studies. His first contributions to the defense and war efforts were directly in the consumer credit field, and are detailed in Chapter XXXVI. They included help in solving the small loan problem in Hawaii to protect military personnel, and chief responsibility for drafting Regulation W, giving the Federal Reserve Board power to regulate consumer credit. By shortening the term, increasing downpayments, and controlling charge accounts, this device greatly reduced the demand for automobiles and other expensive durables, releasing much productive capacity for armaments before it was legally possible to accomplish this end by direct order.

After Pearl Harbor, Mr. Nugent was put in charge of rationing the half-million automobiles remaining after manufacture ceased in January, 1942. He then became chief of the consumer requirements branch of the Office of Price Administration (OPA), and later, director of its credit policy office, under his former chief at the Foundation, Leon Henderson.

In February, 1944, he joined UNRRA, continuing on leave from the Foundation but transferring to UNRRA's payroll in March, 1945. He began work in Washington in the Bureau of Supply, dealing with problems of allocation of food, clothing, and equipment for liberated areas. In the spring of 1944 he spent three months in London working out these problems for European areas. That summer he was sent to Australia by bomber to confer with General MacArthur and others on responsibilities of the military and UNRRA for civilian relief in the Far East, and to discuss with Australian and New Zealand authorities the problems of supplies. He spent the first half of 1945 in Yugoslavia and Italy, as deputy chief of UNRRA's Yugoslav Mission, with responsibility for the supply functions, including programing of requirements, industrial and agricultural rehabilitation, shipping and internal transport, and distribution. He returned to the United States in August, just after V-J Day.

The assistance of his secretary, Miss Eleanor Nissley, on a leave-of-absence basis was granted him in November, 1945; the Department of Consumer Credit Studies, having no personnel on duty, was closed. Mr. Nugent went to Europe on a brief mission to England, France, and Germany, and then he, followed by Miss Nissley, started on what was planned as his final UNRRA assignment, to the Philippines and China. While on his way from China to Manila via Japan, he met with a fatal accident while swimming in the surf near Yokohama in July, 1946.

It has been noted[1] that the Trustees of the Foundation were charged by Mrs. Sage with administration of the income of a fund of $10,000 in behalf of the Susana Hospital on the Island of Guam. The Island was captured by Japanese forces in the first month of the war, and it was known only that the hospital "had been bombed." After recapture by United States forces, it was discovered that the hospital had been entirely destroyed. In the spring of 1946, the Navy reported its plan to construct a general hospital on Guam with 300 beds, to be known as the Guam Memorial Hospital, and suggested that the funds at the Foundation's disposal be devoted to the support of a Susana Maternity Section within this hospital. The Trustees accepted this proposal, with an agreement that the Navy will place in this section a tablet reciting Mrs. Sage's gift.

[1] See p. 37.

XXXIV

RECREATION: 1932-1937

AS HIS department was beginning its final period, Mr. Hanmer wrote: "The enlarging conception of recreation is constantly widening the scope of this department's work. We have proceeded from play for children to athletics for youth and adults of both sexes, and to music, dramatics, and the whole range of cultural arts, as resources for the constructive and satisfying use of free time."

These words summarized rather well the expanding interests which two earlier chapters have recorded. His next sentence was prophetic of the final period in a sense he neither desired nor intended: "Leisure is no longer the gift to the rich, but is rapidly becoming the possession of all economic classes on an extensive scale."

It was, indeed. In the fall of 1931 depression and unemployment were already severe, but their full depth and duration were not yet guessed. Practically the whole of the remaining period of the Department of Recreation, from 1932 to its discontinuance on September 30, 1937, was a period of deep depression, with many millions of the unemployed desperately needing recreational outlets for their enforced leisure.

DEPRESSION ACTIVITIES

The program of the Department was profoundly altered to meet the emergency needs of the depression. The first and nearest workshop was New York City itself, where Mr. Hanmer and other members of the Department contributed ideas, advice, material, and frequently personal service to a recreational program which expanded rapidly to supply profitable occupation for the increased leisure arising from unemployment, partial employment, and shortened hours.

502

The initial step was to spread information about facilities already available. Bulletins prepared by the City Recreation Committee (recently affiliated with the Welfare Council) were widely distributed for posting in schools, libraries, settlement houses, relief offices, and elsewhere, and were reprinted by the Police Department for use of patrolmen.

Many of the summer camps were an early casualty. As a substitute for those camps for poor children which were forced by lack of funds to close or shorten their season, "day camps" in specially equipped areas in outlying parks were developed (five by 1935), to which playground leaders took children for a day at a time of simulated camping experience. The Children's Aid Society held athletic tournaments for older boys. Greenwich House devised a "block recreation" experiment, supplying gangs of boys with empty stores for club headquarters, with graduate students from Columbia to supervise their activities, but this project was itself seriously hampered by lack of funds. In these efforts the Department assisted as it could.

Assistance in camping activities was not only local, but national. When the Camp Directors' Association undertook a Camping Exposition with a "real woods camp" set up on the roof of the Pennsylvania Hotel in the spring of 1932, the Department participated in the planning. Mr. Hanmer made a trip to Suffern which resulted in a personal appearance by Dan Beard, and gave a radio talk a few days before the Exposition opened. It was "an unexpectedly successful occasion." Next year, when the Camp Directors' Association held its annual conference in New York City, Mr. Hanmer was in charge of the program. In 1934–1935 he helped re-establish the Association's magazine on a self-supporting basis. In the spring of 1937 he assisted in the Camp Pow-Wow held at the George Washington Hotel in New York, co-operatively undertaken by New York University and Camping World Magazine.

For older groups, local agencies such as the YWCA sought to develop new vocational resources and free-time interests for their own clientele. The Society for Experimental Study on Education arranged a course of lectures on "Guidance for Leisure." The

Leisure League of America held a Hobby Show in the Port Authority Building.

Mr. Hanmer and the Department undertook further support for the Sportsmanship Brotherhood, which he had helped establish. Financial backing for the Brotherhood had always been hard to get, and from the beginning of the depression the difficulty increased. To help out, the Department supplied clerical assistance to its executive, Daniel Chase, who was "temporarily without a secretary" through much of the depression period. Meanwhile, under Mr. Chase's leadership the Kiwanis Club sponsored a baseball tournament in the summer of 1932, in which teams of boys from various parts of the city engaged. The idea was adopted by the Police Department's Bureau of Crime Prevention. This was the origin of the "sandlot" baseball tournament, later conducted by the New York City Baseball Federation and under other auspices; by 1936, nearly 3,000 boys were enrolled in 220 teams, playing throughout the summer. In 1934 the Department joined with the Brotherhood, the American Athletic Union, and the National Collegiate Athletic Association, to arrange for a visit of 300 Italian students to America, including a tour of several universities and ending with a grand field day at Yankee Stadium on Columbus Day. In the last year of the Department's existence, Mr. Hanmer carried still more responsibility when Mr. Chase was incapacitated for many months by an accident, and endeavored to obtain an assured income for the Brotherhood's future.[1]

Mounting concern for unemployed young people showed itself in various other ways. About the middle of the decade a three-day Boys' Exposition was held at the Hotel Commodore, sponsored originally by the Madison Square Boys' Club but enlisting participation of practically all agencies in the city engaged in work for boys. At this exposition a medal was presented to Mr. Hanmer for "outstanding service to boyhood." Further manifestation of concern for youth, this time nationwide, was the appointment in 1935, by the American Council on Education, of the American Youth Commission, to make a five-year

[1] It appears to have become a war casualty.

investigation of the care and education of persons between the ages of twelve and twenty-five. Mr. Hanmer was a member of its advisory committee. His office supplied bibliographies, lists of persons, memoranda, and sundry other material for the use of the Commission. A bulletin on Youth Movements Here and Abroad was prepared by Miss Williams and published by the Foundation as Library Bulletin No. 135 in February, 1936.

Depressed conditions, which made increased recreational facilities important, led most municipalities at the same time to reduce their appropriations for recreation, education, health, and general social welfare. Mr. Hanmer took an active part in setting up Citizens' Councils for Constructive Economy under the auspices of the National Municipal League for the purpose of studying budget problems, discovering new sources of revenue, and suggesting economies that would not jeopardize essential services. In specific instances, as in Newark in the depths of the depression, the Department helped prevent serious cuts in the budget for recreation.

The situation of the recreation worker was another anomaly of the depression. Reductions in budgets threw many competent workers out of jobs. Meanwhile, work-relief projects, first under private and later under public auspices, were creating many new playgrounds and other recreational facilities where trained workers were needed. But usually no regular salaries were provided for these positions, which were filled by the work bureaus from the relief rolls, at no cost to the city or the private agency. The trained worker who was unemployed could not take these jobs until he was in such reduced circumstances as to "qualify for relief," to use the current euphemistic phrase. As time went on, many did so "qualify," but the size of the program and the difficulties in obtaining experienced workers made training courses a requisite. The department personnel gave substantial assistance in such courses, which were conducted under the auspices of the Welfare Council and the Emergency Work Bureaus of the Prosser and Gibson Committees. The training of recreation leaders grew later into a WPA project offering courses to some 1,500 relief workers in a Training School for Recreation

Leaders conducted by the School of Education of New York University. Mr. Hanmer was a member of the supervisory committee of this Training School, and both he and Mr. Perry gave lectures. They also advised the Work Bureaus on selection of persons for assignment to recreation centers, playgrounds, boys' and girls' work organizations, and other agencies engaged in providing wholesome occupation for leisure time.

The Department was closely associated with the Adjustment Service of 1933–1934, a demonstration in personal counsel and guidance for the unemployed conducted by the American Association for Adult Education with the help of a grant of $100,000 from Carnegie Corporation of New York made through the Gibson Committee, which also assigned staff. Mr. Hanmer was a member of the advisory committee. Mr. van de Wall was a consultant in the field of music, and was assigned space in the Foundation building for interviews with his clients. The Department also assisted in plans, designed largely for the benefit of unemployed musicians, for presenting operas at popular prices at the New York Hippodrome.

When the Works Progress Administration began its operations in New York City in 1935, General Hugh S. Johnson appointed Mr. Hanmer a member of the committee charged with reviewing all "white-collar" projects under way; they examined 334, disapproving 24.

In the wider area of national programs, conferences were attended on plans for recreation and avocational pursuits in the Civilian Conservation Corps, in camps for homeless men, in colonies of the Resettlement Administration; on plans of the National Park Service for extending facilities for active recreation by providing more hiking trails, nature trails, campsites, and hostels. As a member of the National Parks Association, Mr. Hanmer took part in discussions on many such topics, and on the financial problems of the future entailed by the vast expansion of facilities. He added his voice to the others that were warning public and private agencies of the necessity for facing questions of cost of administration and maintenance of these new facilities when the "free ride" on emergency relief funds came to an end.

OTHER SERVICES

Beyond emergency services growing out of the depression, the Department continued a heavy program of assistance to persons, projects, and organizations in the general recreational field. The "organizations with which we have co-operated most closely during the year" listed in the annual reports of the Department usually ran to 50 or more names. Co-operation meant "chiefly participation on programs of meetings and in program-making, development of policies and plans within the organizations, some minor contributions of funds in a few instances but more often contributions of services, work on committees, preparation of articles for publication, and so forth."

Final revisions of reports of the White House Conference had still to be completed in 1933–1934. The President's Conference on Home Building and Home Ownership, held in 1931, involved both Mr. Hanmer and Mr. Perry in committee meetings and preparation of reports that were published in 1932. Arthur E. Morgan, chairman of the Tennessee Valley Authority, asked for suggestions as to persons and agencies who would be helpful in his task of community planning. Paul M. Pearson, a personal friend, was given requested help on recreation and community-welfare projects when he was Governor of the Virgin Islands, and on some phases of housing when he later became assistant director of housing of the Federal Emergency Administration of Public Works.

The annual Recreation Congress of the National Recreation Association[1] remained an event in which the Department took active part, as it had since 1907. Acting as the Association's center for information on research, the Department in 1930 began systematic compilation of a list of research projects under way or recently completed. By 1932 there were 800 on the list. In co-operation with the Association a study of requirements in both space and equipment for children's play was rounded out in 1933–1934 for publication by the Association. In the same year, with the help of an assistant assigned by the work-relief

[1] Until 1930, the Playground and Recreation Association of America.

507

bureau, plans were drawn for low-cost field houses and other recreation buildings.

When the Boy Scouts had in preparation a history of the first twenty-five years of the movement in America, Mr. Hanmer, who helped organize it, was called upon for information about the early days.

Improvement in the quality of motion pictures and promotion of their use for educational purposes continued to be part of the Department's program. Assistance was given in the early thirties to the Harmon Foundation in developing its Religious Motion Picture Foundation, and to the dean of the graduate school of Boston University in plans for a motion picture service for religious, educational, and character-building agencies. When the National Recovery Administration in 1933 undertook to increase employment and improve working conditions through codes of fair competition, the framing of the code of the motion picture industry offered an opportunity to get formal recognition for some of the principles long advocated by various unofficial bodies. Mr. Hanmer participated in drafting provisions for the code and in defending them at hearings before the deputy administrator in Washington. These provisions related to good taste in production and advertising; greater freedom in program-making by local exhibitors in response to requests from the community; encouragement of use of travelogues, newsreels, and other educational features; free film service to shut-ins; and arrangements to facilitate use of films for non-theatrical purposes.

Community activities for recreation and education continued to be a major interest. In 1931 Mr. Perry published, in collaboration with Miss Williams, a pamphlet entitled New York School Centers and Their Community Policy, describing development of community programs in New York's school buildings, beginning with the public lectures instituted in 1890. He devised a plan (and submitted it to 200 institutions) for using extension departments of universities to bring more young people into contact with the universities and to increase social opportunities of a community nature. He proposed for discussion (in Camp Life) a plan for what he called "Circus Guilds," composed of local dramatic groups which would provide opportunities for participation by large numbers of persons; but this suggestion seems to have met with little response.

Publication in 1933 of Mr. Perry's book, The Work of the Little Theatres, was most timely. Not only had the disappearance of road shows, driven out by the competition of movie theatres, left the greater part of the population of the country without opportunity to see "legitimate" dramatic productions in their own communities, but the "new leisure" was creating a demand for a broad program of cultural activities as well as physical recreation. As one way of providing shelter for amateur dramatics Mr. Perry suggested (in articles in Library Magazine and The American City in 1935) accommodations in branch libraries, whose buildings might be adapted or enlarged for such purposes as part of the public works program.

The Department's long-continued interest in music in institutional programs culminated in 1936 in publication of a book of nearly 500 pages on the subject, Music in Institutions, by Willem van de Wall, assisted by Clara Liepmann.[1] Mr. van de Wall was only occasionally on the Foundation payroll, but interest in, and assistance to, his work in music[2] was constant. After the Department of Recreation was discontinued, and his book had finally gone out of print, Mr. van de Wall received an assignment to prepare for the Foundation a pamphlet on institutional uses of music, which was published in 1946 under the title Music in Hospitals.

In the closing years of the Department, substantial further steps were taken toward better co-ordination of the public recreational programs in New York City. Chicago in the middle thirties had unified its 17 district park administrations, organizing a non-administrative recreation commission of citizens. Mr.

[1] Who became Mrs. van de Wall in August, 1937.

[2] These activities included a study of music in community life for the American Association for Adult Education published in 1938 under the title The Music of the People; a project for promoting community music throughout the state of Kentucky financed by Carnegie Corporation, during which he was a faculty member of the University of Kentucky; a professorial assignment at the University of Louisiana; and his present work in occupied Germany with the public health and welfare branch of the United States Office of Military Government.

Perry made two visits to Chicago to study this development. The Department was asked by Mayor LaGuardia of New York whether the Chicago plan would be advisable locally. About this time a three-day conference on recreation problems in New York was held under sponsorship of New York University, with Mr. Hanmer presiding and a member of the findings committee. A copy of the findings was sent to the Mayor, with recommendation that an advisory and planning commission be set up by the city authorities. In co-operation with the Welfare Council and local welfare agencies, Mr. Hanmer drafted a proposal for creation of a New York City Recreation Commission.[1] The Department also assembled recommendations of the welfare agencies for provisions to be included in the new city charter, most of which were favorably received by the Charter Revision Committee.

CITY PLANNING

Planning for parks and playgrounds, community center promotion, and particularly studies for the New York Regional Plan, involved the Department deeply, in its final period, in the problems of city planning.

Much of this work dealt specifically with recreational facilities. For example, assistance was given to the Regional Plan Association in a park-planning project for the Navy Yard district in Brooklyn, a playground at Greenwood Lake, New York, a housing and recreation project of Prudential Life Insurance Company at Newark, a plan for parks in the Borough of Richmond. Both the Long Island and the Westchester park commissions consulted the Department on the extensive developments they had under way, as did the landscape architect for the new Marine Park in Brooklyn. The Department assisted the Englewood, New Jersey, school board in planning its new high-school site.

But some of this interest, especially on the part of Mr. Perry, extended to more general aspects of housing and city planning problems. He served on the committee on slum clearance of the Tenement House Department of New York City. He wrote a monograph on The Rebuilding of Blighted Areas, a study of the

[1] Not yet appointed (1946).

neighborhood unit in re-planning and plot assemblage, which was published by the Regional Plan Association in 1933. He re-planned a section of the Cord-Meyer Development in Forest Hills to show how it might be made more favorable to neighborhood life, and his study was published in January, 1935, by the Regional Plan Association, as Information Bulletin No. 22, Planning for the Improvement of Your Own Neighborhood.

Both Mr. Perry and Mr. Hanmer were members of the Community Activities Committee of the City Housing Authority. A detailed plan for the Williamsburg project was proposed; many of its features were incorporated. Advice on space required for recreation was given the Slum Clearance Committee of the State Housing Authority. Relations between structural plans and community life were outlined for the housing division of the Federal Emergency Administration of Public Works, and on this topic various addresses were given and papers prepared. Mr. Perry took part in courses at New York University, and in conferences discussing Forest Hills Gardens (where he lived) at the City Planning School of Harvard University. He was chairman of a local committee which worked out plans for four neighborhood units in a residential area of the Forest Hills section, adjoining the site of the World's Fair. One concrete result was that the site for the new high school in that section was expanded from the 2.3 acres originally proposed to 9.3 acres.

Difficulties in assembling land for large-scale housing projects constituted a serious obstacle to the development of neighborhood units. After years of study and conference on this problem, Mr. Perry proposed a legal procedure for land assemblage, many of the principles of which have been included in recent legislation.

When time for official retirement came, he had drafted two chapters of a definitive book on the "neighborhood unit," an important principle in modern city planning in the development and popularizing of which his name stands foremost.

Closing of the Department

In 1936 Mr. Hanmer sent to the general director a memorandum pointing out that both he and Mr. Perry would reach retirement age the following year. "With the development of the National Recreation Association," he wrote, "an agency now exists that should be able to provide the services in the field of recreation that the Department has helped to bring into being. During the coming fiscal year our Department work can probably be rounded up so as to make this transition possible in the main if the Foundation so desires." Mr. Perry's community planning work could not so conveniently be taken over by another agency; however, Miss Williams, assistant to the director, could ease the transition through her own further service.

So it was decided. The final year was a busy one. In addition to the "rounding up" of which Mr. Hanmer had spoken, a new responsibility looking toward the future was undertaken. New York was to open its World's Fair in 1939. Mr. Hanmer was named chairman of a committee representing some 80 agencies, which drew up a detailed memorandum for the World's Fair management and urged appointment of an official recreational planning committee for the Fair. Meetings and consultations, preparation of lists of names and collection of information for the World's Fair staff, including an account of what was done in this field at the recent San Francisco Golden Gate International Exposition and the lessons to be learned from it, took a substantial amount of Mr. Hanmer's time for his last year or two in the Foundation, and after his retirement.

On June 30 1937, Mr. Hanmer "retired from recreation to work on a farm."[1] At the National Recreation Congress the previous month a Service Award was presented to him in recognition of his thirty years' work for recreation. Movie Makers, the magazine of the Amateur Cinema League, which he had been instrumental in founding, referred to him as "the senior recreational counselor of the United States."

Mr. Perry retired on September 30 of the same year. The Department was officially closed, though Miss Williams continued

---

[1] Even in his official retirement, at Merrylea Farm among his apple trees and his farm animals, Mr. Hanmer maintained an active community life, serving as member of the school board, chairman of the local selective service board, organizer of a rural chamber of commerce, member of the Grange, promoter of a rural hospital, trustee of the New Hurley Reformed Church.

to handle correspondence, assist Mr. Perry in his continuing work on the neighborhood unit book, and extend some of the service of the Department through several years.

After his official retirement, Mr. Perry completed the work on his book, which was published in 1939 under the title Housing for the Machine Age, rounding out the major interest of his final period with the Foundation, the neighborhood unit in city planning. His death occurred in September, 1944.[1]

[1] The funeral, at which impressive tributes were paid to his contributions to recreation and city planning, was held at the Church-in-the-Gardens, which Mrs. Sage had presented to the residents of Forest Hills Gardens.

Architectural detail from the north façade,
Russell Sage Foundation Building

XXXV

CHARITY ORGANIZATION: 1931-1946

IN NOVEMBER, 1928, two months after the death of the Department's founder, Miss Richmond, Miss Joanna C. Colcord was appointed director of the Charity Organization Department. She was not able to assume her office, however, until the following August, and much of her first year was occupied with preparation of The Long View, a collection of the papers of Miss Richmond, with biographical notes.

Certain plans and even beginnings had been made toward a new program for the Department, but these were soon swept aside by the strong winds of national events. The period of this chapter, which begins in October, 1930, is therefore substantially the complete record of the directorship of Miss Colcord, who retired in 1945. She was the daughter of a sea captain, herself born in the South Seas and receiving much of her early training on shipboard. Experience with gales and hurricanes, and the need to change course in heavy weather, was a useful background for piloting her department through a tumultuous fifteen years.

The Great Depression

The depression which began in 1929 and continued for nearly a decade affected all phases of the Foundation work, but none quite so intimately as that of the Charity Organization Department. Provisions for relief and social welfare, which are the core of the Department's interest, underwent changes in the decade which can only be described as revolutionary, and in their extent unequaled in any other period of the history of this country.

At first it was generally believed that this depression, like many predecessors, would be brief. Prosperity was "just around the corner." To meet the immediate emergency, nearly every city organized its special mayor's committee, or citizens' committee.

Private welfare societies conducted special drives for funds, and tried to carry the load. It was a period of improvisation and experiment, all on the local level—breadlines, commissaries, share-the-work, subsistence gardens, work relief, self-help co-operatives. President Hoover did appoint a national committee (in November, 1930) named the President's Emergency Committee for Employment, but merely for co-ordination and stimulation of local efforts.

The depression deepened. Local communities in many instances could not meet the bare subsistence needs of their citizens. Many states set up emergency relief administrations. In a political upheaval, the Roosevelt administration and the New Deal came to Washington. Federal loans to states were succeeded in 1933 by outright federal grants for relief. The Civil Works Administration mushroomed briefly as a gigantic federal experiment in work relief, to be succeeded in 1934 by national programs of work and direct relief under supervision of the Federal Emergency Relief Administration (FERA). During much of this period the important administrative units were the state ERA's (Emergency Relief Administrations), which administered federal as well as state funds and, under some federal guidance, established most of the local standards. Workers—trained, semi-trained, and untrained—flocked to the public agencies. Government assumed vastly increased responsibilities for relief. While assistance granted by voluntary agencies remained fairly constant, it represented a rapidly decreasing proportion of total relief.

In 1935 was launched the Works Progress Administration (later called the Work Projects Administration, but in either event the WPA). In August of the same year the Social Security Act became effective, constituting probably the most important single act of social legislation in our history.

In all these changes the Department was deeply involved, sometimes as adviser on method or center of information on what was being done; sometimes as critic of an inadequate program, or protagonist for a new one. "The Department's program," Miss Colcord wrote, "became a breathless rush to keep abreast of the changes and their implications. Constant field work, and much public speaking, all with promotional as well as research emphasis, became necessary. The output of periodical articles by members of the staff doubled and trebled; there was no time for the preparation of books and pamphlets which would have been out of date before they saw print."

First Years, Community Relief Efforts. In the winter of 1930–1931 the Department found it necessary to follow up its autumn conference on Facing the Coming Winter with reports to the participants on further developments in the various communities as the depression deepened. A projected handbook for casework supervisors was set aside; for "refinement of method," as the director noted in her report for 1931, "had to be abandoned by the caseworkers of the country; in city after city they were being faced with the development of community-wide relief committees."

The first project toward meeting the new needs was the pamphlet, Community Planning in Unemployment Emergencies, summarizing the best experience that could be found. It was prepared at great speed as a co-operative undertaking for the President's Emergency Committee for Employment, and was ready in January, 1931. Over 9,000 copies were distributed free, chiefly through the President's Committee, and 1,800 copies were sold. A special publicity campaign brought it to wide notice.

It was now evident that a major emergency faced the country, though its duration was not yet guessed. The Department cleared decks for an intensive study of community organization for unemployment relief, which would include three phases: a history of unemployment relief in the past; a continuous study of developing methods in selected cities; and a special study of work-relief methods and results. To the regular department budget was added an Unemployment Emergency Fund.

The historical study was assigned, in the spring of 1931, on an honorarium basis, to Miss Leah Feder, an experienced social worker and teacher, who was studying for her doctor's degree at Bryn Mawr. She found that records of earlier depressions were often buried in dust-covered files and out-of-print publications, and their collection and presentation, in combination with teaching duties, proved a longer task than had been anticipated. Her book, Unemployment Relief in Periods of Depression, was published in October, 1936. It included records of relief methods in the principal depressions from that of 1857–1858 to that of 1920–1921.

Miss Mary Johnston was appointed research assistant in November, 1931, to maintain files on current developments. The material she kept indexed and abstracted flowed from field visits, correspondence, copies of regular reports, and clippings from one newspaper in each of the 25 to 30 cities which were being studied.

The program of field visits was conducted by Miss Colcord and two assistants, one for only a brief period.[1] The second appointment of a field representative brought to the Foundation in September, 1931, Russell H. Kurtz, who had held a joint position as general secretary of the Family Service Society and as director of the Department of Public Charities in Akron, Ohio, and before that had served as a personnel manager in industry.[2]

Field work, shared by Miss Colcord and Mr. Kurtz, was for several years a very important part of the program. During 1932 and 1933 Miss Colcord made one long field trip and several shorter ones; Mr. Kurtz was constantly in the field, or in his office working on reports.

It proved impossible to limit field visits to fact-finding; community leaders were eager to hear what was being done in other communities, and to submit their own situations and plans for critical comment and advice. The Department's field contacts, therefore, in many respects resembled those of a national functional agency, except that collection of factual material was the chief emphasis.

Examples of this broader service abound in the Department's annual reports. "Advice was given in Seattle," said Miss Colcord

[1] William C. Koplovitz, from June through September, 1931, gathered material for Emergency Work Relief, of which he was a co-author.

[2] Mr. Kurtz became successively assistant director of the Department (May, 1935), editor of the Social Work Year Book (November, 1935), and assistant general director of Russell Sage Foundation in September, 1943.

in her report for 1932, "to chest and family society representatives on difficulties in co-operation with the Unemployed Citizens' League; in Portland on the avoidance of a commissary system; in Salt Lake City on distribution of Red Cross flour, and on plans for the care of the homeless; and in Omaha on the formation of a citizens' committee . . ." while Mr. Kurtz "was able to assist the chest executive [in New Orleans] in marshaling the vital factual information from other cities that helped to put across a $750,000 bond issue . . . [and] in Toledo, discussed work relief with a group of engineers who had ill-considered plans."

By 1934 financial stringencies within the Foundation reduced the funds available for travel, but field visits were continued on a smaller scale, usually in connection with addresses, institutes, or other outside activities.

A chief purpose of field visits, and other related activities of the Department, was the study of work relief which the Department had set for itself as a part of the threefold program. Such projects were examined in 26 different communities, some under municipal, some under private agency or committee auspices. Preliminary conclusions could be presented by the fall of 1931, in Miss Colcord's article,"This Winter's Work Relief" in The Survey for September, in duplicated copies of her address on "Municipal Work Relief" before the American Society of Municipal Engineers, and in her pamphlet, Setting Up a Program of Work Relief, preprinted from the full study. About 14,000 copies of this pamphlet were distributed, chiefly through the President's Emergency Committee for Employment. The complete study was published in book form in August, 1932, under the title Emergency Work Relief, by Miss Colcord, assisted by Mr. Koplovitz and Mr. Kurtz.

In 1933 Miss Hertha Kraus, director of the Department of Public Welfare in Cologne, Germany, arrived in this country as a refugee, and was commissioned to prepare the pamphlet, Work Relief in Germany, which was published in 1934.

Many improvisations of the early depression period received special study. One of these was subsistence gardens. During 1932 community sponsorship of gardening programs for the unemployed appeared in a number of places. Information on these programs was gathered in field trips and by correspondence, and the material digested into a pamphlet under the joint authorship of Miss Colcord and Miss Johnston[1] which appeared early in 1933 under the title Community Programs for Subsistence Gardens.

Organized self-help was another phenomenon of the early years of the depression, emerging, particularly in the West, in the form of groups of unemployed persons bartering labor and services for the means of livelihood. This revival of the pioneer spirit among the unemployed roused the sympathetic interest of the Department, whose workers made contact with many of the groups and leaders in the course of field trips, and constituted the Department an informal center for circulation of material such as bibliographies, lists of self-help centers, and descriptive articles. This movement could not withstand certain economic factors, including the pull of the cash wages which became increasingly available under federal work programs.

The need for record forms during the emergency period resulted in a face sheet (CO69) and a financial data card (CO70) drawn up by a committee appointed by the Family Welfare Association of America, and published by the Department in 1932. These were the last of a considerable series of face sheets and record forms published by the Department for the use of social workers and social agencies. Their publication and widespread use, together with continuing use of some of the older forms, established in 1932 an all-time record for Foundation sale of forms and record sheets, 448,489—nearly half a million in one year. The Family Welfare Association of America seemed the logical agency, however, for continuance of such service, and the Department transferred to that association its interest in this project, together with stock of its remaining forms, on October 1, 1937.

Some of the measures taken to meet the emergency called for the Department's disapproval and opposition. In spite of long experience with the evils of commodity distribution, both bread-

---

[1] Miss Johnston remained with the Department until May, 1936, when she suffered an attack of rheumatic fever, which proved fatal in January of the year following.

lines and commissaries made their appearance early in the depression, and for a time spread and flourished. The Department advocated relief in cash instead of "in kind," and opposed the spread of commissaries with all the means available. Miss Colcord's article in The Family attacking "The Commissary System" was given wide free distribution in pamphlet form, producing, she later reported, "embarrassingly fervent commendation from wholesale and retail grocers' associations!"

This opposition to commissaries and advocacy of cash relief grew under later stimulus into a quick study of several of the larger cities in the country which during 1934 and 1935 abandoned the practice of giving relief in kind or in grocery orders, and boldly went over to a cash-relief basis. In the belief that a factual account of their experience might aid in inducing other administrations to adopt the same policy, field visits were made in the late summer of 1935. Miss Colcord's resulting report, Cash Relief, was published in book form in July, 1936. Even before publication, galley proofs forwarded to Los Angeles were used in successfully opposing a plan proposed by the county supervisors to return to commissary distribution. The availability of this report doubtless had general influence on relief policy.

Expansion to State and Federal Programs. As the depression continued and one state after another set up state emergency relief administrations, the Department's unit of study gradually shifted from the individual city to the state.

Releasing accumulated information was an appropriate and important part of the Department's work during this period of enlarging scope. The earliest regular effort in this direction was the four-page section in Survey Midmonthly called "Unemployment and Community Action" in which Miss Colcord and Mr. Kurtz presented highlights of the relief picture for three years, beginning with the issue of November, 1932. "As a public service it has been outstanding," wrote Editor Paul Kellogg when this series was concluded in December, 1935.

A second service of information, this time purely on the state level, was begun in January, 1934, in the form of duplicated monthly bulletins, sent free to state relief administrators, containing excerpts from state reports of the previous month which included novel or interesting features. Neither the emergency relief division of the Reconstruction Finance Corporation nor its successor, the Federal Emergency Relief Administration, developed channels for exchange of experience and methods between states—all their output was from Washington. State relief administrators expressed great appreciation of this service, which was continued until March, 1936, when the "emergency" bodies within state governments began to be absorbed into permanent state departments of public welfare.

As the signs became unmistakable that state emergency relief administrations should be replaced by permanent, well-organized departments of public welfare, and a more permanent structure would have to be organized on the federal level, Mr. Kurtz prepared a pamphlet entitled Looking Toward a Public Welfare Plan. It digested expressed opinions and arguments on this point. It was widely circulated, with some 8,000 copies distributed by a dozen interested agencies to their members. Much favorable comment, in letters and in the press, resulted.[1]

Before the first large federal attack on unemployment was launched, in the Civil Works Administration program of 1933, Miss Colcord was called to the Federal Emergency Relief Administration's office in Washington for a two-day session with an invited group to advise on the future of this project. After the plan was in effect, she helped interest historical and genealogical societies in setting up programs in their fields to employ white-collar workers.

By the end of 1935, the interlocking federal programs of WPA and Social Security had been established; the Department program was adapted to the larger setting. Donald S. Howard, formerly area statistician for the Works Progress Administration in the Colorado area and director of research and statistics for the

[1] A further reporting service on state relief and public assistance developments was conducted some years later when the Department, in co-operation with the Social Work Year Book, of which Mr. Kurtz became editor in 1935, conducted field visits during 1938 to nearly all of the states in preparation of the special section, "Public Assistance in the States," which was published in the Social Work Year Book 1939.

Colorado Relief Administration, was appointed research assistant in August, 1936.

Throughout this period the Department was increasingly a center of information and advice in the whole area of unemployment relief. A heavy schedule of articles, addresses, conferences, and consultations was undertaken. Numerous articles by the several members of the Department appeared in The Survey, The Family, The Annals of the American Academy of Political and Social Science, the various issues of the Social Work Year Book, one—"But People Must Eat," by Mr. Howard—in The Atlantic Monthly, and scattering contributions elsewhere.

Sometimes personnel from the Department was briefly lent to outside agencies, as in 1934 when Mr. Kurtz assisted the national Committee on Care of Transients and Homeless to make a study and report on FERA transient camps. Mr. Howard was lent for the last three months of 1937 to serve as executive secretary of the (New York) Mayor's Board of Survey on the Transfer of Relief Administration, charged with planning the incorporation of New York City's emergency relief functions in the permanent Department of Public Welfare.

Speeches varied from formal addresses before such organizations as the National Conference of Social Work, usually printed in the Proceedings and often circulated in reprint form, to informal luncheon talks before local groups. Among the more important were Miss Colcord's National Conference of Social Work addresses on "Relief—Style 1936" and "Necessary Supplements to Unemployment Insurance," the latter at the 1937 meeting. Some of her speeches pointed out possible dangers in the new setup and were frankly critical of the policy of the federal government in withdrawing from general relief and completely categorizing the relief program. This resulted in what she described as "an abatement in the cordial relations previously maintained with the FERA in Washington."

Services outside the Department included teaching assignments, at special institutes or in courses in schools of social work; committee service, of which one of the more important examples was the committee on current relief objectives of the American

Association of Social Workers, with Miss Colcord serving as chairman of the committee and Mr. Kurtz as its secretary; attendance at, and usually participation in, numerous conferences called by such organizations as Family Welfare Association of America, American Public Welfare Association, American Association of Social Workers, National Conference of Social Work, and various state conference groups.

Service within the Department included reading, review, and editorial advice on publications in the relief field by various individuals and organizations, and growing use by outside research workers and agencies of the Department's extensive files on unemployment relief problems. A worker from FERA spent several weeks in the Department unearthing copies of its own documents no longer available in the Washington files. Faculty and students of the New York School of Social Work were especially frequent visitors, a relation which later assumed semi-official status.[1] These research uses were greatly assisted by the addition to the staff, in June, 1937, of Miss Sigrid Holt, a trained librarian.

With the great increase in public social work and the Department's interest in it, the development of satisfactory civil service standards became a matter of concern. In June, 1938, Mrs. Alice Campbell Klein, a social worker with experience in personnel work and in placement services for social workers, was commissioned to make a study of merit systems. An advisory committee was appointed for the study, composed of social workers with special interest in personnel problems and of civil service administrators with experience in selection of social workers. This committee held two all-day meetings, in addition to individually reading and criticizing the material submitted to them. The report grew from the planned small manual to a full-length book. Civil Service in Public Welfare was published in March, 1940, which turned out to be a strategic time since it followed closely the passage of federal legislation requiring, as a condition for

---

[1] From October, 1945, the public welfare files of the Department, expanded by additions from the School, were made available to the School students in the Department's file room. In 1946 this collection was expanded to include international welfare materials.

federal reimbursement to states, the setting up of a merit system for selection of state and local welfare personnel to administer the special forms of public assistance.

Some departmental attention was also directed to the federal food stamp plan, announced in 1939 as a means for distributing federal surplus commodities to relief recipients. Miss Colcord made visits to several eastern and midwest cities to study the plan, and the Department collaborated with the American Association of Social Workers and the American Public Welfare Association on a project maintaining current information on its progress. As it worked out, the plan did not justify the apprehensions earlier felt about it, and the data assembled were not published. The plan itself was curtailed and then abandoned with the coming of lend-lease shortages.

The chief occupation of the Department at this period, however, was the WPA study. To Mr. Howard fell the task of digesting the voluminous material already on file, and collecting needed new data by correspondence, field visits to the larger centers of WPA employment, and conferences with the Washington directors of the program. Shifts in eligibility requirements, in procedures, and in scope were constantly occurring, complicating the problem. The very processes of collecting material led to opportunities for service in particular situations related to other interests of the Department which could not be overlooked.

The WPA and Federal Relief Policy was published in September, 1943, just as the WPA program was being liquidated in view of the heavy employment demands of World War II. It is therefore a substantially complete record of federal relief policy during the latter half of the depression decade, and the definitive report on the largest works program ever undertaken by any government for the relief of unemployment.

OTHER ACTIVITIES

Charity Organization Department found it possible, during this period, to include in its program a very few activities which had little or no direct relation to the depression. One such project was preparation of the study outline, Your Community.

The Department's little best seller, Miss Byington's pamphlet, What Social Workers Should Know About Their Own Communities, had last been revised in 1929. That it was seriously out of date had been realized for years, as also the need for a much more comprehensive guide to community studies; but in the rush of trying to keep up with the relief picture, time had never been available to revert to the Department's earlier interest in community organization, and produce an up-to-date text. Work was begun by Miss Colcord during the summer of 1937, and completed by the end of the following summer. Much willing and valued help was received from authorities in the various fields of community effort discussed.

The book, Your Community, appeared in January, 1939, and was immediately in wide demand. It was adopted by the Delaware State Conference of Social Work as the basic text in educating citizens of the state regarding their home communities. Schools used it widely. Civic organizations, or groups of organizations, made it the basis for community self-surveys, one of the most extensive of which was conducted in Portland, Maine, in 1941 under auspices of the community chest. No book published by the Department except Miss Richmond's Social Diagnosis has had such wide distribution. In 1941 a revised edition was published. By October, 1946, sales had exceeded 23,000 copies, and a second revision, by Donald S. Howard, was about to be published.

Miss Colcord's welfare knowledge and her seafaring interests[1] were happily combined in her appointment by President Roosevelt to membership on the advisory council to the Government of the Virgin Islands. This membership resulted in a visit to the Islands in 1934, an article for The Survey, testimony before a congressional committee, correspondence, and consultation.

Miss Colcord was chairman of the American Division on Broken Homes in connection with the International Conference

[1] In addition to her social work writings, Miss Colcord managed in her own time many contributions to the literature of the sea, among which were Roll and Go, a book of sea shanties published in 1924 and issued in revised edition as Songs of American Sailormen in 1938 (Norton); Sea Language Comes Ashore, in 1945 (Cornell Maritime Press); and various articles on maritime subjects in Neptune and other comparable magazines.

of Social Work, and presented the Division's report at the second meeting of the Conference in Frankfurt am Main in 1932. She also presented a paper on "The Significance of Unemployment for the Family." She was in attendance at the third session, in London in 1936. In 1938 she became chairman of the American Committee, whose plans for a fourth session in Brussels in 1940 were interrupted by the advent of war in Europe.

Various members of the Department took active part in such organizations as the National Conference of Social Work (Miss Colcord served two terms on its executive committee) and the American Association of Social Workers.

Another activity which took a substantial amount of the director's time through the depression years was a forerunner of the greater catastrophe, not yet foreseen. In 1933 Miss Colcord served on "an unnamed committee on the plight of German social workers." In 1934 she became secretary of this organization, by this time christened Hospites, the work of which became concentrated in Charity Organization Department offices. Its program included hospitality to refugee social workers who managed to reach America, together with scholarship aid and assistance in finding work, and a highly secret program within Germany itself which sometimes took food and other aid to social workers in concentration camps.

The Foundation was related to this program in many ways. The chairman, so long as her health permitted, was Mrs. John M. Glenn; Miss van Kleeck served continuously on its executive committee; Mr. Harrison was for some time acting treasurer; in addition to her early service as secretary, Miss Colcord became chairman of Hospites in 1941. The Foundation itself financed early organization expenses and granted scholarship honoraria to several German social workers.

Perhaps this close relation to some of the results of fascism abroad gave Miss Colcord the prophetic view of what lay ahead which led her to write in her report for 1939:

In the event that this country enters the war . . . some wholly different role would have to be played by this Department; a role which cannot now be envisaged, and which would develop and be revealed with the progress of events, as was our ten-years' preoccupation with unemployment relief.

War and Rehabilitation

The war that broke out in Europe in September, 1939, soon ended any remaining vestiges of unemployment in the United States. We became the arsenal of democracy, and also a potential target for hostilities. The Council of National Defense was revived early in 1940 from its dormant state since World War I. Passage of the Selective Service Act in September of that year began to alter the social and economic patterns of our society.

With the WPA, which the Department had studied so long and carefully, on the way out, a breathing spell seemed available, and the Department revived the idea of an old project—a short history of social work in the United States. But events moved too rapidly. In December, 1941, came the attack on Pearl Harbor, and our country entered the war. Once again the Department shifted its program radically to meet needs of a new emergency.

The most immediate task was civilian defense—organization of the "home front." Miss Colcord accepted service in Washington in the period January through March, 1942, as consultant to committees on family security and on community organization of the Office of Defense Health and Welfare Services. She later made an extended field trip, studying the impact of civilian defense on community organization for health and welfare. Programs for federal aid to civilians who were victims of enemy action, development of plans to evacuate civilian populations in case of need, and the actual procedures in removal of persons of Japanese ancestry from the Pacific Coast area, were made subjects of special study.

The chief wartime project of the Department, however, took shape in late 1942, after our invasion of Africa made it apparent that we would soon have on our hands severe problems in the administration of relief and in the rehabilitation of liberated

527

territories, problems closely allied to the earlier work of the Department.

Military and naval schools were established to train officers in the civil administration of these territories, and civilian colleges began to offer courses for persons seeking relief work abroad. Little teaching material was available. Mr. Howard, who had become assistant director in December, 1942, turned to examination of recorded experience of American agencies and workers in administering relief abroad, and began to plan a series of pamphlets, presenting in condensed form material which was out of print or difficult to obtain, and also a book of readings, arranged topically. In preparation for this work he visited the school for army officers at Charlottesville, Virginia, and conferred with the interested government departments in Washington.

A series of eight Occasional Papers resulted, the first of which was a bibliography compiled by Miss Holt, with the co-operation of Miss Hertha Kraus. The remaining seven pamphlets, all edited by Mr. Howard, consisted of excerpts from published or manuscript material.[1]

The book of readings was not completed for publication, for Mr. Howard, shortly after publication of the eight Occasional Papers in the fall of 1943, was drawn into the program of the United Nations Relief and Rehabilitation Administration (UNRRA), for which his work in the Department had been excellent preparation. However, these readings in typescript form, and the published pamphlets, had considerable use in the training of Service and civilian administrators of relief operations abroad.

---

[1] These papers on "Administration of Relief Abroad" consisted of the following titles:

1. Foreign Relief and Rehabilitation—A Bibliography
2. The Near East Relief, 1915–1930, by James L. Barton
3. The American Red Cross in the Great War, 1917–1919, by Henry P. Davison
4. American Aid to Germany, 1918–1925, by Sidney Brooks; together with The Long Mile Beyond Berlin, by Shelby M. Harrison
5. The American Friends in France, 1917–1919, by Rufus M. Jones; together with Problems Involved in Administering Relief Abroad, by Clarence E. Pickett
6. The American Relief Administration in Russia, 1921–1923, by H. H. Fisher
7. Recent Relief Programs of the American Friends in Spain, 1937–1939, by John Van Gelder Forbes;—in France, 1941–1942, by the American Friends Service Committee
8. American Red Cross Famine Relief in China, 1920–1921, from the Report of the China Famine Relief, American Red Cross.

Both Miss Colcord and Mr. Howard, before his foreign assignment began, made substantial contributions to the organization of the "home front" through field work, addresses, articles, conferences. For the period, 44 addresses and 7 published articles are recorded. Special assistance was given the American National Red Cross toward improving service in military camps; to the American Association of Social Workers in the adaptation of program to war needs, and on internal organization; to the American Friends Service Committee; and to many other agencies.

But some of the work the Department might have undertaken was curtailed by the declining health of its director. After the summer of 1944 Miss Colcord was unable to return to the Foundation or resume any of her duties, and submitted her resignation in July, 1945, after more than fifteen years of active service as director of Charity Organization Department.

Illness of the director and absence of the assistant director largely suspended the operations of the Department. However, Miss Dorothy Kahn had been added to the staff on a temporary basis in June, 1944, to prepare a report on problems of policy and procedure in preparation for the expected development of a general assistance program with federal aid, which would not be related to emergency needs but might become a permanent, nationwide program. Work on this project, which was begun under the guidance of Mr. Kurtz as acting director of the Department, is not yet completed.

Mr. Howard's services with UNRRA are more fully recorded in the general section on the Foundation's wartime services.[1] He began this work in October, 1943, at first on loan, but soon on leave of absence. His duties took him to England, France, and China, from which he returned to his work with the Department in March, 1946.

On May 16, 1946, Mr. Howard was made director of the Department, which at the same time ceased to be called the Charity Organization Department and became the Department of Social Work Administration, representing more accurately

[1] See p. 499.

the scope of its work. Mr. Howard has proposed studies in three areas, community organization, public welfare, and international and foreign welfare measures. Emphasis in the last-named is to be upon ways in which American social work practices and United States participation in international social welfare measures can be improved through knowledge of international and foreign service.

One of the earliest projects under this program was preparation of a report on the plight of the approximate million displaced persons. The Department engaged on a short-time basis Pierce Williams, who prepared a preliminary report which was released to United Nations personnel and other interested persons and organizations in September, 1946. Mr. Howard, through articles and addresses,[1] has continued to bring to social workers and other audiences his special knowledge of foreign and international relief needs and welfare problems in the postwar world.

As this record closes in October, 1946, progress has also been made in the study of state and local general assistance programs, and in obtaining personnel for the study of community organization.

[1] Including one of the principal evening addresses on "Welfare Problems and Program in China" at the May, 1946, meeting of the National Conference of Social Work.

XXXVI

CONSUMER CREDIT STUDIES: 1932-1946

THE DEPARTMENT of Remedial Loans did not officially change its name to Department of Consumer Credit Studies until February, 1938, but this change in name reflected only belatedly a progressive broadening in sphere of interest that began in 1929. Previously, its activities centered around the promotion and enforcement of small loan laws and the development of low-cost loan agencies, especially remedial loan associations and credit unions. In the late twenties the Department was impressed with the increasing interrelation between the small loan problem and other areas of consumer credit, such as industrial banking, the personal loan departments of banks, charge accounts, and installment selling. It therefore began to broaden its own program to include the whole of consumer credit.

First steps in this expansion were taken while the Department was still under the fighting and colorful leadership of Leon Henderson. But Mr. Henderson's effective tactics as a member of the Consumers' Advisory Board of the National Recovery Administration, in behalf of consumers who were also borrowers, brought him to the favorable attention of General Hugh S. Johnson, NRA administrator, to whose assistance he went in January, 1934.[1] Rolf Nugent, who had been assistant director of the Department since 1926, was appointed associate director in April, 1934, and director in November. With Mr. Nugent's appointment, the change of emphasis in the Department's work became pronounced. Legislative work in the small loan field was minimized and research was emphasized.

[1] At first on leave of absence, but with his resignation following in September. He became director of the Division of Research and Planning in NRA. A succession of important governmental jobs followed, including service as consulting economist, WPA; executive secretary, Temporary National Economic Committee; Securities and Exchange commissioner; member, Advisory Commission to the Council of National Defense; and administrator, Office of Price Administration.

Mr. Nugent's directorship covered a period of unparalleled economic stress, at first as the result of depression and then under the compulsions of war. The Department of Consumer Credit Studies, in its key position in the economic field, was often called upon to meet special emergencies, which altered or interrupted some of its planned program. These dramatic interludes deserve their large place in the history of this period, but the central purposes of the Department could still be stated in the words of the new director in the introduction to his annual reports:

Improvement of the conditions under which credit is available to families of limited means.

Protection of small debtors against harsh and abusive contracts and collection practices.

Development of adequate consumer credit statistics.

Interpretation of the social and economic significance of events in the field of consumer credit.

The Small Loan Series

In 1922 the Trustees of the Foundation had voted a special appropriation for a comprehensive survey of the small loan business under the direction of Louis N. Robinson.[1] Ten years later, at the time this chapter begins, one pamphlet and one book had been published,[2] and the remaining planned volumes were well advanced.

Final revision on the next volume, Small Loan Legislation,[3] was done by Geoffrey May, and the book was published in May, 1932. It included an account of early small loan legislation and the theories on which it was based; the devising of the Uniform Small Loan Law; the struggle for its adoption in the legislatures of various states; and its gradual revision into the Fifth Draft adopted in 1932, which appeared as an appendix.

The following year Moneylending in Great Britain[4] was published. This study covered British experience in this field from

---

[1] See p. 339.

[2] The Regulation of Pawnbroking, by R. Cornelius Raby (1924), and Ten Thousand Small Loans, by Louis N. Robinson and Maude E. Stearns (1930).

[3] By David J. Gallert, Walter S. Hilborn, and Geoffrey May.

[4] By Dorothy Johnson Orchard and Geoffrey May, 1933.

the earliest days, when all forms of interest were forbidden under church law as usury, to the operation of the Moneylenders Act of 1927.

The next volume of the series took longer to prepare. It was to be the summary volume, putting into historical perspective the development and regulation of the small loan business in the United States. But the Department was just in process of developing important statistical data on the business, particularly with relation to the controversial question of maximum rate of charge. Mr. Nugent heavily revised the original manuscript to include this information, and it was not ready for publication until May, 1935.[1] This book became the standard reference work in the small loan field. It went out of print in 1945.

An additional title,[2] not contemplated in the original series, was published in June, 1938, under the authorship of F. B. Hubachek, for many years chairman of the law committee of the American Association of Personal Finance Companies. The legal work on the manuscript was done by the author without compensation from the Foundation, but the Department assisted in preparation of the non-legal text and the editing. Annotations on Small Loan Laws was intended primarily to assist prosecutors and state supervisors in interpreting the law; it gave special attention to decisions involving devices to evade laws regulating interest rates. The American Association of Personal Finance Companies, which had originally intended such a volume as its own publication, assisted in its distribution, and it went into two printings.

The six titles of the Small Loan Series, as it was finally completed, represented a rounded presentation of the problem, in relation to an enlightened social policy. What a reviewer said of one book[3] might have been applied with even more pertinence to the series as a whole: "None of our perennial proposers of unsound small loan laws can be excused for his ignorance when the truth is at hand in this plain, adequate, authoritative volume."

[1] Regulation of the Small Loan Business, by Louis N. Robinson and Rolf Nugent.

[2] Annotations on Small Loan Laws, by F. B. Hubachek.

[3] Review of Regulation of the Small Loan Business, by LeBaron R. Foster, in Journal of the American Statistical Association, December, 1935, p. 766.

The Uniform Small Loan Law

Ignorance, unfortunately, was not the only, or the chief, source of unsound legislation. In every state where an effort was made to introduce the Uniform Small Loan Law, it met bitter opposition from loan sharks and the loan-shark chains, which knew very well what would happen to their own unconscionable profits if credit became legitimately available to the needy borrower. Where satisfactory laws already existed, attempts to "amend" them into unworkability, usually under the pious pretense of aiding the small borrower, were unending. Although the Department announced its intention of concentrating upon research and avoiding active promotion of legislation, and had turned over to the American Association of Personal Finance Companies the task of policing the laws in force, it was unable to avoid involvement in legislative problems. The volume of proposed legislation, on which the Department's opinion was usually asked, was enormous. In 1933 alone, 282 bills affecting small loans were introduced.

On January 1, 1932, the Department released the Fifth Draft of the general form of the Uniform Small Loan Law. It provided for greater supervisory powers than any of its predecessors, and certain new regulations for the licensed business to meet the problems arising since the Fourth Draft was adopted nine years earlier.

At the beginning of 1932 the number of states with satisfactory small loan legislation was 24, but during that year long battles in New York and New Jersey ended favorably, bringing the total to 26. The line between "satisfactory" and unsatisfactory legislation was not always definite. A law might be proposed which purported to be the Uniform Law and copied nearly all of its words, but omitted or altered some cardinal provision so as to make it undesirable or even unworkable.[1] In 1933 modern small loan bills were enacted in Wisconsin and Indiana. Kentucky joined the list in 1934.

[1] As in Puerto Rico, where a bill purporting to be based on the Uniform Small Loan Law, but allowing unconscionable charges, was passed by the Territorial Legislature in 1940. Information concerning the bill did not reach the Department until it had been passed, but its objections were at once forwarded to Governor Leahy, who vetoed it.

On January 1, 1935, the Department issued the Sixth Draft of the Uniform Small Loan Law. The principal change was the adoption of a graduated rate: 3½ per cent a month on the first $100 of any loan and 2½ per cent on balances in excess of $100; moreover, this was recommended as an initial rate subject to further revision by state authorities after a period of experience.

In 1937 the Uniform Law was enacted in Vermont and the Territory of Hawaii. California and Minnesota joined the states with similar legislation in 1939, and the Dominion of Canada also enacted a regulatory small loan law which incorporated most of the principles of the Uniform Law. Washington and Oklahoma were added in 1941.

A Seventh Draft of the Uniform Law was issued in mimeographed form on June 1, 1942. It had been in preparation and under discussion for several years; an effort was made to coordinate its provisions with the draft of a model installment sales act upon which the Department was at work.

In 1943 Colorado, Idaho, and Nevada joined the states with reasonably satisfactory small loan legislation; in 1945 Utah was added.

The Law provided for a licensing and supervising official, who in practice was usually one of the officials of the state banking department. In 1934 the Department invited these officials together for a discussion of examination policies, proposed changes in the Uniform Law, and use of a uniform report form. The meeting was so successful that the following year the National Conference of State Small Loan Supervisors was formed, and has continued to the present with a growing membership. Annual meetings are held for discussion of problems of supervision and enforcement, to which all persons in attendance contribute from their own experience. Discussions are technical, intimate, and off the record, rendering the Conference a remarkably effective device for making available to each state the combined experience of all the states. For the first two years, Mr. Nugent served as secretary of the Conference, but the Department has withdrawn as rapidly as possible from its position as sponsor. Since 1936 the Conference officers have been state officials, with the Department furnishing only a secretariat for arrangement of the annual meetings and handling of correspondence.

Maximum Interest Rate

Most of the legislative maneuvering of this period, however, did not concern mere adoption of the Uniform Law, but the question of maximum rate of interest on small loans. In the early period of regulation, the problem had been to establish a rate high enough to make profits possible on loans of $300 and less, so that capital might be attracted to this field. In the absence of such capital, the needy borrower had no one to turn to but the loan shark, to whom he often paid rates exceeding 1,000 per cent a year. To keep the field to themselves, the loan sharks frequently joined forces with well-intentioned but ill-informed persons to defeat small loan legislation establishing rates above the "legal" 6 or 8 per cent per annum, or—where small loan legislation already existed—to reduce the rate allowed to a level which did not permit the legitimate business to survive.[1]

The maximum rate first agreed upon, and included in the Uniform Law as late as the Fifth Draft of 1932, was 3½ per cent a month on unpaid balances. No accurate statistics on the cost of the business were available, and this initial maximum rate was the result of a compromise between the licensed lenders and the existing Department of Remedial Loans: the lenders agreed to support the supervisory and regulatory features of the model Law and the Department agreed to the inclusion of this rate as the proposed maximum. It was expected that competition for small loan business would bring the actual rate down to whatever level proved efficient under changing conditions and in various states. Experience disproved this expectation. The maximum was, for practical purposes, also the minimum.

Meanwhile, the Department's studies on costs of the small loan business were indicating that at least on the larger loans, above $100, a smaller maximum rate would afford adequate profit.

[1] "In Georgia," reported the Department in 1935, "a rate reduction to 1½ per cent a month led to the virtual destruction of the licensed small loan business there." Similar disasters occurred, or were narrowly avoided, in many other states.

The lenders proved to have a different conception of adequacy of profit. Relations became "somewhat strained, due mainly to the division in opinion as to proper maximum rates to be allowed commercial lenders."

Experiments were tried. With the Department's encouragement, laws were passed in Indiana and Wisconsin in 1933 delegating rate-making to a permanent commission with power to fix the rate of charge for different classifications of loans. In Michigan in the same year Governor Comstock took an unprecedented action when the legislature passed a bill fixing the rate at an unworkable 1¼ per cent; he called the licensees together and agreed to veto the bill if rates were voluntarily reduced. They were—to 3 per cent on loans up to $100 and 2½ per cent for larger loans.

The Sixth Draft of the Uniform Small Loan Law, released in 1935, was issued on sole authority of the Department, without joint action with the lenders' Association. As already noted, this draft reduced the recommended maximum rate to 3½ per cent a month on the first $100 of any loan and 2½ per cent on balances in excess of $100, and this merely as an initial rate subject to further revision after experience. It was the first of the various drafts which the American Association of Personal Finance Companies failed to approve. In the same year the Department published, in Regulation of the Small Loan Business, its extensive statistics on costs. The current Seventh Draft represents a further reduction, recommending a maximum rate not exceeding 3 per cent a month on the first $100, and 2 per cent a month on the portion of an unpaid balance which is above $100.

Efforts to decrease the cost of loans to needy families were not limited to attempts at rate reductions within the licensed field. These needy families suffered most from the illegal lenders, the loan sharks, whose rates often started at 20 per cent a month, who collected by strong-arm methods, and who sometimes prevented payment of principal to keep the debtor constantly in their toils, paying many times over the amount he originally borrowed. As the depression deepened in the early thirties, the number of families in financial difficulties greatly increased, and loan sharks redoubled their efforts to obtain the profitable business, and to outlaw the licensed lenders.[1]

The loan sharks often adopted devices to conceal the true interest rate, in attempts to evade the law. Loans were disguised as purchases of wages, insurance, store coupons, charges to cover a special "hazard," or even jewelry sales.[2] The Department uncovered many of these instances in the course of its studies, gave information to the authorities, and sometimes participated in actions as *amicus curiae*.

The situation in New York City became particularly bad in the late years of the depression, when the end of Prohibition brought many New York bootleggers into the loan-shark racket. After Thomas E. Dewey was appointed special prosecutor for New York County to attack organized crime, the Department described to him the conditions and turned over the accumulated evidence. The director of the Department, after receiving anonymous telephone calls, was advised to go armed. By October, 1936, 130 lenders were convicted in New York County alone under the penal provisions of the Uniform Small Loan Law, and the racket was virtually destroyed in that locality.

At the request of the Attorney General of New York State, the Department participated as *amicus curiae* in a case involving the use of the hazard agreement as a means to evade the small loan law.[3] This case was decided in favor of the Foundation's position. The decision permitted criminal actions by the Attorney General which in 1939 resulted in repayment of about $100,000 in cash to borrowers, and reduction of borrowers' notes by a similar sum.

[1] Early in the thirties an identical bill to eliminate small loan companies mysteriously appeared in some 20 states, together with propaganda in favor of the bill, addressed to every legislator in those states, from "the Congressional Information Service, Room 219, National Press Building, Washington." Room 219 proved to be the office of a public stenographer; the manager of the building knew of no such organization.

[2] In 1937 the Department assisted in analyzing garnishments against New York City employes. It was discovered that about 2,100 of these garnishments were brought by so-called jewelry lenders, who delivered a diamond ring instead of cash to the borrower. The borrower then pawned the ring for less than one-fifth the contract price, and the lender proceeded at once to collect by garnishment the principal involved. Interest costs under this racket ranged from 200 to 1,500 per cent a year.

[3] Common in securing high rates on loans against automobiles. The charges were claimed to be an insurance and not a loan contract.

At the request of the Comptroller of the Currency of New York State, the Department prepared a memorandum on legal aspects of the Vee Bee System[1] which "insured" unendorsed personal loans from banks. The Comptroller in 1940 issued a ruling to the effect that the System was usurious and, even if not usurious, contrary to public policy. This led in 1941 to a suit for $1,500,000 damages by the Vee Bee Service Company against the Foundation, Mr. Nugent as director of the Department of Consumer Credit Studies, the Household Finance Corporation, and its president. Three years later the referee appointed by the court held the Vee Bee lending system wholly invalid, and his report was sustained in later court actions; the suit for damages was disallowed.

In the face of this continuous record of efforts, usually successful, to reduce the cost of loans to the needy borrower, the Foundation is frequently subjected to charges of attempting to maintain high rates, or even of participating in the small loan racket for its own profit, by interests which desire to discredit its recommendations and open the field to their own illegal operations. Russell Sage Foundation has had no investment in any company in the small loan field, other than the Provident Loan Society of New York and the Chattel Loan Society of New York, limited dividend corporations organized to assist needy borrowers. Its own carefully considered investment policy has recently been given general statement.[2]

MISCELLANEOUS SERVICES

In addition to its major projects usually centering in a departmental publication, the Department rendered many general services of which no complete record can be given.

[1] Organized by Vernon Buchman.

[2] "Certain other types of investment are unwise, not for financial reasons, but because of effects on the foundation program or reputation. Obviously, no investment will be made in a business or enterprise generally regarded as anti-social. Also, any operating foundation having investments in, or whose executives have investments in or derive profits from, a business which is a subject of its surveys is in serious danger of having the objectivity of its findings challenged." From American Foundations for Social Welfare, by Harrison and Andrews, 1946, p. 73.

At the beginning of the period here recorded, the Department had a considerable but diminishing interest in credit union activities, particularly in New York State. Its tasks in assisting in the orderly liquidation of distressed credit unions at the beginning of the depression were nearly over by 1932, but it continued to study causes of credit union failures and to collect national statistics on organization. Mr. Nugent served as executive secretary of the New York State Credit Union League until 1936, when he insisted upon the acceptance of his resignation, and the Department's active participation in this field came to an end. It did, however, assist in setting up a credit union for employes of the Foundation itself and associated agencies, in 1939.

A large program of addresses, conferences, and correspondence was maintained. In 1934, for example, calls for special assistance came from nine agencies of the federal government alone: the Consumers' Council of the Agricultural Adjustment Agency, on policy toward credit agencies; the Commissioner of Labor Statistics, on a proposal to lend government funds to consumer applicants; the Committee on Government Statistics, on the Kuznets memorandum on consumer credit statistics; the Consumers' Advisory Board, on plans for dealing with delinquent debt; both the Department of Agriculture and the Farm Credit Administration, on rural credit unions and administration of the federal credit union act; the Federal Housing Administration and the National Emergency Council, on methods of financing home repairs; and the NRA, on a master code for all consumer credit institutions. Assistance to non-governmental agencies was still greater, and exceedingly varied. It ranged from aid in editing a scenario, I Promise to Pay, for Columbia Pictures Corporation, to consultations with the Family Welfare Association of America on the consumer debt problems posed by its member agencies.

The director of the Department usually gave the address on developments in the small loan field at the annual meetings of the American Association of Personal Finance Companies. He and his associates contributed many articles to such periodicals as The Annals of the American Academy of Political and Social Science, Banking, Harvard Business Review, Journal of the

American Statistical Association, Law and Contemporary Problems, Retailing, and the World Almanac. Many of these addresses and articles were reprinted as separate pamphlets, and distributed or sold by the Department, outside the regular publication program of the Foundation.

Mr. Nugent assisted in planning or revising, or contributed sections to, a number of publications in his field of interest issued under other than the Foundation's auspices. Among such enterprises was his chapter on "Consumer Credit and Consumers' Capital Formation" in Capital Formation and Its Elements,[1] and his co-authorship of The Volume of Consumer Instalment Credit, 1929–1938.[2]

Consumer Credit

When Mr. Nugent took over the direction of the Department in 1934, one of the first major requests to reach him fell directly in line with his resolve to expand the area of interest to the whole field of consumer credit, and to concentrate upon research. In June of that year he was asked to direct the work of a special committee appointed by the Consumers' Advisory Board of the NRA to study consumer debt and its retarding effects upon industrial recovery. The Foundation authorized him to devote a major part of his time to this work.

A preliminary survey indicated that, on balance, the liquidation of consumer credit had stopped, and that many consumer obligations were being invalidated by the statute of limitations. A recommendation was therefore made against emergency action by the federal government, but for a long-term study of the economic effects of consumer credit fluctuations and the social consequences of the widespread use of consumer credit. The committee accepted this proposal.

The Department was assigned four statistical workers by the New York Emergency Relief Bureau and some of the needed data were independently developed by the United States De-

[1] A symposium published by the National Industrial Conference Board, New York, 1939.
[2] By Holthausen, Merriam, and Nugent. National Bureau of Economic Research, New York, 1940.

partment of Commerce and the United States Bureau of Labor Statistics. But unfortunately, the Consumers' Advisory Board furnished neither the funds nor the advice that were anticipated. When the Supreme Court invalidated the National Recovery Administration in May, 1935, responsibility for completion and publication of the "consumer debt" study—as the depression lifted it became, significantly, the "consumer credit" study— passed to Russell Sage Foundation.

As the study developed, its main purposes became (1) development of over-all statistical measurements of consumer credit; (2) analysis of economic consequences of consumer credit fluctuations; and (3) appraisal of the social consequences of the extensive use of consumer credit. The field work included the collection, in co-operation with the United States Department of Commerce, of information concerning outstanding accounts from 900 representative credit merchants and professional men; gathering data, in co-operation with the Bureau of Labor Statistics, on wage executions for debt; tabulation of garnishment actions in four selected areas; a survey of outstanding loans of all types in four diversified cities; and an intensive study of records of the courts and consumer credit agencies of Detroit, partly as a basis for a separate report for the NRA on request of President Roosevelt.

John E. Hamm, formerly assistant to Mr. Henderson in the NRA, was drawn into the Department as assistant director in August, 1935. He helped in the consumer credit study, with emphasis on installment credit. His first publication was a bibliography on Credit for the Wage Earner, published in the regular Library series of the Foundation in October, 1935.

As analysis of the accumulating data progressed, it became evident that there were involved both an economic study of the relationship between fluctuations of outstanding consumer credit and the business cycle, and a social study of problems arising in the wake of increased consumer debt. It was decided to develop the economic study first.

A major historic shift in the influence of consumer credit seemed to have occurred. During the nineteenth century its volume was small, and seemed to vary inversely with wage payments; that is, in "bad" times the grocer and small businessman allowed accounts to run, increasing purchasing power and cushioning depressions. But at least by the twenties of the present century consumer credit was relatively large in volume and varied directly with wage payments; that is, in good times people bought houses on mortgages, and automobiles and other expensive durables on installments, and when times turned "bad" installment sales greatly decreased and current purchases dropped even more than wages; for people had to pay off previous installment contracts, made when prospects were bright. This, concluded Mr. Nugent, following in part the Keynes theory, gravely accelerated booms and deepened depressions; consumer credit had become a key factor in the business cycle, exerting an influence far beyond its dollar position in the economy. Therefore, control of consumer credit might prove one of the more hopeful means for leveling out cyclical changes.

His book, Consumer Credit and Economic Stability, was published in November, 1939. War in Europe had started; the book contained several last-minute observations on possible use of consumer credit controls in a national emergency which soon had national repercussions. It was well received, and its thesis generally accepted by economists.

Completion of the material for this book meant only more time to spend on other aspects of consumer credit. The National Bureau of Economic Research, under large grants from the Rockefeller Foundation and the Reserve City Bankers Association, conducted a group of studies in the general area of consumer credit. Mr. Nugent served on a committee to outline the research program; between 1937 and 1940 the Department contributed heavily of its time and material, and reviewed each of the publications at some stage prior to publication. Mr. Nugent's co-authorship of one of the resulting volumes has already been noted.

Assistance was given to the United States Department of Commerce in setting up machinery for collecting monthly figures on consumer receivables, and to the United States Business Census in development of census items to measure retail receivables in census years.

In other areas of consumer credit, the Department has made attempts to formulate "model" laws after the general pattern of the Uniform Small Loan Law. When personal loan departments were developing in banks in the early thirties, the New York Superintendent of Banks requested the Department to draft a bill to authorize and regulate the making of personal loans by state banks. The primary features of the bill were permission to lend at 12 per cent a year, subject to authorization by the Superintendent of Banks, segregation of records of personal loans, statement of rates of charge in simple interest, limitation of fines, and revocation of authorization for cause. Interest might be discounted, subject to disclosure of the true interest rate. With some compromise amendments arrived at in discussions with a committee of bankers, this bill was introduced in 1936 and became law. The Department prepared formulas and tables for conversion of discount rates into interest rates.

The existence of the dual banking system, state and federal, offered obvious difficulties in efforts at control, and the Department delayed development of a general model law pending experience under the New York law and solution of this problem. It later appeared, as a result of a test in Nebraska, that no legal obstacles exist to prevent regulation by the state of creatures of the federal government if such regulation represents an exercise of the state's police power and is not in conflict with pertinent federal statutes.

Early in 1943 the Department completed and circulated for criticism a preliminary draft of a model law to regulate personal loans of banks. The draft was applauded in many quarters, but vigorously objected to by some bankers. Wartime duties of the Department prevented further development of this proposed bill.

Regulation of installment sales became a major concern of the Department. Both the high interest cost of many installment contracts and the large total volume of such sales made installment selling an important area of consumer credit. Investigation of British efforts at control resulted in the publication of a pamphlet on the subject.[1] The Department began work on its model law in 1938, and when Mr. Hamm entered governmental service in June, 1940, other members of the Department continued the project. Walter Robinson, son of Louis N. Robinson, was retained for a short period to deal with certain legal problems. Toward the end of 1940 a preliminary draft was circulated for discussion. This tentative draft was introduced in the legislatures of three states in 1941, but the bills were not pushed and none was enacted. The New York legislature, however, did enact in that year 13 bills directed at various abuses in the installment field, proposed by a committee of which Mr. Nugent was a member.

The following year J. Glenn Donaldson[2] prepared an analysis of existing installment-selling legislation and a revised draft of the proposed installment sales act on the basis of criticisms which had been received. Further action was prevented by war activities.

In 1941 work was begun on a revision of the Department's Uniform Pawnbroking Law, which had not been changed since it was first drafted in 1924. After analysis of the pertinent laws of each state, a tentative draft was prepared and sent for criticism to the officials of the five states which had the most effective regulatory statutes, and to others. Helpful criticisms were received, and work was begun on a final draft.

WARTIME SERVICES

From 1940 to the end of this record in 1946 the problems of national defense, total war, and then international relief were the central concerns of the Department of Consumer Credit Studies, depleting its personnel, overriding its regular program, and finally costing the life of its director.

One pre-Pearl Harbor service of this sort went unheralded at the time. Early in 1940 Mr. Nugent undertook a western trip which included a visit to Hawaii. While there he conferred with intelligence officers of the armed forces, who were gravely con-

[1] The English Hire-Purchase Act, 1938, by John E. Hamm, 1940.

[2] Mr. Donaldson joined the Department as counsel in June, 1941. He resigned in November, 1942, to become state attorney for the OPA in Colorado.

cerned over the numbers of our military personnel in the Territory who were in the toils of Japanese loan sharks. Other forms of consumer credit were suggested—safer for our military secrets.

Mr. Hamm's services were requested, and granted, for a study of the movement of prices being undertaken by the Temporary National Economic Committee in the fall of 1939. He was on leave from mid-October to January. After the Advisory Commission to the Council of National Defense was created his services were again requested, and he departed on a new leave in June, 1940, and did not again return to the Department.[1] The later sequestration of Mr. Donaldson by the OPA has already been noted.

At the request of the United States Army, Mr. Nugent submitted a confidential memorandum in July, 1940, on the control of consumption in time of war, which proposed regulation of installment credit terms and the imposition of excise taxes on goods which competed with armaments for skills and materials. When the Council of National Defense took over from the War Department responsibility in this area, Mr. Nugent was appointed economic consultant, charged with amplifying his memorandum in co-operation with a committee of economists. After the middle of May, 1941, Mr. Nugent began a series of leaves for governmental service which took substantially all his time. The Foundation continued his salary, but he did not again appear in his office except for occasional days.

His first such service was in helping draft Regulation W, an executive order giving the Federal Reserve Board power to regulate consumer credit. Though the United States was not yet at war, the need was apparent to throw most of our heavy industry into war production. But just at that time the higher wages of "defense" production and the fear of later scarcities were causing a buying boom. It seemed not legally possible, nor politic, arbitrarily to shut down certain plants or industries and transfer them to war production by direct command. The President, however, did have power to regulate "banking institu-

---

[1] Resignation followed, and he became senior deputy administrator of the OPA under his former chief in the NRA, Leon Henderson.

tions" which might include all institutions extending consumer credit. If down-payments were made heavy and the term short, a large percentage of the purchases of such expensive durable goods as automobiles, refrigerators, and the like—precisely those which competed most seriously with armaments for materials and manpower—would be cut off. Mr. Nugent assisted officers of the Federal Reserve Board and the Office of Price Administration and Civilian Control[1] in framing Regulation W to accomplish this purpose. President Roosevelt issued the Order on August 9, 1941, and Regulation W was promulgated by the Federal Reserve Board on September 1, 1941.

The initial regulation required down payments of varying amounts on installment sales of certain types of consumers' durable goods and limited to eighteen months the period of maturity of installment-sales contracts for these goods, and of installment loans. In the spring of 1942, down-payment requirements and maturities were further tightened, the list of goods covered expanded, and charge accounts were brought within the Regulation. It was estimated that outstanding consumer credit dropped about $3,500,000,000 during 1942. The Department regarded this early application of one of its theories as of "primary importance in the field of consumer credit." As Mr. Nugent reported, "Unlike the controls traditionally exercised by the states, which were directed primarily toward the protection of small debtors, these new controls were directed solely toward national economic objectives."

Mr. Nugent's further governmental service had less direct relation to the work of the Department of Consumer Credit Studies, and has been covered under the general wartime service of the Foundation.[2] It included his work as supervisor of automobile rationing, as chief of the consumer requirements branch, and as director of the credit policy office of the OPA, the last of these terminating in July, 1943, after which he became associate chief, Civilian Requirements Branch, War Food Administration. He joined the United Nations Relief and Rehabilitation Administra-

[1] Of which his former chief, Leon Henderson, was administrator.
[2] See pp. 500–501.

tion in February, 1944, continuing on leave of absence from the Foundation but transferring to UNRRA payroll in March, 1945.

During this period of governmental service he proposed, and vigorously promoted, a Plan for Instalment Selling for Post-War Delivery, which was intended to absorb some of the excess wartime earnings and to help insure full employment after the war through building up purchasing power.[1]

He planned to return to full-time service with his department in September, 1946, but on a final mission as deputy chief of the UNRRA Bureau of Supply, he died in a swimming accident off Yokohama on July 27, 1946, while on the way from China.

His death left the Department with no personnel except the department secretary, Miss Eleanor Nissley, who had for some years carried on such activities as the Department could maintain, in the absence of its director; for example, the arrangements for the annual meetings of the National Conference of Small Loan Supervisors and routine correspondence. But she also was on leave, to serve with Mr. Nugent, through most of 1946.

Two studies, practically completed, were left unpublished. The first was in line with the Department's proposal to study the social consequences of consumer credit; it involved an analysis of legal actions for debt in the lower courts of four Kansas communities for the years 1900, 1910, 1920, 1930, and 1940, and was conducted by Nell M. Reeder.

The second was the result of a unique situation Mr. Nugent discovered in California in 1940. In that state, before passage of its small loan law, there was no restriction upon maximum rate of interest, but the lender was required to report his charges to the Corporation Commission. This offered the only known opportunity for discovering the actual rates of charge which prevailed under conditions of free contract. The data for a typical month in 1938 were transcribed and analyzed, by rate of interest, size of loan, and by communities, but publication of the proposed pamphlet was delayed by emergency work, and then by the tragic death of its author.

[1] His plan was among the 17 that won awards in the Pabst postwar planning contest, which drew 35,766 entrants. It was not adopted, however.

XXXVII

INDUSTRIAL STUDIES: 1932-1946

EARLIER chapters have recorded the development of the Department of Industrial Studies from the Committee on Women's Work which first received a grant from the Foundation in 1908 to the status of a full department of the Foundation, and the broadening of its scope from studies of industrial conditions, particularly among women, to studies of industrial relations between workers and management. The Industrial Relations Series, recording these latter studies, was not limited to labor relations in single companies,[1] some of which, under the name of employes' representation, were later known as company unions, but also included collective agreements between trade unions and groups of companies within a given industry or area.[2]

The present chapter records a further broadening of scope, under the urgencies of a severe depression and a world war, to a consideration of the whole social-economic environment as affecting industrial relations, with emphasis upon the relationship between technological advance and living standards. The Department, throughout these thirty-eight years of its history under the auspices of the Foundation, has been under the direction of Miss Mary van Kleeck.

INDUSTRIAL RELATIONS SERIES

The sixth volume of the Industrial Relations Series returned to the coal mines of Colorado, which had been the setting for Employes' Representation in Coal Mines, initiated in 1919 and published in 1925. This volume, however, presented a factual record of what happened when the miners' union and the Rocky Mountain Fuel Company, under direction of Miss Josephine

[1] As in Sharing Management with the Workers (1925); Employes' Representation in Coal Mines (1925); Employes' Representation in Steel Works (1925); and The Filene Store (1930).

[2] As in Labor Agreements in Coal Mines (1931).

549

Roche, entered into an agreement which not only provided for collective bargaining but undertook "to stabilize employment, production, and markets through co-operative endeavor, and to accomplish through mutual aid other unusual purposes."

Miss van Kleeck's Miners and Management was published in April, 1934, approximately ten years after the earlier Colorado study. The intervening decade, and particularly the onset of the severe depression, had effected great changes in the economic scene. As Miss van Kleeck pointed out in her Foreword:

> The center of interest has shifted from relations between employer and employe in one establishment or even in one industry to the basic problem of industrial depression with unemployment widespread, wages and earnings declining, profit-making problematical, and prices at levels which are unstable and often unrelated to costs of production.

The volume included an early appraisal of policies of the National Recovery Administration with respect to coal together with discussion of the broad questions of whether control by government is to increase and if so what form it shall take; what modifications should be made in the forms of private ownership and its claims upon profits; what place the workers are to have in determining larger economic and industrial policy; and an analysis of the possible application of the idea of socialization to coal mines along with other natural resources in a planned economy.

A further study in this series was projected under the working title Trade Unions and the Government to explore industrial relations under the National Recovery Administration. But the economic kaleidoscope shifted too rapidly, and the base of this study was broadened in several successive steps which will later be described. No further study in the Industrial Relations Series has yet reached publication stage.

OTHER COAL-MINING STUDIES

In addition to Miners and Management, the Department's long-continued interest in the problem of coal found expression in this period in further studies, several of which have been published.

A survey of Germany's experience in regularization of employment in coal mines, based on data from 1890 to 1933, has not been published. Preliminary facts were gathered as early as 1922, when Herbert Hoover, then chairman of the President's Conference on Unemployment, suggested to the Department that it make a comparison of American experience regarding regularity of employment with that in other countries. German coal mines seemed the best choice, and preliminary statistics were gathered. It was unsafe to interpret these data, however, without first-hand acquaintance with the industry in Germany. Opportunity to review and continue this study came in 1934 when, through Hospites,[1] a fellowship was granted to Dr. Felix Hase, a German economist, to carry on his work at the offices of the International Industrial Relations Institute at The Hague. He brought the statistical information up to date, and through his personal contacts with conditions in German coal mines, and his knowledge of pertinent legislation and the development of the coal cartel, he was able to evaluate the material.

After completion of his manuscript on the German coal mines, which was reviewed by the Foundation's Department of Statistics but was not published, Dr. Hase undertook a brief inquiry into material in Great Britain which might show the effect of national legislative policy upon the comparative stability of the industry in that country. It was not found possible to finance a continuation of this study, but even the brief inquiry threw light on the similar problem in the United States.

Further data on the British experience were gathered in 1944–1945, when Miss Roche, on a visit to the British mines, was commissioned both to gather data for the Department and to make the Department's own material on labor relations and productivity available in Great Britain.

Edward A. Wieck, a former coal miner, was appointed to the Department's staff as a research associate in January, 1934. His

---

[1] An organization for the relief of central European social workers, in concentration camps in Europe or as refugees. Miss van Kleeck was a member of its executive committee. See p. 526.

first task was to observe the operation of the National Recovery Administration in the coal mines and in certain other industries. In the course of his work he began a search for data on the early history of miners' organization, and found enough in the Belleville, Illinois, public library to warrant initiating a study of the American Miners' Association. Organized in 1861, the Association may be described as not only the first national miners' union in the United States, but as the beginning of the modern labor movement in this country. Supplemented by a study of local newspaper files in other libraries for the period, and of other available documents, the result was published in book form,[1] as a contribution both to historical record and to perspective on present-day labor policy.[2]

The year in which this book was published, 1940, was marked in mining annals by six disastrous explosions in the United States, resulting in the deaths of 277 miners. This unusually bad record seemed to call for inquiry by the Department of Industrial Studies, particularly as the occurrence of the worst of these fatalities was in mechanized mines, bringing them into the orbit of the Department's further studies of effects of technological change. Mr. Wieck examined the records and analyzed the findings of the investigating boards, publishing the result in a pamphlet entitled Preventing Fatal Explosions in Coal Mines, which included recommendations with regard to ventilation, coal-dust control, electrical equipment and its safe maintenance, explosives and blasting. Participation by the union in establishing and maintaining safety standards was suggested as practicable and helpful.

The pamphlet was issued in May, 1942, and a second printing was required by July. It has had substantial distribution both among local unions of the United Mine Workers of America and among coal operators. It was one of the documents, as was

[1] The American Miners' Association: A Record of the Origin of Coal Miners' Unions in the United States, by Edward A. Wieck, 1940.

[2] While searching for this information, interviewing old-time miners, Mr. Wieck came upon a probably unique collection of documents which had been in the possession of a former union official in the early days of the United Mine Workers of America. These have been acquired for the department library, and may subsequently be used in a history of the United Mine Workers.

Miners and Management, placed in evidence before the fact-finding panel of the National War Labor Board in the 1943 dispute between the United Mine Workers and the operators over renewal of the biennial agreement. What influence Preventing Fatal Explosions in Coal Mines may have had in the miners' strong emphasis on accident prevention in their 1946 negotiations cannot be definitely stated, but must have been substantial.

PROMOTION AND GENERAL SERVICE

The Department, from its beginnings, has directed its studies toward problems on which some practical action can be taken. It has therefore recognized a responsibility for making its findings known through many channels in addition to formal publication. In the period of rapid change which this chapter covers, the economic scene sometimes shifted faster than its record could be published. For this reason formal books were not numerous, and a greater burden fell upon the general service and promotional program.

The purposes of the Department were advanced by a wide variety of means, including membership in other organizations, committee service, addresses, magazine articles, testimony before congressional committees, correspondence, consultations. The detailed record is far too long for inclusion; some idea of the volume of such activity may be gained from a glance at a single year, 1932.

During that year the Department's report records publication of 14 articles by Miss van Kleeck, from an authorized interview in the New York Times to two book prefaces; 36 addresses, including her remarks at Frankfurt am Main in Germany as president of the International Conference of Social Work, a broadcast on "Social-Economic Planning," and numerous talks before labor groups; 45 recorded consultation services on such subjects as unemployment, labor statistics, housing, Negro race relations, women in industry, and international economic relations; attendance at 18 conferences; and service on committees of 12 organizations, including chairmanship of two committees of the American Statistical Association, the vice-presidency of the Church League for Industrial Democracy, and associate director-ship and chairmanship of two committees of the International Industrial Relations Institute.

At the beginning of the 1932–1946 period considerable time was still given to the affairs of the Committee on Governmental Labor Statistics of the American Statistical Association, which until the fall of 1932 had offices within the Department and was supported by an appropriation in the Department's budget. Miss van Kleeck wrote the Foreword to this committee's report on Statistical Procedure of Public Employment Offices by Annabel M. Stewart and Bryce M. Stewart, which the Founda-tion published in April, 1933. Activities of this committee were largely taken over by a new committee appointed by the Amer-ican Statistical Association at the request of Miss Frances Perkins, Secretary of Labor, but interest in the subject continued, par-ticularly with respect to unemployment statistics of the 1930 census and the possibilities for better census procedures in the future.

The earliest interest of the Department, women in industry, recurred from time to time as a subject for special attention. Miss van Kleeck prepared an article on "Women in Industry" for the Encyclopaedia of the Social Sciences. When the Assembly of the League of Nations was urged to embody in an international treaty an "equal rights" amendment which might have pre-vented protective legislation for women workers, the League called upon the International Labour Organization for a report. Miss van Kleeck served in 1936 as one of the correspondents from the United States to report on conditions of women's work to the ILO, and participated actively in the formulation of the Women's Charter, an attempt to reconcile the demand for en-larged opportunities for women with the maintenance of special legislation establishing standards for their employment. This charter was the basis for subsequent resolutions adopted in the International Labour Conference in Geneva, Switzerland, and in the Pan American Conference in Lima, Peru. In 1944 Miss van Kleeck served as chairman of a committee of the Society for the Advancement of Management considering management policies which would contribute to the effective use of women's work in war production.

Particularly in the middle thirties, the department director took a very active part in the meetings of the National Conference of Social Work, where she spoke to overflow meetings on such subjects as "Governmental Intervention in the Labor Movement," "Social Work in the Economic Crisis," and "The Common Goals of Labor and Social Work."

Studies of the Department were also drawn upon in some publications appearing with other than the Foundation's imprint, particularly in publications of the International Industrial Relations Institute and in Creative America: Its Resources for Social Security.[1]

As a member of the committee on unemployment of the American Association of Social Workers, Miss van Kleeck suggested early in the depression the desirability of forming an organization representing various professions to deal with the status of professional workers in social insurance and to win support from these professions for the whole program of social work and social insurance. In 1934 the Inter-Professional Association was organized, and Miss van Kleeck became its national chairman. Within most professional organizations only a small minority concerned itself with the relation of the profession to the general public welfare, but, as the depression deepened, more and more professional workers gained personal acquaintance with problems and conditions to which they had previously paid little attention. The Inter-Professional Association endeavored to direct this new interest into constructive action. It supported the Workers' Bill for Unemployment and Social Insurance, which differed from the Social Security Bill as enacted in 1935 in including professional and independent workers as well as employes in industry, and would have provided funds through the public treasury rather than through payroll taxes. The Association also took a lively interest in the unionization of professional and white-collar workers, which began to develop about 1937.

[1] By Mary van Kleeck, Covici, Friede, New York, 1936.

At the request of Elmer A. Benson, governor-elect of Minnesota, the department director spent ten days in Minneapolis and St. Paul, late in 1936, conferring with representatives of the unemployed, with social workers, governmental administrators, trade union officials, and others. Her recommendations to Mr. Benson dealt with principles appropriate to a farmer-labor government extending and administering social insurance and relief for the unemployed.

The numerous inquiries and requests for co-operation, of which only a few examples have been given, were often opportunities for useful service, but they also represented a serious problem in interruption of regular program, which the Department increasingly recognized. In 1938 this problem was freshly studied and a mimeographed manual prepared, reassigning duties and setting up procedures by which, it was hoped, attention could be concentrated upon productive research without neglect of important outside services.

International Contacts

"While the task of the Department of Industrial Studies is limited to the United States," wrote the director in her report for 1932, "it is important to recognize facts regarding causes which are not limited to any one nation."

The international interests of the Department, already numerous, greatly increased through the depression period. Until World War II limited foreign travel, Miss van Kleeck was in Europe for a part of nearly every year. Studies of coal mining in Germany and in Great Britain have already been mentioned, as has Miss van Kleeck's presidency of the International Conference of Social Work meeting in Germany in 1932. She remained active in the International Conference, and when its meetings were suspended because of the war, she helped continue its organization as vice-president and member of its executive board. Currently, plans are being completed for the first postwar International Conference of Social Work.

A substantial part of the Department's correspondence and advisory service is in behalf of inquirers from other countries, or with respect to international aspects of labor relations. The Beveridge Plan was analyzed with some American comparisons,[1] and Miss van Kleeck gave a number of addresses on the subject. She participated in the Second International Conference on Canadian Affairs held under auspices of the Carnegie Endowment for International Peace at Kingston, Ontario, in 1937; and attended the International Textile Conference in Washington, D. C., the same year.

But the Department's closest association with economic developments in the international field has been through the International Industrial Relations Institute (IRI). Miss van Kleeck's early acquaintance with the Institute and her contributions to several of its reports have been noted.[2] Upon its reorganization in 1932 she became associate director for the United States and chairman of its Research Group, positions which she has held up to the present. Through this group, a committee of engineers, architects, chemists, and educators met with the department director during 1934 to explore the technical basis for social-economic planning in the United States, directed toward prevention of unemployment and raising standards of living. Late that year the IRI held a general conference on the same subject in New York, with speakers discussing various aspects of the National Industrial Recovery Act, then in operation.[3]

Miss van Kleeck usually attended the summer conference of the Institute in Europe. In November, 1937, the relation became still closer when Miss Mary L. Fleddérus, director of the IRI, was given a term appointment as associate in research and administration in the Department of Industrial Studies, to assist in the Department's survey of effects of technology, later to be described. The term was successively renewed, and Miss Fleddérus continues with the Department as this record closes.

Through the Institute, the Department became interested in

[1] "British Plan for Social Security," by Mary van Kleeck, in Lawyers Guild Review, January–February, 1943, pp. 6–11.

[2] See pp. 396–397. The Institute, known as the International Industrial Relations Association until 1932, was organized in 1925.

[3] The proceedings of this conference, published by Covici, Friede (1935) under the title On Economic Planning, were jointly edited by Mary L. Fleddérus and Miss van Kleeck.

557

the work in pictorial statistics of Dr. Otto Neurath,[1] developed at the Social Economic Museum in Vienna. After Dr. Neurath was forced to leave Austria, the IRI and the Department further assisted him in making his work known.

When spreading war in Europe overran the offices of the IRI itself in The Netherlands, headquarters for both its American section and such other activities as could still be carried on became "Room 700, 130 East 22d Street"—which is also the Department of Industrial Studies.

A recent IRI project is a report on Yugoslavia's Resources for Living Standards: A Technological Approach to Post-War Development, prepared by Miss Fleddérus and Miss van Kleeck with the co-operation of engineers and others in the Research Group. A similar study of The Netherlands was initiated, with data gathered by Miss Fleddérus in her visit to that country in 1946.

Industrial Relations and Living Standards

The central, long-term project of the Department of Industrial Studies is perhaps best described under the latest of its working titles, Industrial Relations and Living Standards. As now planned this background study will cover fifteen years, from 1929 through 1944.

When Miners and Management was in process, enactment of the National Industrial Recovery Act brought governmental intervention in industrial relations into new emphasis. One of the stated purposes of this act was to bring about "united action of labor and management"; its famous 7a clause acted as a lively stimulant to the organization of labor. The Department, having drawn in Mr. Wieck as research associate, embarked at once upon a study of the administration of the NIRA[2] and its effect upon labor and industrial relations. This study was planned as the next unit of the Industrial Relations Series, under the working title Trade Unions and the Government: A Study of Indus-

---

[1] Who prepared the charts which appear in Miners and Management.

[2] The more celebrated form of the initials, NRA, stood for National Recovery Administration.

trial Relations under the National Recovery Administration in the United States.

In addition to attendance at code hearings and collection of much documentary material, including newspaper comments and articles, considerable field work was undertaken. Studies of the operation of the NRA centered primarily in coal mining and in the industries of steel in Pennsylvania, Illinois, Indiana, and Ohio, automobiles in Michigan, Wisconsin, and Ohio, rubber tires in Akron, and hosiery and textiles in Pennsylvania. Some attention was also given to labor relations among longshoremen and seamen on the Pacific Coast. The study had three main aspects: (1) provisions for collective bargaining; (2) legislation prescribing minimum wages and maximum hours; (3) the general purpose of raising standards of living.

The Act provided that every code should contain a provision binding employers in its industry to accept the right of employes "to organize and bargain collectively through representatives of their own choosing." The unions immediately grew in numbers as workers understood they were free to organize. At the same time it became the policy of many employing groups to interpret this provision as being fulfilled by "company unions." The Department's earlier studies of employes' representation had indicated the limitations of company unions, and some of the experience with them under the NRA appeared no less than disastrous. Finally the opposition of the unions, supported by many citizens, led to the definite outlawing of company unions in the National Labor Relations Act, passed in 1935.

The Department's study of the National Industrial Recovery Act never received separate publication. The Act itself was declared unconstitutional by the Supreme Court in May, 1935. Field work was necessarily ended. While the report was being shaped for publication, a new situation demanded attention. Industrial conditions had made craft unions a logical development when the American Federation of Labor was in process of formation, and such unions were the basis for its organization. Introduction of mass production greatly limited and modified the craftsmanship which lay at the basis of trade unions. The corporations in control of mass-production industries were almost universally antagonistic to trade unions, and when they were compelled to grant the right to organize, under the NRA codes or otherwise, most of them countered with some form of employes' representation.

Since the craft unions seemed not well adapted to the organization of a whole mass-production industry, the Committee for Industrial Organization[1] was formed. A conflict arose within the union ranks, and the American Federation of Labor suspended the unions included in the CIO. But to the Department the important issue seemed not this immediate conflict, but the whole problem of the status of workers and the conditions of their employment in the highly mechanized industries under corporation control. It was decided not to publish the NRA study until this new material could be added. The scope of the study was expanded to a threefold report covering (1) trends in employment, earnings, and standards of living during industrial depression; (2) governmental action to maintain standards of living and overcome unemployment; (3) the effects of these developments upon the trade unions, and the role of unions in maintenance of standards of wages and income.

By 1937 industrial unionism was in such process of growth and development that it was decided not to attempt a definitive report at that time, but to turn the project into a running record of development. Field work was continued in the steel, automobile, and coal-mining industries, and current material accumulated from newspapers, trade journals, and government documents. A special study was made of sit-down strikes.

The Department's files on labor relations in the building industry were considerably expanded through arrangements to take over the material of D. K. Boyd, an architect, who had worked for many years on these problems. In consideration of an appropriation from the Foundation, Mr. Boyd arranged this material as a permanent file within the Department. It related particularly to technical problems and conditions of employment

[1] After November, 1938, the Congress of Industrial Organizations, but in each case, the CIO.

traceable to changes in machinery, methods of work, and materials used in the construction of buildings.

In 1939 an attempt was again made to set a closing date for the study. War had broken out in Europe, employment was rising, and it seemed logical to handle the accumulated material as a unit—a report on industrial management, labor, and government in a decade of industrial depression, from October, 1929, through 1939. Meanwhile the section of this study which analyzed trends in employment and in standards of living had revealed the fundamental importance of technological change and its social consequences. A separate report on this subject was in preparation, but not as a part of the Industrial Relations Series.

As the war clouds thickened over the United States and the production of war material was speeded, many of the problems which the Department had studied in World War I came again to the fore. The statement of policy and standards for governmental contracts prepared by the Department at that time served as the basis for the policy adopted by the Advisory Commission to the Council of National Defense and was embodied in the President's message to the Congress in September, 1940. The problems confronting management, the unions, and government under conditions of national defense seemed to require treatment, and a new section on Labor in National Defense was proposed for the Department's background study.

Total war, with its rigid controls over manpower, its no-strike agreements, its National War Labor Board, its problems of wage stabilization, was a period of even swifter and more drastic changes, with highly abnormal industrial conditions. The Department embarked upon several brief studies related to wartime developments or postwar problems, but in this whirlpool of events did not attempt to bring to completion the long-term study, now crystallized as Industrial Relations and Living Standards. Present plans are for its early completion as a history of the unions in the period 1929–1945, including the unemployment of the 1930's followed by war with its new developments, both intensifying old issues in social-economic relationships.

TECHNOLOGY AND LIVELIHOOD

Active preparation for the Department's study of technology began in 1937. It was conceived at first as an investigation of speed, mechanization, and output. Miss van Kleeck and Miss Fleddérus, director of the IRI, conferred in Geneva with staff members of the International Labour Office, at The Hague with the secretary of the Confederation of Management Associations in Great Britain, and in Paris with the general secretary of the International Federation of Trade Unions. Keen interest in the subject was everywhere manifested. Mechanization was increasing not only in the United States, but in other countries, in efforts to recover from the depression. It seemed important to bring into clearer view the factors involved in what might be called optimum productivity—the achievement of maximum production of high quality with minimum expenditure of human energy and the most economical use of materials.

As already noted, Miss Fleddérus joined the department staff late in 1937 to advance this study. She produced an initial memorandum on Optimum Productivity in the Workshop[1] after conference with management engineers and union representatives, and this material was discussed at the Oxford (England) Management Conference in 1938 and at the IRI study conference at The Hague in the same year. A large amount of pertinent data was accumulated from reports of the National Resources Committee, the National Research Project of the WPA, the Bureau of Labor Statistics, the Department of Commerce, and other governmental agencies; much of this was incorporated in the book as finally published. Analysis of the material demonstrated a disproportionate increase in production as compared with employment and wages. "Such a development calls for a new orientation of social research," wrote Miss van Kleeck while the study was in progress. "Social research, including economics, must enlarge its concept and become the guide in a new social administration of technology which shall enable society to utilize fully the new productive capacity of all industry."

[1] Reprinted in Technology and Livelihood, pp. 205–211.

Miss Fleddérus and Miss van Kleeck were joint authors of the book,[1] which in addition to the quoted documents and their interpretation, included a statistical analysis of changes in the occupations of the population through the sixty years 1870 to 1930, in which science and invention transformed man's tools. Technology and Livelihood was published in January, 1944, issued at first in paper covers, with a second printing in cloth. It has already achieved the largest sale of any publication of the Department.

Even before the book was off press, the Department was embarking upon its sequel. Technology and Livelihood described the new technology and changes in labor requirements; there remained the task of setting forth its practical implications in terms of existing deficiencies in living standards, the threat of postwar unemployment, and low wages. The first book dealt largely with the technically possible—the potentialities of present-day production, even including the power potentialities of U-235 well before the first atomic bomb exploded over Hiroshima. The second book was seen as an exploration of a social rather than a technical problem, calling for analysis of standards of living and the steps to be taken by the community and nation progressively to improve these standards by full use of our expanded productive capacity.

The working title of this sequel is New Productivity for Living Standards: A Study of the Problem of Social Adjustment to Technological Change. In addition to a general consideration of deficiencies in living standards and the relationship of prices to wages, it is planned to include brief case studies of typical communities and of industries related most closely to essential elements in living standards: agriculture, in relation to food; construction, in relation to housing; textiles, in relation to clothing; and coal and oil, in relation to fuel. Work on this study was begun in 1942; it was still in progress in October, 1946.

[1] Technology and Livelihood: An Inquiry into the Changing Technological Basis for Production as Affecting Employment and Living Standards.

OTHER STUDIES IN PREPARATION

In addition to the fifteen-year study of union history, Industrial Relations and Living Standards, and the sequel to Technology and Livelihood just mentioned, the Department of Industrial Studies has two other manuscripts nearing the stage of submission for publication. One of these is Mr. Wieck's Wage Controls in Wartime, a study of national policy with respect to wages as administered by the National War Labor Board, 1942 to 1945, and the effect of this policy upon labor organization. Largely documentary, this publication will make available the text of executive orders, board decisions, and official pronouncements, for purposes of study of the actual development of the so-called wage-stabilization policy during the war. It is expected to have important bearing upon the postwar problem of wage-price relationships, and on the whole question of how greater productivity can be transformed into security of employment and progressively higher standards of living.

A second study is being brought to completion by Miss Fleddérus, under the working title Industrial Fatigue *vs.* Productive Human Energy. In 1912 Russell Sage Foundation published Josephine Goldmark's pathfinding book in this field, Fatigue and Efficiency. Much additional data have accumulated in the intervening three and a half decades, and marked changes have occurred within industry. The workday and the work week have been greatly shortened, but in many mass-production industries new factors causing fatigue have been introduced in the form of the monotony of single operations endlessly repeated and the speed-up of the assembly line.

The Department recently came into possession of an unfinished manuscript by the late Frederic S. Lee, assembling data from various scientific investigations into fatigue. Drawing on this material together with the Department's own studies of technology, and with the addition of some field work, Miss Fleddérus is preparing an introductory study of the implications of new methods of production for the problem of conserving human energy. The whole subject is an expansion and further development of her earlier memorandum on Optimum Productivity in the Workshop.

At the close of thirty-eight years of activity under the auspices of the Foundation, the Department of Industrial Studies finds itself attacking directly such central problems as full employment and higher standards of living. Earlier studies had a narrower focus, but were likewise concerned with aspects of these central problems, now recognized as significant for the whole nation, and for other nations.

Architectural detail from the north façode,
Russell Sage Foundation Building

XXXVIII

SOCIAL WORK INTERPRETATION:
1932-1946

BY 1932 the long-established Department of Surveys and Exhibits was in process of a three-way division. Functionally, the division had already occurred; official recognition came more gradually, through naming of three distinct departments: the Department of Arts and Social Work, the Department of Social Work Interpretation, and the Department of Surveys.

Work in the social survey was largely suspended during this period. Mr. Harrison, who had become general director of the Foundation, was no longer able to conduct the pathfinding field surveys which had once characterized the work of his Department of Surveys and Exhibits. He was, however, a member of the President's Research Committee on Social Trends which supervised what was in effect a survey of national scope, resulting in publication of Recent Social Trends[1] in 1933. By correspondence and personal interview, he continued to recommend competent persons for projected surveys, to direct inquirers to organizations equipped to undertake surveys, and to give advice on survey procedures. The Foundation's continuing interest in the field was expressed by the maintenance of the title Department of Surveys, when the "exhibits" portion of the earlier department was given separate status as the Department of Social Work Interpretation. But the various problems of depression and war prevented the revival on an active basis of the Department of Surveys; to the end of this period it was without budget, and conducted no program beyond the advisory service already recorded.

A second branching from the original department was into the field of the arts as related to social work. In 1931 the Trustees,

---

[1] Published in two volumes by McGraw-Hill Book Co.; supplemented by many individual monographs.

566

recognizing the work in this area already done by Allen Eaton, appointed him consultant with reference to cultural arts and handicrafts. This work was not given official status as a separate department until 1941, but Mr. Eaton's activities were so completely in this field, even while he remained officially a member of the Department of Surveys and Exhibits or the Department of Surveys, that they are discussed as a unit in the chapter that follows.

The remainder of this chapter is devoted to the growth, and change, of the "exhibits" interest of the original Department of Surveys and Exhibits into the full-fledged Department of Social Work Interpretation. Publicizing the findings of surveys through exhibits and other devices had early been recognized as necessary; the emphasis now became the more thoughtful planning of the whole content of information given the public. For this the term "interpretation" seemed more nearly adequate than either "exhibits" or "publicity."

INTERPRETATION IN THE DEPRESSION YEARS

The Department of Surveys and Exhibits remained in official existence up to October 1, 1934, with Mr. Harrison as its head. The activities in the field of social work interpretation, however, were the special province of Evart G. Routzahn, associate director of the Department to the time of his retirement in October, 1934, and Mrs. Mary Swain Routzahn, at first staff associate, then consultant in social work interpretation[1] from the spring of 1934 to 1936, and finally director of the Department of Social Work Interpretation from 1936 to the close of this record in 1946.

Rapid changes and developments in social work were occurring during the period of the depression. The public had already been left far behind in its understanding. Supporters were usually aware only of the primary needs for food and shelter; social workers had moved on to a concern with the maladjustments of family life, vocational training, and many other secondary problems. As the depression deepened, more and more

[1] An additional title Mr. Routzahn also bore from the spring of 1934 to his retirement that autumn.

people came into direct contact with social work and social workers; they frequently distrusted and disliked their methods and were bewildered by the differences between public and private social work.

A negative attitude of defensiveness was marking the interpretation efforts of most social agencies, public and private. Community chests in their annual campaigns devoted much of their publicity to defending the continuance of privately supported social work in the face of broad and expensive governmental relief programs. Social workers had to defend both themselves and their clients from political attacks. Government agencies were constantly called upon to defend their programs and their budgets before legislative bodies. And although they all felt a great urgency to interpret their work, they had little time to do it.

The Department recognized that the changing conditions called for a new emphasis on interpretation. True, concern for content as well as method of presentation had from the beginning been a policy of the Department, but in the twenties the emphasis had been on the techniques of spreading information; in the thirties, its content took on new importance.

The Department's assistance to the United Educational Program was one example of this emphasis. The Program was organized by the National Social Work Council in 1932 "to enlist all fields of social work in a co-operative movement to bring about public understanding and support of essential social services during these difficult times." Mrs. Routzahn was a member of the administrative committee and chairman of a group of five committees on basic materials, in the fields of character building, public health, social casework, child welfare, and emergency relief. These committees collected facts, figures, statements, and examples for use in magazine articles and speeches. They discussed in their meetings the need for arousing public interest, situations that required most emphasis, and misunderstandings and prejudices on the part of the public which might be corrected.

Beginning in October, 1932, the United Educational Program prepared a series of Behind the Front Lines bulletins containing source material for publicity, edited by Miss Mabel Ellis under Mrs. Routzahn's supervision. These bulletins were intended to strengthen support for social work through broadened public understanding of social conditions, quite apart from direct appeals for funds; they were widely used. Working with Miss Ellis and Miss Louise Franklin Bache as a special magazine committee, Mrs. Routzahn helped to interest established magazine writers and editors in social work material. Mr. Routzahn, meanwhile, gave much time and direction to the committee on interpretation of public health, which prepared articles for syndication, and special bulletins, on a number of subjects within its field.

The United Educational Program continued until April, 1934. The Foundation's contribution included office space, as well as time from Mr. and Mrs. Routzahn. Some of the Program's materials and methods were afterward used by the Mobilization for Human Needs, a project of Community Chests and Councils which developed from the United Educational Program and continued until the beginning of the war.

Money-raising, especially important under depression needs, remained a concern of the Department. This concern did not take the form of studies or publications on the techniques of money-raising. Service consisted, first, in advocating much more information addressed to the public as a means of securing a more intelligent and convinced body of supporters, and, second, collecting and exchanging among financial secretaries and other fund raisers facts about costs and methods, and examples of mail appeals and campaign publicity.

The group of financial secretaries of New York social agencies which Mrs. Routzahn organized in 1928 continued to meet throughout the depression years, with Mrs. Routzahn at first chairman, and later a member of the steering committee up to 1940. One of its early projects was development of a record form for use in mail appeals, in which Mr. Hurlin assisted. Such a form was completed and published by the Foundation, but the group has never persuaded enough members to keep uniform records to provide data adequate for conclusions.

The Department's further services in this field have included talks on money-raising, criticism of letters of appeal, advice on books and articles, vocational advice to persons interested in this work, and general counsel.

The close association of publicity with money-raising has greatly retarded the public's understanding of modern social work. Because it is easiest to get money through simple, familiar, highly emotional appeals, aspects of social work lacking these elements tend to be overlooked in social work publicity. The Department has therefore been much more concerned with efforts to interest agencies in educating the public on these problems and services than in improvement of fund-raising skills.

Exhibits, upon which the Department had focused much of its early attention, remained a special interest of Mr. Routzahn's until his retirement. He held many consultations and prepared memoranda of suggestions for exhibitors, particularly in connection with the meetings of the National Conference of Social Work, the American Public Health Association, and the American Economic Association. A social work conference was scarcely official without the presence of "EGR," green eyeshade low on his forehead, starting a snow of helpful memoranda scribbled on paper scraps, or investigating some new gadget. His last important service in the exhibit field was as member of a committee to organize an American museum of hygiene. Although this project was not carried through, the purposes of the committee were realized in the establishment of the Cleveland Health Museum with Dr. Bruno Gebhard as director.

The Department was called upon for assistance in developing exhibits for the two world fairs which occurred during this period, each of which included in the initial plans extensive social and educational exhibits. At the Chicago Century of Progress Exposition in 1934 the ambitious plan became finally a small but good exhibit of social service prepared by a Chicago group of social workers, and much of the space in the so-called Social Science Building was sold to any exhibitor who would pay for it. The social work committees for the New York World's Fair, opening in 1939, began hopefully with large plans, but did not in the end produce an exhibit.

Exhibits in the social field, the Department has felt, have been increasingly in the direction of incidental use in connection with intensive campaigns, conventions, fairs, and meetings. Social and health agencies have not had funds to pay for work comparable with many commercial exhibits. Only government departments and a very few private agencies have made enough use of exhibits to justify exhibit workers on their staffs.

The health field remained an important area of department interest and contribution, particularly on the part of Mr. Routzahn. His most significant contribution was continuation of his special section on "Public Health Education" in the American Journal of Public Health[1] with its discussion of principles and reproduction of examples. Begun in 1923, this department of the Journal was continued by Mr. Routzahn even after his retirement from the Foundation in October, 1934, and practically to the time of his death.[2]

INTERPRETATION IN ITS BROADER SENSE

In 1936 Mrs. Routzahn became director of the newly created Department of Social Work Interpretation. Only the name was new; it expressed the change which had already taken place, from a chief concern with the techniques of publicity to a broader consideration of the whole problem of the interpretation of social work, with emphasis on content.

A few of the special services linked to the depression began to be dropped, and more attention to research linked to departmental publications became possible. Some of Mr. Routzahn's special interests received less attention. But many of the services and interests of the Department continued throughout the fifteen years of this chapter.

[1] See p. 362.

[2] Mr. Routzahn died on April 24, 1939. "His contributions to the public welfare," wrote Mr. Harrison, "cannot be expressed in any measurable terms; they can only be described in terms of a lifetime spent in incessant activity in putting in the hands of others, far and wide, something which he thought would do them some good."

Instruction in publicity was an important part of these activities. For more than twenty years the Department took active part in the training of publicity workers in the social field. In the New York School of Social Work members of the Department continued active teaching assignments begun in 1923. In general two types of courses were given, an introductory course first called publicity for social work, and later social work interpretation; and a course offering practical experience in presenting social information, publicity practice, which later became social work writing. For some years Mr. and Mrs. Routzahn taught for three terms, but this proved too heavy a program. After the loss of Mr. Routzahn, Mrs. Routzahn continued her teaching. For the past few years she has been relieved in part by Miss Viola Paradise, a former student of the New York School of Social Work, former staff member of the Children's Bureau, United States Department of Labor, and now a free-lance writer. Miss Paradise took over the writing course and one of the two classes in social work interpretation.

The Department has given advice to directors of schools of social work, or to teachers in those schools, on plans and material for courses in social work interpretation. For several years, at a meeting held at the National Conference of Social Work, Mrs. Routzahn brought together teachers of such courses, and also of courses in community organization and social work administration.

The Department prepared teaching and textbook material. The fundamental textbook by the Routzahns, Publicity for Social Work, first published by the Foundation in 1928, remained in print until 1942 and was widely used. In 1932 the Department issued experimentally, in mimeographed form, a Brief Course in Social Work Publicity, consisting of six study outlines designed for use in either institutes or educational institutions by teachers who might not have much training or experience in the subject. This material was later expanded into 12 lessons or sessions, much illustrative material was added, and published in 1937 under the title How to Interpret Social Work: A Study Course, with Mrs. Helen Cody Baker and Mrs. Routzahn as joint authors. It went through several editions, being widely used in classrooms, in institutes, and by individuals. As this record closes, a revision is being completed, to be issued under the title How to Interpret Social Welfare.

The instruction program of the Department has included conducting many institutes, securing instructors for others, and helping such instructors with reference material and outlines for their brief courses. Institutes of this sort have been conducted by the Department at state conferences of social work in Connecticut, Illinois, Maryland, Massachusetts, Missouri, New York, Pennsylvania, and Ohio. Similar courses have been given as local projects, or for staff training, usually by Mrs. Routzahn. An outstanding service of this kind was the participation of Mr. and Mrs. Routzahn in developing the Health Education Institute of the American Public Health Association, which began with arbitrary limitation to 25 students in 1932 and reached a registration of more than 300 ten years later.

Some attention has been given to outlining courses on special aspects of publicity and public relations. Twice, courses in public speaking were arranged in New York City. Miss Paradise was assisted in developing a course for executives of social agencies.

Individual assistance to students included supervision of the projects of several students of the New York School of Social Work each recent year, occasional supervision of field work for students specializing in this area, and some training to help students to specialize in publicity work through service as temporary staff members of the Department, usually for three- to six-month periods. Students from various schools of social work have been helped with thesis material.

Another department product which has had much teaching value, though its widespread other uses are at least as important, is the portfolio library. These portfolios are collections, arranged by subjects, of publicity material—annual reports, news releases, material on health, child welfare, character building, use of illustration, radio talks, financial campaigns, and countless other special topics. By the middle thirties, these portfolios were usually

573

about 100 in number, and their care and revision involved many hours of work each year.

Until recently, when responsibility for these portfolios has been turned over to the National Publicity Council for Health and Welfare Services, the Department of Social Work Interpretation prepared and housed them, devoting a special room to their display where they were examined by many practitioners of publicity and students from the New York School. Most of them have been transported annually to the National Conference of Social Work and to the annual meeting of the American Public Health Association, where many visitors spend hours studying them. Selections from the collection are sent to state conferences of social work, lent to schools of social work, and to various other groups who have need for them. This current library of publicity practice has been not only one of the most useful of the Department's services to outside agencies, but has served to bring into the Department a great amount of material valuable in its own research.

This was a period of rapid development of several new media of communication, which needed to be followed and sometimes guided. When Publicity for Social Work appeared in 1928, the silent film was giving way to the "talkie" in commercial entertainment, but sound synchronized with pictures had only begun to be used educationally. The book devoted little attention to motion pictures, and less than three pages to radio. The use of both of these media in the field of propaganda and public information expanded tremendously in the thirties. Other technical developments included great advances in the art of photography and in the use of photographic processes in printing. Increased attention was given to improving the appearance of printed matter.

The Department continued its interest in dramatized interpretation, noting particularly the Federal Theater Project of the WPA with its Living Newspaper and the rise of the "documentary" film. Up-to-date descriptive lists of social work plays were maintained, and made available through Social Work Publicity Council. The development of the documentary, in

574

particular, Mrs. Routzahn hailed as "a great boon to social work whose statistical material, human interest stories, and records of changing conditions and methods can be presented to advantage through such dramatic combination."[1]

In these and many other fields a large part of the service of the Department was rendered through speeches, articles, advisory service, committee membership, and co-operation with Social Work Publicity Council, a relationship which will receive detailed treatment. The general advisory service was highly varied. In one year, 1938, "the Department staff answered approximately 300 requests for service or consultation. These varied from simple factual questions, easily and quickly disposed of, to requests for advisory service which involved many hours of work and several interviews or letters." The range of this service is suggested by a few items, also from Mrs. Routzahn's report for 1938:

> Assistance to the author of a book on money-raising. This included detailed criticism of the manuscript and help in preparing a bibliography.
>
> Assistance in revising several chapters of Miss Colcord's new book, Your Community.
>
> Advice on the organization of a projected course in public relations at Syracuse University.
>
> Critical comments on the outline of a handbook on community chest publicity in small cities.
>
> Conference to discuss content and treatment of a book on adult health education.
>
> Critical comments on the Handbook for State Conference Secretaries recently published by the National Conference of Social Work.

Another form of advisory service, and one which the Department found very time-consuming, was vocational. In the absence of any clearinghouse of information as to positions or qualified workers in social work publicity, many persons turned to the Department for help. In 1937, for example, 19 positions were

[1] "Publicity and Interpretation in Social Work," in Social Work Year Book 1941, p. 459.

reported vacant and 53 persons requested vocational assistance. Five years later, in 1942, the number of interviews about placement had increased to 114. Where possible, the Department referred both workers and employers to Joint Vocational Service, and later to other placement agencies. But many requests for vocational advice continued to be handled.

The Department maintained a strong interest in planned, year-round programs of interpretation, broadly conceived. The Social Work Publicity Council's two bulletins on program planning, both prepared by Mrs. Routzahn, were best sellers among its technical bulletins. A large demand existed for articles, talks, and institutes on this subject. Agencies became increasingly aware that "the public" consists of many separate publics, each having a different relationship with the movement or agency. Publicity generally recognized these differences by adapting material and method of presentation to group interests. But examples of preparing and using year-round programs of interpretation remained disappointingly few.

SPECIAL STUDIES

When Philip Klein undertook the Pittsburgh Social Study, the Pittsburgh Citizens' Committee requested Russell Sage Foundation to include social work interpretation in Pittsburgh as a part of the survey. The Department undertook this project, dividing its study into three parts: discovery of the resources for interpretation; analysis of the content of public information on social work over a ten-month period; and a plan for a future program of joint interpretation by public and private social agencies. Work was begun in 1935 and completed the following year. The report of 106 typed pages was presented at special meetings to both the Citizens' Committee and the Pittsburgh Social Work Publicity Council. Both groups accepted the report and voted to take steps to put the recommendations into effect. It was later published in mimeographed form and included in an abbreviated version in Mr. Klein's book.[1] Mrs. Routzahn's study marked the

[1] A Social Study of Pittsburgh. Columbia University Press, New York, 1938.

inclusion for the first time of interpretation as a subject for study in a community survey.

Also in 1936 the Department completed a bibliography on social work interpretation which was published by the Foundation Library as No. 140 in its regular series.

The main research project for the Department for this period, however, was a series of studies of positions in interpretation and public relations. The project had been pending since 1929, but it was not until late in 1936 that work could be started; progress was further interrupted by staff changes,[1] other demands upon the Department's time, and rapidly shifting situations in the agencies studied.

The objective of the studies was described by the director as "stabilization of interpretation as a function in organized social work." The Department hoped to influence social agencies to provide for a continuing service of interpretation to the public by including such interpretation in their budgets, staff assignments, and programs. The approach to this objective was to secure and publish information about personnel and positions in this type of work, training facilities (especially in schools of social work), and specific examples of the ways in which public relations service was set up in selected organizations. As the studies went forward, the early emphasis upon personnel shifted to "case studies" of public relations operations.

Part I of the study, completed in 1939, was a census of positions in interpretation and public relations. Its findings confirmed statistically the Department's belief that publicity was a definite staff assignment in very few social agencies. The questionnaire was sent to 4,000 agencies. Only 434, of 2,800 agencies which replied, reported the employment of full-time publicity workers. Moreover, most of their 846 workers were concentrated in a few large cities; in smaller cities, and even in a majority of agencies in the larger cities, publicity work was combined with

[1] Mrs. Natalie W. Linderholm was added to the staff as assistant director in April, 1937, to help with this study, but left at the end of December, 1938, to accept appointment on the staff of the Greater New York Fund. Harold P. Levy, publicity director of the National Conference of Social Work, was engaged on a temporary basis as research associate in February, 1939.

other duties. Approximately 1,800 staff members of over 900 agencies gave about one-third of their time to publicity or money-raising. Staff members devoting less than this amount of time to publicity activities were not counted, but were undoubtedly numerous. Results of this census of positions were published in a special section in Channels,[1] and reprinted by the Department.

The small number of full-time jobs available offered little encouragement to schools of social work to provide training or stress specialization in publicity work. But a second conclusion, valid at least for the time being, was that since social workers frequently must carry responsibility for publicity work along with other major assignments, some instruction in its principles and techniques is highly desirable as a part of every social worker's education. With this situation in mind, the Department brought up to date information Arthur Dunham had been commissioned to prepare in 1937 on the teaching of this subject in schools of social work, and since that time has maintained a file of existing courses. Only 10 courses in 9 schools were found in 1939; by 1943 this number increased to 14 courses in 13 different schools. Correspondence with the schools indicated that more courses might have been introduced, but qualified teachers were hard to secure.

By 1940 the Department was deep in a series of case studies in public relations and interpretation. These were all intended to help agencies define more clearly the function of public relations in the whole agency program. The first step was to make ten brief studies, based principally on personal interviews, of the publicity job in as many agencies. Interviews were supplemented with examination of records and materials produced by the agencies under study. Background information on the history of the agency, and particularly the development of its concepts of public relationships, was also gathered.

As this information accumulated, it became clear that the public relations job was so bound up with agency philosophy and structure that it could be presented effectively only in its relations

---

[1] "A Census of Positions in Interpretation and Public Relations," in Channels, June–July, 1939, pp. 147–160.

to the agency program as a whole. The field was narrowed to five agencies, to be studied in greater detail: the Social Security Board, the Boy Scouts of America, the Pennsylvania Department of Public Assistance, the New York State Department of Social Welfare, and the National Board of the Young Womens Christian Associations. This selection was later modified, for various reasons. In one instance the excellent plan for a public relations program which had called attention to the agency was not carried out. This made the report too negative to be suitable for publication. In another instance major changes in staff and program took place owing to war conditions so that the records were concerned chiefly with rapid change and uncertainty about the future. Nevertheless, these studies were constantly useful for comparison and contrast with the program in the four studies which were chosen for further development. The studies brought to final completion in the period of this record were those of the Pennsylvania Department of Public Assistance and the Boy Scouts. Both were published under the authorship of Harold P. Levy.

The Pennsylvania study presented a documented story of five years' experience of the Pennsylvania Department of Public Assistance, covering its adjustments to economic depression, a period of prosperity, and the war era. The book was published in April, 1943, under the title A Study in Public Relations: Case History of the Relations Maintained Between a Department of Public Assistance and the People of a State. Its two printings brought it to a rather wide audience, including professional workers, executives, agency staff members, students, educators, and others concerned with public relations.

The second volume in this series of Studies in Public Relations was published in June, 1944, under the title Building a Popular Movement: A Case Study of the Public Relations of the Boy Scouts of America. In this study Mr. Levy analyzed the public relations of a national movement, showing how, in the particular instance of the Boy Scouts, assets for public understanding and good will, already existing in its program and organization methods, reduced a formal public relations program to a comparatively minor role.

For the remaining studies, the Department decided to turn from state and national agencies to the local scene. One was to deal with public relations in several carefully selected local Young Men's Christian Associations, using the public relations program of the National Council of the Associations as a background. This study was incomplete when Mr. Levy resigned at the end of December, 1944, to become public relations director of the newly formed Commission on Community Interrelations, and has not been completed.

The remaining local study was concerned with social casework interpretation in Cleveland, Ohio. It dealt, not with the program of a single agency but with what the public needs to be told, and is told, about casework in the community by both public and private agencies, working individually and co-operatively. This study was undertaken by Miss Paradise, appointed research associate for the Cleveland study in September, 1944. It was nearing completion in October, 1946.

Through these publications, the Department plans to make available a type of fundamental literature heretofore missing in the field of social work publicity and public relations: material that tells how the job actually is accomplished and the kinds of planning, production, and personnel needed to do it. Such material, it is believed, will possess value for courses of study in this subject as well as stimulate agencies to clarify and stabilize their own public relations programs.

THE NATIONAL PUBLICITY COUNCIL

The close relationship between the Department and the fledgling Social Work Publicity Council has been discussed in an earlier chapter.[1] The Council's address was the Department's own suite of offices. Mrs. Routzahn often devoted as much as half her time to Council matters, as its executive secretary, adviser, author or editor of many of its pamphlets,[2] and in several emergencies the editor of its bulletin. Staffs of the Department

[1] See pp. 362, 368.

[2] In the period beginning in 1932 these included Tell It with Exhibits (1936); Appraising Your Interpretation Program (1938); How to Plan a Public Relations Program (1940); and Annual Reports and How to Improve Them (1941).

580

and the Council were to some extent interchangeable, and not infrequently the department staff carried on activities in the name of the Council.

It was an arrangement which was certainly necessary in the early years of the Council, and had substantial advantages for the Department. To a considerable extent the Council served as a laboratory and a service agency for the Department. A stream of publicity material flowed into the department offices as entries for the various awards of the Council, or for criticism in the Council's clinics. The Council's "how-to-do-it" bulletins supplemented department publications, providing an outlet for information about rapidly changing techniques, such as radio and exhibits. But without doubt the large share of responsibility for administrative, organizing, and editorial work for the Council frequently interfered with the progress of department studies. By 1931 the hope was being expressed that the Council might "soon" achieve complete independence. This section records the steps by which that goal was finally reached.

Hopes for early independence received a severe depression setback. Membership in Social Work Publicity Council had shown growth every year, reaching a high of 1,000 in 1931; but by 1934 it had fallen to 850. Income from membership was not sufficient for achievement of independent status. The next year Russell Sage Foundation increased its aid to the Council to permit employment of a membership secretary, and membership began again to climb.

In 1938 the Council changed its News Bulletin, which had been appearing in mimeographed form for fifteen years, into a printed magazine called Channels. In 1939 the Council moved from the Department of Social Work Interpretation rooms to its own offices on the third floor of the Foundation building, and its staff was increased to five persons. On January 1, 1942, the Social Work Publicity Council achieved the status of an independent national service agency, the goal toward which the Department of Social Work Interpretation had guided and helped it during twenty years of increasing usefulness. This final step was made possible by increases in contributions and membership dues and a substantial grant from Russell Sage Foundation. In February of the following year the Council formally changed its name to National Publicity Council for Health and Welfare Services "because of the conviction that the term social work was neither sufficiently inclusive nor sufficiently specific to describe the work of the Council as it has been developing during the past few years."[1]

Mrs. Routzahn was made honorary chairman of the National Publicity Council in 1945, in recognition of the services which she, and other members of her department, had rendered to the Council for a period of more than two decades.

CLOSE OF THE PERIOD

In November, 1944, a distinguished awards committee from the public health field voted the first presentation of the Elisabeth S. Prentiss National Award in Health Education to Mary Swain Routzahn and posthumously to Evart G. Routzahn. Although the award was specifically in the field of public health, and to two persons as individuals, the presentation at the Cleveland Health Museum, and the comment which followed it, was a happy occasion for summarizing some of the wider contributions of the Department. Said Channels:

> All Publicity Council members have a proprietary interest in the Routzahns, the redoubtable pair whose talents and enthusiasms and hard work pioneered in the twin fields of health education and social work publicity for more than thirty years. . . . [They], who separately or together founded the public health section of the American Public Health Association, organized the first travelling exhibit campaign on tuberculosis, developed the Department of Social Work Interpretation of the Russell Sage Foundation which Mrs. Routzahn now directs, founded and continued to guide our own National Publicity Council, discovered and encouraged many of the country's other leading health educators, have long been appreciated by their colleagues.[2]

[1] Channels, December, 1942–January, 1943, p. 14.

[2] Ibid., December, 1944, p. 12.

In October, 1946, the Department was completing work on the study of social casework interpretation in Cleveland and on the revised edition of How to Interpret Social Welfare. The former heavy program of service and consultation had been considerably reduced, through transfer of most of these requests to the independently functioning National Publicity Council. Although Mrs. Routzahn had reached retirement age, she continued to supervise completion of the studies just mentioned.

Architectural detail from the north façade,
Russell Sage Foundation Building

XXXIX

ARTS AND SOCIAL WORK: 1932-1946

IN THE introduction to each of his annual reports, Mr. Eaton states that "the purpose of the Department of Arts and Social Work is to study the influence of the arts in everyday living, and to bring a larger measure of beauty, either created or enjoyed, into the lives of all people."

To an extent unusual even in the Foundation, this department is the lengthened shadow of special talents and interests of an individual, Allen Eaton. Its official history is relatively brief, for the activities which Mr. Eaton had long been conducting became a separate department only in 1941; yet its work can best be understood in the light of the full story, some parts of which have already been mentioned.

Mr. Eaton joined the staff of the Department of Surveys and Exhibits of Russell Sage Foundation in 1920 at the close of a series of exhibitions of the Arts and Crafts of the Homelands which he, as field secretary of the American Federation of Arts, had first suggested, then organized and conducted in several cities of New York State. His early activities with the Department of Surveys and Exhibits, particularly in arranging exhibits of immigrant cultural contributions, color prints, and other art objects, and his deep interest in rural life, have already been recorded.[1]

The first step toward later creation of a separate department came in March, 1926, after Mr. Glenn, then general director, had asked Mr. Eaton what he would rather do for the Foundation than anything else. The reply was a 45-page letter, outlining "some thoughts on the relation of art to social work, with a few suggestions as to how the Russell Sage Foundation might help to relate the two." Although no separate department was then created, Mr. Eaton's proposal had a sympathetic hearing, and

[1] See pp. 369–376.

his time was increasingly freed for work in his chosen field. For several years a portion of his time, at first a third and later a quarter, was reserved for work outside the scope of the Foundation, chiefly with the American Federation of Arts; this arrangement continued until 1939, when he came on full time for the Foundation.

Immigrant Gifts Through Their Arts

Soon after Mr. Eaton came to the Foundation, the Department of Surveys and Exhibits decided to publish a report on the Arts and Crafts of the Homelands exhibitions which Mr. Eaton had helped initiate and in which he maintained a continuing interest. This book was to describe the first of these exhibitions, at Buffalo in 1919, in detail; outline chief features of the later exhibitions in this field; include a chapter on the techniques of organizing and conducting an arts and crafts exhibition; and, as finally published, added a long and useful chapter on resources available for future exhibitions showing work done and achievements by foreign-born citizens after settling in this country.[1]

Under Mr. Eaton's authorship this book, Immigrant Gifts to American Life, published in July, 1932, became much more than the contribution to exhibit techniques which had been its origin. It was an addition to art knowledge, and an effective presentation of the viewpoint that "Americanization" should not be a process of remaking immigrant cultures into the established pattern, but should conserve the rich gifts, of which the arts are symbols, that the new Americans bring to our shores.

[1] Among many examples of the artistic achievements of foreign-born citizens, Mr. Eaton mentioned the ten- and twenty-dollar gold pieces, designed by Augustus Saint-Gaudens, born in Ireland; the dime and half-dollar, by Adolph Weinman, native of Germany; the furniture of Duncan Phyfe, born in Scotland; the wood engravings of Timothy Cole, born in London; the Culebra Cut painting, The Conquerors, by Jonas Lie, born in Norway. And as a suggestion and a symbol of an America made up of the population strains of every homeland of Europe he described the New York Philharmonic Symphony Orchestra which had a personnel of 114 men and four staff members. Of this number, thirty-four were American born. Seventy-two were American citizens, born in the following countries: Austria, two; England, one; France, two; Germany, ten; Holland, six; Hungary, four; Italy, thirteen; Lithuania, one; Palestine, one; Rumania, one; Russia, twenty-nine; Scotland, one; Spain, one. Twelve were aliens, coming from the following countries: Belgium, two; France, five; Holland, three; Hungary, one; Italy, one.

The book ran through two printings; before it went finally out of print in 1944, much evidence accumulated on its varied uses and wide influence. It was an aid in citizenship courses in schools and colleges. It stimulated many exhibits, festivals, and special occasions featuring the contributions of immigrants to American culture; examples were a Fourth of July pageant of foreign-born citizens at Oglebay Park, Wheeling, West Virginia, and a long series of Festivals of Nations in St. Paul, Minnesota. As time went on, the Department was called upon for increasing services in this field, sometimes more than it was able to render in view of other commitments. Its report for 1939, after indicating the necessity for many refusals, nevertheless includes a record of Mr. Eaton's services in suggesting materials and other aids for the National Folk Festival, Washington, D. C.; the Folk Festival, St. Paul, Minnesota; folk festivals at the New York World's Fair; the Service Bureau for Intercultural Education; a teaching unit on races and nationalities in the New York City public schools; the Hall of Nations of the American University Graduate School, Washington, D. C.; the Immigration and Naturalization Service, Ellis Island; a New York City conference on the immigrant and the community. The Federal Office of Education broadcasts entitled Americans All—Immigrants All used extensive quotations and material from Immigrant Gifts to American Life.

During that and the following year Mr. Eaton served as a member of the American Common Committee for the New York World's Fair, which arranged the Hall of Fame at the American Common, stressing contributions from the foreign born, and planned the nationality programs given at the Fair.

HANDICRAFTS OF THE SOUTHERN HIGHLANDS

The Department has given attention to the work of professional artists through fostering exhibitions of reproductions of famous paintings for homes and schools and similar activities, but its abiding concern has been for artistic expression among all the people, which often flowers in objects that can be roughly classified as handicrafts. "Art in its true sense," said Mr. Eaton, "is

586

just the best way of doing something that needs to be done; hence the studies will often be concerned with those expressions commonly called handicrafts which hold untold satisfaction and inspiration for those who are engaged in them."

When the Southern Highland Handicraft Guild was first organized at a meeting in Penland, North Carolina, in 1928, Mr. Eaton was present and assisted by working on its organization problems. At that time the group passed a unanimous resolution requesting Russell Sage Foundation to "conduct an early survey of the handicrafts in the schools and homes of the Southern Mountains as a fact basis for the association's wisest development." Other projects made such a study then impossible, but early in 1933 Mr. Eaton was authorized to make it the major project of his expanding work.

Much material was already in hand, and activity was redoubled. The area was mapped, many producing centers visited on field trips, and the book outlined. A special project of 1933, in which Mr. Eaton was largely responsible for bringing together examples of handicraft from the producing centers of the Southern Highland Handicraft Guild to be circulated by the American Federation of Arts, proved helpful for the general study. From some 800 articles examined, 584 were selected, ranging from sometimes rough but useful "old timey" brooms, "settin' chairs," baskets, and coverlets, to excellent examples of modern work in wood, metal, fibers, and other materials, and especially weavings produced largely for sale.

For the specific purposes of the book, Mr. Eaton visited many individuals working in some form of crafts and many handicraft centers. Data gathered included the location of the industry; the name of the center or individual working in handicrafts; how long work had been established; names of directors and personnel; number of workers; types of articles made; training and skill required; whether articles were made at home, at school, or in the shop; extent to which machinery, water, or other power was used; relative use of native and imported materials; extent of original designs; information on marketing and how returns from sales were used; standards of craftsmanship; and something of the history and environment of each center. A bibliography on handicrafts was assembled and included in the report.

Several years earlier, Mrs. Doris Ulmann, an outstanding American photographer, had made a few fine portraits of native people in the mountains of Kentucky and Virginia. Later, she expressed to Mr. Eaton a desire to make a definitive collection of photographs of the people of the mountains, especially the older types who were fast disappearing. Being well acquainted with people in the Highlands, he made arrangements for a large number of special portraits including many craftsmen at work, with the agreement on her part that any of these might be used in the book. Some 2,000 plates were thus exposed, from which were selected 58 outstanding Ulmann photographs which appear in the published volume. Other illustrative material was included from various sources showing a variety of handicraft objects and handicraft processes, some in color.

While this study was in progress the continued economic depression made it advisable to give more attention to the use of handicrafts in communities. Mr. Eaton became a member of the committee considering collaboration between the Tennessee Valley Authority and the Southern Highland Handicraft Guild for the advancement of handicrafts in the entire region. The result was the organization of a co-operative group in the TVA area which called itself the Southern Highlanders, Inc. Later Mr. Eaton assisted this co-operative and the Southern Highland Handicraft Guild in leasing quarters at Rockefeller Center, New York, and helped work out the selling concession of the Guild with the Shenandoah National Park, Virginia.

The Department at the same time maintained interest in and contacts with handicrafts in various other parts of the country, which are later discussed. This wider interest received attention in the book, focused though it was on developments in the Highlands, through the addition of Part III, "The Rural Handicraft Movement and the Wider Use of Handicrafts," which dealt with the growth of the movement throughout America, and included discussions of handicrafts as instruments of adult education and recreation.

Handicrafts of the Southern Highlands was published in August, 1937. It was one of the few opportunities the Foundation has had for artistic bookmaking with fine illustration; the effort was apparently successful, for the volume was chosen by a distinguished jury of the American Institute of Graphic Arts for The Arts of the Book in the United States, a traveling exhibit for the Latin-American countries. Reviews were enthusiastic, and use of the book widespread, not only in the Highlands, but generally. It is now in its fourth printing. Many people have used the book as a guide in their travels through the Highlands, and it has brought substantial assistance and co-operation to the handicraft workers of the region.

Bibliographical material collected in the study was far more extensive than could be used in the book. A separate bibliography was therefore prepared and published in the regular series of Library Bulletins as No. 145, Handicrafts in the Southern Highlands. Subsequently, beginning in 1938, Dr. Ernst Harms, a student of and writer on handicrafts, was engaged for a short period to advise with Mr. Eaton on various aspects of the subject and to prepare bibliographical material on the more important publications on handicrafts in languages other than English.

The extent to which the Department's study of handicrafts in the Southern Highlands and its more general studies and services may have influenced a national movement cannot be definitely stated. However, three steps have been taken toward formation of a national handicraft organization that would serve handicraft workers in various ways, particularly through bringing their products before the public and creating a desire for their use. The first was the National Handicraft Conference, which convened at Camp Kehonka, Wolfeboro, New Hampshire, in 1937 under sponsorship of the League of New Hampshire Arts and Crafts. Representatives attended from the most important organizations in the eastern area "to work out together what we cannot do alone," as one delegate expressed it. Mr. Eaton helped prepare the agenda and presided at all the sessions. The Second Conference was held in August, 1940, at Penland, North Carolina; Mr. Eaton gave the opening address, conducted several of the discussions, and assembled an international handicraft exhibit from displays at several of the foreign pavilions at the New York World's Fair.

In 1938 a group in New York City formed a committee to organize in behalf of handicrafts of the whole country. Miss Anne Morgan was chairman, Mr. Eaton a member. However, the war emergency and other factors made it seem advisable in 1942 for this group to merge with the American Craftsmen's Cooperative Council, Inc., which had already launched a distribution center and retail shop, America House, in New York City, and is undertaking the monthly publication, Craft Horizons. Mr. Eaton is a member of the Board of Directors.

The philosophy underlying the interest of the Department of Arts and Social Work in relation to the arts and especially handicrafts, that large division of the arts with which the Foundation has been concerned, is perhaps best expressed in the Preface to the book, Handicrafts of the Southern Highlands:

> The time will come when every kind of work will be judged by two measurements: one by the product itself, as is now done, the other by the effect of the work on the producer. When that time comes the handicrafts will be given a much more important place in our plan of living than they now have, for unquestionably they possess values which are not generally recognized.

RURAL ARTS

Rural arts in the sense of Mr. Eaton's definition, "Art is just the best way of doing something that needs to be done," had long been a subject of special interest. A significant early date in his activities in this field was the 1933 meeting of the American Country Life Association at Blacksburg, Virginia. For this meeting Mr. Eaton had assembled two exhibits, one of color prints of rural scenes and country life, the other of handicrafts of the Southern Highlands, and was principal speaker at a session on rural cultural arts, choosing as his subject "Woodpiles and Haystacks, A Talk on Art in Rural Life." This address, emphasizing that even a well-built haystack or woodpile may be a creative and artistic expression, roused wide interest, and was repeated as a radio broadcast and in various other forms. An immediate result was a request from the president of the American Country Life Association that Mr. Eaton direct a countrywide study of rural arts. The handicrafts study then prevented, but his department has accumulated much information about rural arts and has done much work in this field.

Mr. Eaton's interest in this and related fields led to his participation in the schools for extension workers conducted by the Department of Agriculture for which a small faculty went into different states and developed programs and discussion groups for extension workers of a state or a region. Mr. Eaton spoke on one of these programs at the University of Maine, his subject being some phases of rural art. The result was that he later took part in similar schools in Maryland, Kansas, Iowa, New Mexico, and Michigan. These contacts led to invitations, which were accepted, to speak at the Annual Farmers Week held in Columbus, Ohio, in 1937; and at Farm and Home Weeks at Kansas State College of Agriculture and Applied Science in 1938, and the University of Wisconsin in 1941.

The most fruitful contribution of this work was the assistance which was given in preparing the first exhibition ever held on a national scale of the Rural Arts of America, displayed from November 14 to December 5, 1937, in the patio of the administration building of the United States Department of Agriculture during the celebration of its seventy-fifth anniversary. Mr. Eaton organized and directed this exhibition. Every state, territory, and possession, except small islands which were uninhabited when we acquired them, was represented by handicrafts, by photographs, or by both. The arts of the American Indian were shown not as artifacts of an odd people but as the arts of a part of our rural population. The decorations used were plants of the farm and the forest, thus rooting the exhibition in the soil. The inside gallery was given over to the exhibition of handicrafts; the outside gallery was the background for probably the finest group of enlarged photographs of American country scenes and country work ever brought together. Among distinguished visitors were

President and Mrs. Franklin D. Roosevelt and Mr. and Mrs. Henry Wallace.[1] In addition to the interest the Exhibition aroused among those able to attend, it was the subject of illustrated articles in many newspapers and was featured in at least 16 magazines.

Out of this Rural Arts Exhibition grew two specific governmental projects for which Mr. Eaton helped develop the survey plans. The first was a comprehensive survey of handicrafts in the Works Progress Administration and the National Youth Administration, a joint undertaking carried out in 1938 by WPA staff. Its results were not published; before the WPA could complete the quantitative study the organization was disbanded. The second was a survey of handicrafts and rural arts conducted by the Extension Service, United States Department of Agriculture. Publication of results of this survey was delayed by the war, but it was finally issued in 1946 as Rural Handicrafts in the United States, a bulletin by the Department of Agriculture in cooperation with Russell Sage Foundation. In addition to Mr. Eaton's contribution to its subject matter, it contains many illustrations from the Foundation's collection of rural arts photographs.

When in 1936 the Associated Country-Women of the World held their international conference in Washington, D. C. under the auspices of the United States Department of Agriculture, Mr. Eaton was asked to act as adviser to the conference on handicrafts. He spoke to several groups and assisted the American section in planning their exhibits. At this conference it was decided to build a five-year program around rural arts and handicrafts based upon the conviction that such a program would contribute more than any other to better understanding among all rural peoples; but World War II defeated this purpose, and no meetings of the Associated Country-Women of the World have since been held.

When the British Craft Exhibition was sent over to the United States and Canada in 1942 and made an extensive tour of both countries, Mr. Eaton was invited to represent the States at the

[1] Mr. Wallace was then Secretary of Agriculture.

opening of the Exhibition in the Canadian capital at Ottawa; and he arranged through the Smithsonian Institution at Washington for the final showing of the Exhibition in our country.

EXPERIMENTS IN CREATIVE EXPRESSION

Through a temporary staff appointment from March, 1939, to March, 1944, the Department has also provided an opportunity for Professor Henry W. Schaefer-Simmern to continue in America a method of teaching art expression which he had tried out in his native Germany. The theory upon which his work rests is that all normal human beings are capable of artistic expression in the visual arts, such as drawing, painting, modeling, or in any of the handicrafts, if certain natural laws are followed. The person is encouraged to draw or model "out of his head," using his own powers of conception as opposed to the conventional methods of copying or following the instructions of others. As the inner concept clears, the ability to express the mental image will advance.

The first group of pupils selected were two old sailors, some refugees, a metal worker, a broker, a social worker; later, several first offenders in prison and certain persons with subnormal intelligence at a New England state training school. In many cases unexpected growth has been recorded, and the pupils themselves experienced a great lift through a sense of achievement. Exhibits of the work of pupils were held in the Foundation building, and Professor Schaefer-Simmern has prepared a report covering his educational theory and his experiments in America which probably will be issued by another publisher but with credit to the Foundation auspices under which the work was conducted.

OBJECTS OF BEAUTY FOR THE BLIND

Mr. Eaton has long felt that much pleasure could be derived by sightless persons experiencing different beautiful objects in nature and in art through the sense of touch. This idea resulted in his assembling within the Department an exhibition of beautiful handicrafts chiefly for the enjoyment of the blind. These objects

593

were selected from a wide field of handicrafts including many kinds of materials and various techniques with representation from many countries and every continent. The objects were of a kind and size which a sighted person would not only be interested in seeing, but would enjoy taking in his hand. This double test was based on the belief that objects appealing strongly to the touch of sighted persons would bring tactile pleasure to the blind, and if the object was also visually interesting, it would stimulate pleasant communication between the sighted and the blind.

Collection of such objects into an exhibit of 40 to 50 pieces has proceeded for several years, and experiments have been conducted during the past two years. Results have been encouraging, establishing beyond doubt the power of many blind persons to enjoy beautiful objects through the sense of touch. While many more experiments will be completed before the results are published, Mr. Eaton claims that every blind person has within his reach a kingdom of beauty so vast that he cannot exhaust it in a lifetime; but, of course, this privilege is one of education and opportunity with the blind as with the sighted.

Some Special Services

In addition to the Department's main continuing projects, it has rendered special services, advisory and participating, in many activities related to its interests. The WPA had developed a linen project at Parksley, Virginia, in which some 20 women raised flax, prepared it by hand for spinning, spun the thread, and wove it into some of the most beautiful fabrics that have been made in this country. When the WPA was forced to close the project in 1942, the Department saved some samples of the spinning and weaving, made a photographic record of the operations, and found outlets for the thread, which permitted some of the women to continue in the work.

John Ousta, an American citizen of Turkish birth, came to this country imbued with the idea of helping it become a silk-producing nation. His experiments in sericulture included importation of silkworm eggs, raising the worms, developing and improving the cocoon, and finally, on a machine of his own construction, reeling the silk fiber into usable form. When he found most of the interest in this country centered on selling stock in such projects rather than making a serious attempt at organizing modest industries, he accepted Mr. Eaton's advice to develop it along handicraft lines.

The Department's interest in the graphic arts has found expression not only in the Department's own books but in advice on format of other Foundation publications and in Mr. Eaton's activities in the American Institute of Graphic Arts, of which he has been a director and vice-president.

Briefer services, often by correspondence or a single interview, have covered wide fields. In one year, 1940, they included the following range, which may be regarded as fairly typical: advice on an international exhibition of handicrafts, on a handicrafts exhibit at the Museum of Modern Art, and on murals for the American Common at the New York World's Fair; information furnished to a director of handicraft work in Kentucky, to a teacher of weaving considering employment with the Farm Security Administration, to a director of arts and crafts in a settlement in Pittsburgh, to the United States Department of Agriculture on a handicraft program for the extension division; consultation with writers on material on the Southern Highlands, on folklore, on the League of New Hampshire Arts and Crafts, on handicrafts at Arthurdale, West Virginia, on publication of explorations in Mexico, on a unit of the Visualized Curriculum Series on contributions to America of the foreign born; aid to workers in the field with respect to photographing rural scenes, weaving, metal working, co-operative workshops for the National Youth Administration, activities of the Lutheran Mission in North Carolina, activities of the Farm Security Administration; consultations with a representative of the All Indian National Congress and with students of handicrafts in Scandinavia.

NEW ENGLAND HANDICRAFTS

The Department's main project, as the period of this record draws to its close, is a study of New England handicrafts. In 1930 Mr. Eaton had accepted an invitation to become adviser to the

New Hampshire Commission of Arts and Crafts. The Commission created the League of New Hampshire Arts and Crafts which was the first example of state support of handicrafts through taxation. Even earlier, requests for a special study of New England handicrafts had come to the Foundation, but the Southern Highland study was given precedence. Mr. Eaton maintained his active interest in handicraft developments in this section of the country, however, and by 1941 the study was decided upon.

Field work began in 1942 on an intensive schedule. Late that year, however, it was interrupted by travel restrictions imposed by World War II. Miss Doris Day of Connecticut, engaged by the Foundation as photographer for the New England study, enlisted in the Army and received a California assignment. However, limited field work was later revived, and Mr. Eaton was frequently able to arrange for adequate photographs from other New England photographers. Maine remained a problem in this respect until the war was nearly over, when the services of George French were obtained.

Research for the study was much advanced through the fortunate occurrence of the Exhibition of Contemporary New England Handicrafts held at the Worcester (Massachusetts) Art Museum from October through December, 1943. Mr. Eaton assisted in planning the Exhibition, helped select the objects shown, which represented probably the largest number of handicraft objects ever assembled from New England, wrote the Introduction to the catalogue, and had an excellent opportunity during his visits to the Exhibition to collect additional data for his study. The exhibit itself, by increasing interest in handicrafts throughout New England and giving to them the accolade of recognition by an art museum, seemed to Mr. Eaton "one of the most important and far-reaching events in which our Department has had a part."

Additional field work occupied parts of three years, including visits both to organized groups and to individual craftsmen working alone. One such trip was made by boat up the coast of Maine and to the adjacent islands. Since it was necessary to represent the frequently differing conditions of six states, the task of selection from material which would have filled "several volumes" became difficult. Through 1945, field work was greatly reduced and work on the manuscript became the chief emphasis. It became evident during the war that handicrafts would have broadened uses as occupational therapy for veterans and others; therefore an effort was made to include material on this subject.

As this record closes in October, 1946, the manuscript of the New England handicrafts study has been substantially completed, and early publication is anticipated. It will add another important chapter to the record of the Foundation's services to the arts of the people of America.

Architectural detail from the east façade,
Russell Sage Foundation Building

XL

SOCIAL WORK YEAR BOOK: 1932-1946

AN EARLIER chapter[1] has recorded Fred S. Hall's original proposal in 1928 for a "Social Work Annual and Who's Who," modifications of this idea, and the appearance in the fall of 1930 of the first volume of the Social Work Year Book, based on these altered concepts. When the book was named, annual publication was contemplated, as its title implies. This ambitious program was soon abandoned, however, and the Preface to the very first volume proposed biennial publication, which has been the practice since 1933. This initial volume, too, established the general content pattern for its successors, with a first section devoted to signed topical articles and a second section containing directories of agencies in social work and related fields. Refinements and modifications have been introduced, but in its main elements the original plan proved sound and has been continued.

EDITORSHIP OF MR. HALL

The first three editions of the Social Work Year Book were brought out under Mr. Hall's editorship. These were the issues bearing the dates 1929, 1933, and 1935. The second volume, it will be noted, did not meet the proposed biennial publication schedule. Staff changes[2] caused Mr. Hall to undertake sole editorial responsibility for the topical article section, and he found the task more time-consuming than had been anticipated. This resulted in an unavoidable delay in publication.

Meanwhile, a change in conception of the Year Book resulted in a change in the dating of the volumes. The first issue had been

---

[1] See pp. 429–430.

[2] Miss Mabel B. Ellis resigned as assistant editor on July 1, 1931. Miss Margaret B. Hodges joined the staff as assistant to the editor on January 1, 1932, with primary responsibility for the directory section.

designed to record particularly the events of 1929, and was therefore called the Social Work Year Book 1929, even though published on November 1, 1930. Beginning with the second volume, the emphasis changed to recording the status of activities in the various fields as close as possible to the date of publication. When the second volume was published in April, 1933, it therefore bore the title Social Work Year Book 1933. Somewhat less than two and a half years had elapsed between publication dates, though the respective titles suggested four years.

The 1933 volume introduced few innovations beyond the increased emphasis upon current status already noted. Most of the topical articles continued from the 1929 volume were reassigned to the same authors, with standing type used where possible—a practice later abandoned in favor of complete resetting of each edition and frequent shifts in authorship to provide variety of viewpoint. A limited index was introduced. The edition of 2,518 copies sold somewhat more slowly, under conditions of deep depression in 1933, than its predecessor, but was sold out in 1934.

The third issue, the Social Work Year Book 1935, appeared in April, 1935, exactly on the biennial schedule. It followed previous patterns, with some expansion in size and the addition of a section on statewide private agencies to the directories section. Demand improved, and two printings totaling 3,554 copies were required.

Work of the Department throughout this period was concentrated on the problems of initiating and developing the Year Book itself. Mr. Hall followed a general policy of declining invitations to serve on committees, write articles, or address conferences, though he did write one article on his old topic, "Marriage and the Law," for the Annals, maintained membership on several national committees, took an active part in the depression problems of his home community, Montclair, and found time to edit a pamphlet by Jeffrey R. Brackett which the Foundation subsequently published.[1] After his work on the 1935 Year Book was completed, he prepared a Manual showing details of policies and

[1] The Transportation Problem in American Social Work, issued in 1936.

599

procedures for the guidance of the editor who would succeed him. His retirement took place on October 1, 1935.[1]

EDITORSHIP OF MR. KURTZ

Russell H. Kurtz was appointed to succeed Mr. Hall as editor of the Social Work Year Book on November 1, 1935. He transferred from the Charity Organization Department, where he had been assisting Miss Colcord in making relief studies[2] since joining the Foundation staff in September, 1931. A few commitments to his former department remained, and he continued a teaching assignment on public relief problems at the New York School of Social Work; but he was soon deep in the problems of the new Year Book, the volume for 1937.

The Social Work Year Book 1937 was published in March, 1937, with its two printings totaling 4,337 copies. The new editor made no radical changes in plan or content. Different authors were selected for many of the topical articles, and the content reflected the almost revolutionary shift of relief responsibilities to federal and state auspices and early operation of the Social Security Act; but the general plan of the volume continued the series along the lines established by Mr. Hall.

The new editor, however, sought opportunities for his department to serve as more than the producer of a biennial Year Book. He saw it as a potential center for development of social work literature in selected areas. Preparation of the Year Book itself brings to a single office a perhaps unrivaled opportunity for an over-all view of the varied fields of social work, the available literature, and the more serious gaps in this material. Mr. Kurtz believed his office could serve usefully as a stimulus to others in production of needed material and sometimes, in the off years when its own work was lighter, as itself the producer of material in some neglected field. Conversely, it was hoped that these

[1] His "retirement" was into very active voluntary service for his fellow man, particularly among the Negroes of Winter Park, Florida, which became his winter home. Upon his death on January 31, 1946, a fellow citizen declared at the memorial service, "God must be advertising 'Men Wanted' in Winter Park today; for there are at least six jobs which Fred Hall did which are now in need of a successor."

[2] See Chapter XXXV.

broadened contacts and experiences would enrich the content of the Year Book.

Consequently, Mr. Kurtz and his assistant, Miss Hodges, have welcomed opportunities to participate in social work activities within the limits of their time schedules. Mr. Kurtz served on the editorial committee of the National Conference of Social Work in 1936 and in all subsequent years, the Year Book editor becoming substantially an ex officio member of the Conference editorial committee. He has served on publishing committees, or as critic of particular publishing projects, for the Family Service Association of America, Survey Associates, American National Red Cross, Columbia University Press, the American Association of Social Workers, the Committee for the Study of Community Organization, and others. Miss Hodges edited a community self-study in Portland, Maine, based on the Foundation's book, Your Community, and has served in other editorial capacities. In such advisory services the stimulation of publications in neglected fields has often been prominent.

The preparation of special studies by the Department itself has met with both success and failure. The first attempt, made in the spring of 1937, was from most points of view a substantial success. Rapid expansion of public social work had exhausted the supply of trained social workers. Full professional training was not possible for many of the new workers, and in-service training and special short courses became the order of the day. To help fill this and other needs, the Year Book Department prepared The Public Assistance Worker. This was a symposium of 225 pages, following the pattern of the Year Book itself in consisting of six carefully integrated assigned chapters, one of which was written by the department director. Its emphasis was on the "human" rather than the routine aspects of public assistance. Published early in 1938, it required three printings in the course of a few months.

The Year Book for 1939 contained an innovation, not afterward repeated, that reflected the still depressed conditions of its year of preparation. This was a special 96-page section consisting of state-by-state descriptions of public assistance programs, compiled under the general direction of Miss Joanna C. Colcord of

601

the Charity Organization Department, with field trips to 39 state capitals by Miss Colcord, Donald S. Howard of her department, and the Year Book editor. The Social Work Year Book 1939 was published in an edition of 5,020 copies; it went out of print late in 1940.

Another special study followed in the ensuing off year, this time growing out of the director's activities on the Council on Interstate Migration. Heavy displacements caused by the depression, the severe drought in the "dust bowl" states, conditions in the "cut-over" areas and elsewhere, together with conflicting settlement laws which left many of these persons citizens of no state, without rights to state assistance benefits, had raised problems which needed both study and action. When the Council was dissolved in 1939, its executive secretary, Philip E. Ryan, was employed by the Foundation on a temporary basis to prepare a pamphlet on these problems, under direction of the Year Book Department. The booklet, Migration and Social Welfare, paperbound but running to 114 pages, was published in February, 1940, and shortly required a second printing.

The 1941 Social Work Year Book reflected the feverish activities of the "defense" period. War was raging in Europe. Defense industries and Selective Service were resulting in special social problems, including the "boom" town. Aside from articles reflecting these changes, the Social Work Year Book 1941 followed the pattern of its predecessors. It required two printings, totaling 6,774 copies, and exceeded in sales any previous volume.

Following publication of the 1941 volume, the special studies program ran into difficulties. A volume on servicemen's benefits and legal rights seemed timely and was partly written, but final legislation on these subjects moved too slowly while events moved too fast, and this project was abandoned. A symposium on the "whence, why, whither, and how" of social work, based on a forum discussion by four social work practitioners, failed of publication because "only one of the four participants fulfilled his promise to provide us with a manuscript."

Indeed, the Year Book Department was to issue no further special studies, as formal publications, until the end of the period of this record. We were fast swinging into active participation in World War II. The editor and his associates were soon on frequent loan to government agencies directly concerned with the war. Mr. Kurtz had additional responsibilities as active head of the Building Safety Committee which organized floor wardens and a Red Cross emergency unit within the Foundation; in connection with building employe relations; as acting head of the Charity Organization Department after the illness of Miss Colcord; and, beginning in September, 1943, as assistant general director of the Foundation. He did, however, complete a 28-page mimeographed memorandum for limited circulation on Social Work and War Industry, following a brief survey in that field.

In spite of war, the difficulties of getting manuscripts from contributors (most of whom were working overtime in Washington agencies), staff problems, in spite of printing bottlenecks, the Social Work Year Book 1943 was published as usual, in February of that year, in an edition of 5,545 copies. It reflected the tremendous shiftings in social work personnel and programs as the nation geared itself for all-out war. The edition sold out by May, 1944; meanwhile severe paper restrictions had been clamped down and no reprinting was possible.

The 1945 volume was planned in an atmosphere of still more severe restriction and difficulty. To meet the obvious large demand with the limited poundage of paper available, articles were abbreviated, the page redesigned, the state directory section omitted. Through these economies an edition of 6,986 copies was made possible. Toward the close of 1945 even this large printing was nearly exhausted, but by this time World War II had ended with unexpected suddenness, restrictions on paper were lifted, and a further printing of 1,010 copies was made. Continued heavy demand exhausted this supply, and the 1945 volume went out of print in October, 1946.

In the late summer of 1946 the Year Book office undertook supervision of another of its special publications. With the end of the war, many communities began to consider appropriate memorials. Considerable sentiment sprang up in favor of "living" war memorials—something people in the community could use.

James Dahir came to the Foundation with a proposal for a pamphlet dealing with community centers as memorials, and was commissioned to prepare it as a part of the Year Book program. Community Centers as Living War Memorials was published late in 1946. It was prepared, not as original research, but as a connected commentary on the subject, based chiefly on digests and quotations of appropriate published material.

By October, 1946, the Social Work Year Book 1947 was already partly in type. It is the ninth issue in the series, the sixth published under the editorship of Mr. Kurtz, and the print order for 10,000 copies is the largest initial printing the Foundation has made. The combined sales of its eight predecessors amount to 36,269 copies. The Social Work Year Book has established itself as the primary reference work in its field.

XLI

STATISTICS: 1932-1946

THROUGHOUT the period represented by this chapter the Department of Statistics remained under the direction of Ralph G. Hurlin. Its activities continued to include assistance to other departments of the Foundation on statistical portions of their work, preparation of its own statistical studies, and service to outside agencies, which ranged from isolated interviews and memberships on committees to full responsibility for conducting extensive surveys. The general pattern did not greatly differ from preceding years, but the onset of the severe depression brought unusual demands upon the Department.

During most of this period a series of studies in professions was conducted within the Department by Miss Esther Lucile Brown under Mr. Hurlin's direction. This work grew into the separate Department of Studies in the Professions in October, 1944, and the record of this activity has been reserved for the chapter which follows.

Some Unemployment Surveys

As the depression deepened, the need increased for accurate figures on unemployment, and for other statistics related to relief. The Department had conducted in 1931 a pathfinding study in New Haven, Connecticut, chiefly as a means of developing methods for such studies. Its results were published in Miss Hogg's book, The Incidence of Work Shortage. Exactly two years later, in May–June, 1933, Miss Hogg directed a second survey of unemployment in New Haven, again in collaboration with the Yale Institute of Human Relations. Although New Haven was not so severely hit as some other industrial cities, the resurvey showed that unemployment had almost doubled in the two-year interval, with one earner not working but wanting work for every two earners actually working. One child in every six was in a family with all earners idle.[1]

Miss Hogg's services were requested by the Committee on Government Statistics and Information Services, and were granted for a period of eight months in 1933 and 1934. Her principal work in Washington as its staff member was to advise this committee in its investigation of the Bureau of Labor Statistics indexes of cost of living and retail prices, to which there will be later reference. She also assisted the Bureau in planning special unemployment censuses of Bridgeport, Connecticut, Lancaster, Pennsylvania, and Springfield, Ohio, and supervised the tabulation and analysis of the data of these studies made by the United States Bureau of the Census. She returned to the Foundation in June, 1934, but continued consultation services to the Committee and the Bureau of Labor Statistics so far as her failing health permitted. The following summer, while en route to her former home in England, she died at sea.

Early in 1934 the Department began a survey of unemployment in New York City at the request of Commissioner of Welfare William Hodson, at first confined to sample areas in Manhattan but later including similar portions of the Bronx. In addition to supplying needed information, this project was designed to furnish employment to Civil Works Service employes. During the enumeration and main tabulation period, January through May, the department staff supervised some 60 Civil Works Service employes in an emergency office which the Foundation set up for them in East Hall. Nearly 54,000 workers were questioned and tables were prepared, detailing information on unemployment by section of the city, occupation, industry, and family situation. This information was of immediate value to the New York (City) Department of Welfare in formulating its relief policies. Some of the results were published in the Report of Mayor LaGuardia's Committee on Unemployment Relief, issued in 1935.

[1] The findings were reported in "Ebb-Tide of Employment," by Miss Hogg, in The Survey, August, 1933, pp. 279–280; also summarized in Monthly Labor Review, October, 1933, p. 811.

THE EMERGENCY RELIEF BUREAU

In October, 1934, Commissioner Hodson came to the Foundation with a further request. New York City was spending for relief purposes some $18,000,000 a month, but uncertainty on the details of its own vast operations, problems in obtaining adequate funds, and the many abrupt changes in policy of the state and federal relief administrations, made planning difficult. Deficits were a regular occurrence, in spite of every effort to forecast needs and plan expenditures within the appropriation made each month by the city Board of Estimate. Would the Foundation lend Mr. Hurlin to the Emergency Relief Bureau (ERB) to organize and conduct for a time a new statistical service? The request was granted. Mr. Hurlin became director of a reorganized division of statistics of the ERB, with Miss Geddes director of the report section of this division. For the first three months their salaries were met by the Foundation; thereafter by the ERB.

The task proved "herculean."[1] Mr. Hurlin set up a new plan of statistical reporting covering all activities of the Bureau, including work-relief projects, home relief, relief to unattached and transient persons, commodity distribution, personnel, and finance. Full weekly reports were issued to Commissioner Hodson, other members of the board, and to administrative heads of all divisions and of some 45 large district offices. Daily controls were established whereby it was possible to report at any time the amount of unobligated funds for the proper planning of further expenditures. The scope of this work is suggested by the fact that the relief cases of the ERB had reached 340,000 by the summer of 1935, when the WPA program got under way and the work-relief projects of the ERB began to be transferred.

The central and district office statistical personnel under Mr. Hurlin's direction numbered 63 persons, partly recruited from the project on unemployment he had earlier directed. In addi-

---

[1] In a letter to the Foundation, Miss Charlotte E. Carr, on taking over the responsibilities of director of the Home Relief Bureau, wrote of Mr. Hurlin's work: "Because of the groundwork which he has done under herculean odds, we shall have finished by the 15th of August the foundation for a statistical service that can give to the public for the first time a real picture of the social and economic involvements of our relief program."

tion, he set up a badly needed central index of all cases, for which a staff of 165 persons was required at one period. During the summer of 1935, also, a further temporary staff of 113 workers was set to the task of verifying district case records and preparing the detailed statistics of cases required by the Federal Emergency Relief Administration. For a short time, at its peak, the statistical project was employing 341 workers.

Miss Geddes left this project at the end of April, 1935, to become senior research analyst for FERA's division of research, on leave from the Foundation.[1] Mr. Hurlin remained at this task until the end of September, and then officially returned to the Foundation though he continued to give service to the ERB office for an additional month.

CONSUMERS' EXPENDITURES

Relief administrations throughout the country were using federal indexes of cost of living and family expenditures in revising their relief budgets, giving to such indexes a new critical importance. Miss Hogg had earlier pointed out a logical fallacy in the cost of living index of the United States Bureau of Labor Statistics, and one of her assignments in her association with that bureau in Washington in 1933–1934 was to help make a detailed analysis of the statistical problems relating to measurement of changes in living costs.[2]

Commissioner Isador Lubin of the Bureau of Labor Statistics requested the Department to undertake in New York City a preliminary experimental study of consumers' expenditures which would be of service in laying plans for a national project in this field to be started in the fall of 1934. Planned by Miss Hogg, work was begun in June, 1934, with a field staff recruited from CWA workers, under the supervision of Miss Regina Stolz, who had come to the Department in December, 1927, as statistical

---

[1] After extension of this leave for a further FERA study, she resigned from the Department of Statistics in August, 1936, to join the statistical staff of the newly established Social Security Board.

[2] Reported in "Revision of Index of Cost of Goods Purchased by Wage Earners and Lower-Salaried Workers," by Faith M. Williams, Margaret H. Hogg, and Ewan Clague, in Monthly Labor Review, September, 1935, pp. 819–837.

assistant.[1] Consultants on this project were Dr. Gertrude Schmidt of the Bureau of Labor Statistics and Miss Hogg. About 40 investigators compiled schedules from 400 families, which were analyzed by the Bureau.

In September the same staff started a more comprehensive similar survey in Manhattan and the Bronx. It was begun as a co-operative study by the Bureau of Labor Statistics, the Foundation (which for a time assisted in supervision and gave office space to the workers), and the New York Department of Welfare, which furnished the investigating staff. This was the first of the two important series of local studies of consumers' expenditures conducted by the federal government, the urban studies issued by the Bureau of Labor Statistics and the rural series by the United States Department of Agriculture. The New York study was published by the Bureau under the title Family Income and Expenditure in New York City, 1935–36.

RELIEF STATISTICS

The Department became, and has remained, a center for advice and information in the whole field of the statistics of relief. Private agencies, professional associations, and governmental agencies and departments at all levels were assisted, sometimes through the performance of sample studies such as those already described, more often by service on policy-making committees. The Department concerned itself not only with the techniques of relief statistics, but with pointing out the need for them.[2] But Mr. Hurlin was equally ready to condemn the multiplication of unnecessary statistics, and to recommend the economies of sampling procedures.[3]

[1] Miss Stolz resigned in September, 1934, to join the staff of the Bureau of Labor Statistics.

[2] See, for example, Mr. Hurlin's paper, "Need for a Permanent Program for National Relief Statistics," in This Business of Relief, American Association of Social Workers, 1936, pp. 120–127. The Department also prepared the statistical appendix on the relief situation for this volume.

[3] "At the risk of being misinterpreted I would suggest that our statistics in the field of relief have already reached a stage at which they should be examined for overproduction," said Mr. Hurlin at the National Conference of Social Work in Seattle in June, 1938. Printed in "Statistics in the Administration of a Public Welfare Program," Papers on Relief Statistics, No. 5, November, 1938, p. 9.

When Secretary of Labor Frances Perkins appointed an advisory committee to co-operate with the Committee on Government Statistics and Information Services, Mr. Hurlin served as a member from 1933 through 1935, and was acting chairman part of this time. In this connection he acted as consultant to the Committee in the preparation of the portions of the "COGSIS" report[1] relating to welfare statistics of the Department of Labor and the Children's Bureau.

Further co-operation in the field of federal relief statistics included his membership in 1935 on a committee appointed by the American Public Welfare Association to prepare statistical plans for the anticipated program of the Social Security Board (SSB), chairmanship in 1936 of the federal Central Statistical Board's committee on relief statistics which assisted in the transfer of statistical functions from the FERA to the new SSB, and chairmanship in the same year of a committee on relief statistics of the American Statistical Association. In 1936–1937 he served as chairman of a joint committee of the SSB and the WPA charged with the co-ordination of all federal statistics of relief and public assistance. Since the latter year, he has acted as an official consultant on welfare statistics to the SSB.

The American Statistical Association's committee, already mentioned, joined with the American Public Welfare Association's committee to become the Joint Committee on Relief Statistics, which from 1936 to 1943 served important functions in stimulating the interest of state and local welfare administrations in the improvement of statistics of assistance and the provision of adequate personnel for their development. It was soon made an official advisory committee to the Social Security Board. One of its early projects was the inauguration of current comparative reports of operating statistics on the part of large-city relief administrations, beginning with 14 and growing to 19 cities. Collection of these data was soon taken over by the SSB, and has since provided a timely index of changing relief conditions. Between 1938 and 1940 the Committee issued 16 Bulletins of

[1] Government Statistics: A Report of the Committee on Government Statistics and Information Services. Bulletin 26, Social Science Research Council, April, 1937.

Information for Relief Statisticians. A second publishing enterprise was its series of Papers on Relief Statistics, begun in February, 1938, and concluded with Paper No. 11 in May, 1940. The series was edited by Mr. Hurlin, who was also author of Paper No. 5, Statistics in the Administration of a Public Welfare Program. The Joint Committee was dissolved in 1943, in the belief that its purposes had largely been accomplished.

SOME ENUMERATIONS

The inadequacy of some census data, particularly of workers in the welfare field, has remained a concern of the Department. In 1933, with the co-operation of the National Conference of Catholic Charities, Mr. Hurlin undertook an examination of the occupations of religious sisters of the Catholic Church with reference to their treatment in the 1930 census of occupations. All sisterhoods in the United States were canvassed, and the analysis covered 123,304 such sisters.[1]

The Fifteenth Census of the United States (for 1930) included "social and welfare workers" for the first time as a separate category among occupations. This census reported 31,241 such workers. Mr. Hurlin analyzed these figures, which did not include all categories of social workers, and reported that the probable number of persons in social work positions in 1930 was between 40,000 and 42,500, without inclusion of public health nurses. About one quarter were men. There were about twice as many dentists as social workers, and thirty times as many teachers.[2] However, the number of social workers was already showing evidence of rapid growth, which was to be greatly accelerated by the depression.

With a view to insuring a more adequate enumeration in the 1940 census, Mr. Hurlin in 1939 suggested to the American Association of Social Workers certain steps it might take. He was appointed chairman of a committee on enumeration of social

[1] "Results of an Occupational Census of the Sisterhoods in the United States," in Proceedings, National Conference of Catholic Charities, 1934, pp. 369–375.

[2] St. 7, The Number and Distribution of Social Workers in the United States, by Ralph G. Hurlin, 1933.

workers, which made recommendations to the Bureau of the Census on the positions to be included in the social work category, and later, through an article in The Compass, advised social workers on proper co-operation in securing accurate tabulations. The number of social workers reported by the 1940 census was 72,528, an increase in one decade of approximately 80 per cent over Mr. Hurlin's estimate of 40,000 in 1930.

The Department also planned and tabulated the results of a check-census of social workers taken in June, 1941, in Rhode Island by a local committee of the Association, which indicated under-identification of social workers in the federal occupational census of the previous year.

SALARY STUDIES

The Department conducted an extensive series of salary studies for various agencies in the social field during the critical decade and a half of depression and war, during which social work was more than doubling its personnel, with demand for trained workers consistently far outrunning the supply, but with budgetary limitations on salaries offering little encouragement to prospective workers to secure needed academic training.

In 1932, at the joint request of the Family Welfare Association of America and the American Association of Social Workers, a study was made comparing salaries in 1931 and 1932. In 1934 a group of studies covered various family casework agencies, including Jewish agencies, agencies in New York City, Catholic agencies, and also some public agencies. In 1936 new tabulations were completed, continuing the series for casework agencies made at approximate two-year intervals since 1925. The study analyzed salaries as of March, 1936; vacations, hours of work, and sick leave; and changes in salaries, 1929 to 1936; it was published as a pamphlet by the Family Welfare Association of America[1] in addition to its appearance in issues of The Family and The Compass.

[1] Salaries, Vacations, and Sick Leave in Private Family Case Work Organizations in March, 1936, by Ralph G. Hurlin. Family Welfare Association of America, 1937.

Salaries in settlements in New York City were surveyed in 1936 at the request of the United Neighborhood Houses, with the findings issued in a mimeographed report. A second survey, covering 88 settlements in other cities, was issued in 1938 in a mimeographed report, Salaries in Settlements in 1937. The salaries and education of probation officers in New York State, studied at the request of the State Division of Probation, were the subject of a report by Mr. Hurlin at the Probation Officers' Conference in October, 1940. A study of professional workers in branches of the 379 Young Women's Christian Associations throughout the United States was undertaken in 1942, and resulted in a department pamphlet, St. 12, Salaries and Qualifications of YWCA Professional Workers.

A series of studies of salaries in medical social work included a comparative study of 450 agencies issued as a mimeographed report, Salaries in Hospital Social Work in 1930 and 1932, and a department pamphlet, written by the director, Salaries in Medical Social Work in 1937. A further study of these salaries, which will include social work positions in mental hospitals and mental hygiene clinics, was in progress in 1946.

The inadequacy of salaries of child welfare workers created a critical situation when World War II, breaking up many homes, placed heavier loads upon child-caring agencies. Repeated requests for salary studies came from the Child Welfare League of America, which occupied space on the tenth floor of the Foundation building and had other close relations with the Foundation. Three studies were undertaken. The reports of two were published as department pamphlets; the third appeared in the League's Bulletin.[1] The data were also used in the book, Institutions Serving Children, prepared for the Foundation by the League's executive director, Howard W. Hopkirk, and published in 1944.

A study concentrating on qualifications of caseworkers newly

---

[1] St. 11, Salaries and Qualifications of Child Welfare Workers in 1941, by Ralph G. Hurlin, 1943; St. 13, The Recent Trend of Salaries in Child Welfare Agencies, by Ralph G. Hurlin, 1944; and "Current Salary Quotations for Child Welfare Positions," also by Mr. Hurlin, in Bulletin of the Child Welfare League of America, January, 1945.

employed during 1938 was completed in 1939.[1] In 1943, at the request of the Welfare Council, Mr. Hurlin conducted a brief wartime survey of salary standards for the various fields of social work in New York City.[2]

FAMILY CASEWORK OPERATIONS

Throughout this period the Department maintained its series of monthly statistics of family casework operations, begun on an experimental basis in 1926 and thereafter continued at the request of participating agencies because of the important services this series rendered in indicating trends and administrative practices. The existence of this continuing reporting service also made possible the collection of special data in particular years, as for example surveys on cases caused by unemployment in the period 1932–1934, the interrelation between private and public agencies in 1935, and comparisons of statistics of voluntary and public casework agencies thereafter.

Mr. Hurlin reported trends in the casework field in a number of articles and conference addresses, based on the continuing data of this series. Collected at first as confidential data, after 1936 the monthly table of identified operating statistics was published regularly for general distribution, as were annual summary reports, some of which were issued as formal publications of the Department.[3] The plan underlying these statistics was detailed in a 26-page pamphlet, issued in 1946, on Definitions of Terms and Instructions for Reporting Monthly Statistics of Family Casework. In October, 1946, it was planned to transfer the collection of these data to the Family Service Association of America as of January 1, 1947, concluding for the Department a 21-year statistical series which had proved of great value in recording

---

[1] "Recent Hiring Practices of Private Family Agencies," by Ralph G. Hurlin, in The Family, October, 1939, pp. 181–184, and January, 1940, pp. 286–289.

[2] "New York Social Work Salaries," in Better Times, February 2, 1945, pp. 10–12.

[3] St. 10, Statistics of Family Casework Operations, 1937, by Ralph G. Hurlin, published 1938; St. 14, Operation Statistics of Selected Family Casework Agencies, 1943, by Ralph G. Hurlin, published 1944; St. 15, Same title, 1944, published 1945; St. 19, Same title, 1945, published 1946.

trends in family casework and in developing a method for obtaining similar statistics in related fields.

Hospital Social Work Statistics

During the latter part of the period here recorded the Department of Statistics revived a project for collecting data on hospital social work which had been interrupted in 1932. The new series resulted from a request of the United Hospital Fund in New York City, which needed more complete information to guide its allocation of funds. With the co-operation of a committee of the Fund, work was begun in the fall of 1941 with preparation by the Department of a plan for the recording of data on medical social casework needed for administrative purposes. Collection of these data, confined to hospitals in New York City, began in January, 1942; the Department's first analyses of the statistics were issued only to the participating agencies. Annual summary reports of these statistics for 1944 and 1945 appeared as regular department pamphlets.[1] More than 50 hospitals, including both municipal and voluntary institutions, were covered. The pamphlets covering operations of the two most recent years included a section describing the reporting plan and containing definitions. At the time this record closes in October, 1946, a total of 142,970 of the forms developed for these statistics had been sold, and the plan was being adopted by hospitals in other cities.

Various Services

In addition to the particular services already indicated, the Department gave assistance in many special projects, only a few of which can be separately mentioned. It continued aid to the various departments of the Foundation, reviewing all publications containing statistical data and lending its own personnel for collection of data and preparation of charts and tables in many of the Foundation publications issued in this period. Special

[1] St. 16, Statistics of Medical Social Casework in New York City, 1944, by Ralph G. Hurlin, published 1945; St. 18, Same title, 1945, published 1946.

assistance was given the Department of Social Work Interpretation, both in its survey of salaries of public relations workers in social welfare fields and its census of positions. Staff members who undertook much of this detailed assistance to departments were William Drager, Miss Margaret H. Hogg, Miss Dorothea Jung, and Miss Regina Stolz.

Mr. Hurlin served on a Committee on Statistics of the Blind established jointly, in 1930, by the American Foundation for the Blind and the National Society for the Prevention of Blindness. He became chairman in 1937. This committee prepared record forms for the improvement of statistics of agencies concerned with blindness, has set up classification systems for classification of blind persons by degree of blindness and causes of blindness, and has given consulting service in various state and local surveys. Mr. Hurlin prepared for the committee an estimate of blind persons in the United States, placing the figure at 230,000 in 1940; this was much higher than previous estimates, and was influential in hearings before Congress and elsewhere. With the collaboration of the Social Security Board staff, he was completing in 1946 the report of a study of the causes of blindness among recipients of aid to the blind.

Joint Vocational Service, which had been established in 1927 by the American Association of Social Workers and the National Organization for Public Health Nursing to provide a placement service and vocational information in their fields, asked for a review of its records and statistics after a decade of operation, which the Department undertook in the summer of 1937. This study resulted in a recommendation for reorganization of the Service as a membership organization, a plan subsequently adopted.

The Department has accepted some teaching assignments in the fields of statistics and methods of research, with Mr. Hurlin for several years at the New York School of Social Work and the Graduate School of Jewish Social Work and Miss Hogg at the Fordham School of Sociology and Social Service. Addresses before conferences and other appropriate groups on subjects within the Department's field were frequent, as were contributions to a variety of journals, of which only a few have been mentioned.

In any summation of the services of the Department in the period here reviewed, consultation and committee service would represent an important part. Some examples have been given; no complete record is feasible. Substantial pieces of work were done for no fewer than 11 agencies and departments of the federal government, three state governmental agencies, and two local. Voluntary agencies receiving important aid from the Department were no fewer than 16 of national scope, and numerous local, the latter chiefly in New York City.

Architectural detail from the east façade,
Russell Sage Foundation Building

XLII

STUDIES IN THE PROFESSIONS: 1932-1946

THE Department of Studies in the Professions is the youngest of the Foundation's departments, being given official status in October, 1944. Like several other departments, it had its roots in the work of an individual which grew to an importance meriting department status.

Miss Esther Lucile Brown was one of two assistants employed by Mr. Hurlin when he was preparing, with Meredith B. Givens, a chapter on "Shifting Occupational Patterns" for the President's Research Committee on Social Trends. Miss Brown had earned her doctorate in social anthropology at Yale University, was for several years an assistant professor in the University of New Hampshire, and had spent 1929-1930 in France on a Social Science Research Council fellowship for study in anthropology. As a result of work begun in connection with occupations, the Department of Statistics decided to examine developments in various professional groups, including lawyers, physicians, dentists, nurses, clergymen, engineers, teachers, and social workers. Miss Brown became a member of the Foundation staff in February, 1932, and Mr. Hurlin asked her to undertake this study.

By June of that year her comparative examination had progressed to the point where she was able to present at the National Conference of Social Work a paper on "Social Work Against a Background of Other Professions." She left the Foundation in October to serve as educational director of the United Parents Associations of New York City, but came back the following June "for the summer months" to resume work on the comparative study of selected professions, and has remained with the Foundation since that date. While she was officially a member of the Department of Statistics until creation of her own department in 1944, her work has been so thoroughly concentrated in the field of the professions that its whole record is presented in this chapter.

Although all of the professions have a large technical literature, few of them have given adequate attention to the important social problem of how professional service can be made adequate both in quantity and quality, and can be extended to society everywhere in the United States at a cost that can be met either by those persons in need of service or by the use of charitable and public funds. Miss Brown's Department has centered its attention upon conducting and stimulating studies in this neglected field to the end that professional skills may become more widely available to all the people of the nation.

Social Work as a Profession

As study in the various professions deepened, the original plan for a single volume comparing selected aspects of many professions was modified. Education already possessed so exhaustive a literature concerning the adequacy of schools and teachers in the United States that no further supplementation was necessary. On the other hand, several of the professions, especially the younger ones, needed more profound study and detailed treatment than could be provided in the brief chapter originally proposed. The idea of the comparative volume was not yet abandoned, but the range of professions to be studied was narrowed, and their social aspects were increasingly emphasized.

Because of the Foundation's long-continued interest in social work, this occupation was the first to come under the closer scrutiny of the new plan. Was social work, to begin with, a profession at all? Miss Brown examined its origins, schools, national associations, the supply of workers and the demand for them, and their salaries. She reported that, as of 1935, it met most of the criteria of a true profession, and was well on its way toward meeting the remainder.

Her preliminary study was issued in June, 1935, as an 80-page pamphlet entitled Social Work as a Profession. A prefatory note announced it as advance publication of "a chapter of a book on the professions." No such book has been published, but the "chapter" itself grew into a book which had a profound influence on social work in the ensuing decade, and shaped many of the future activities of its author.

One year later a second edition was issued, expanded to 120 pages, and published in book form. In this edition it was announced that the project for a single volume comparing various professions had been abandoned in favor of a plan to issue separately the material on each profession. The series was entitled Studies in Professions, and two other such studies, as noted later, were published also in 1936.

However, Social Work as a Profession continued to demand attention. A third edition, not expanded but bringing statistics to date, was required by January, 1938. A few years later the great growth of social work (partly as a result of the Social Security Act), the availability of new data from the 1940 census, the ferment of change within social work and its professional schools, and the coming of World War II seemed urgently to call for a new appraisal of the emerging profession. The book was completely rewritten, its content greatly expanded, and a section added on the relation of social workers to the war and to the problems of reconstruction which would follow. This fourth edition of 232 pages was published in December, 1942.

Movements within the social work field which these successive editions recorded, and frequently influenced, involved Miss Brown in a widening circle of activities. She was in demand as a speaker before groups of social workers, at the National Conference of Social Work, at state conferences, and in local groups. Her careful studies of the curricula of schools of social work brought many requests for consultations on this subject.

In the early forties difficulties arose between the American Association of Schools of Social Work, whose member schools offered training chiefly on the graduate level, and the increasing number of colleges and universities which, under strong pressure from state departments of public welfare and other agencies, were introducing courses in social work for undergraduates. The long list of these new curricula which Miss Brown included in the 1942 revision of Social Work as a Profession emphasized the extent of undergraduate training, and its publication resulted in many demands for advice about how recognition could be obtained for these curricula.

Shortly afterward a National Association of Schools of Social Administration was formed to represent the interests of schools that were predominantly but not exclusively undergraduate. Immediately, however, a multiplicity of questions arose concerning the desirability of two accrediting agencies, and a possible reconsideration of the entire pattern of social work education. A Joint Committee for Education in Social Work, composed of members of both groups, was therefore created in 1945 to review the respective functions of these two associations. Miss Brown was appointed impartial chairman.

Although the older association rejected several of the proposals made by the Joint Committee and accepted unanimously by the National Association, it did accept two broad general proposals which may have profound influence upon the future of social work education. The first was the formation of a National Council of Education in Social Work which should be composed not only of representatives of the two associations of schools but of the American Association of Social Workers and of national organizations and federal agencies which had a special interest in social work education. The second proposal was for a comprehensive research survey of training for social work, with recommendations for future development.

Miss Brown has been giving informal advisory service to the National Council. With its needs particularly in mind, she prepared her pamphlet, The Use of Research by Professional Associations in Determining Program and Policy, which was used as the feature article in the September, 1946, issue of The Compass, prior to being published by the Foundation in October for distribution to other professions.

In recognition of the growing importance of the public social services and the challenge that they present to educational institutions, the American Council on Education established, in 1944, a Committee on Education and Social Security, the name of which is about to be changed to Committee on Education and the Public Social Services. Miss Brown is an active member of this committee.

Her concern that social work should not merely develop professional techniques but should contribute toward fundamental solutions of social problems found expression in many directions, including membership in the Social Work Action Committee.[1] Her work with this group has included preparation of a pamphlet, Ethnic Democracy and the Social Worker.

THE PROFESSIONAL ENGINEER

The second book to be published in the Studies in Professions was The Professional Engineer, in August, 1936. In this little volume of 86 pages Miss Brown pointed to the progressive growth and strengthening of engineering education on the professional level. She viewed the creation of the Engineers' Council for Professional Development as a medium for raising standards of education and practice, attaining greater solidarity within the profession, and achieving greater effectiveness in dealing with technical, social, and economic problems. She noted the rapid disappearance of the private engineering practitioner with his frequently large income and opportunity to engage in engineering in foreign countries as well as in the United States. But in his place she observed the large numbers of salaried engineers who were occupying responsible positions of a managerial nature, not only in their particular field of engineering but in business and industry.

This book went out of print in 1939. It was not reprinted because a new edition was needed which would reflect a more intensive and extensive examination of the profession, taking note of the growing interest of engineering education in social planning and the increased awareness that competence in managerial positions requires social as well as technical skills. It has not been possible for Miss Brown as yet to give the requisite time to such an examination. Files of recent developments are being built, however, and in her pamphlet on The Use of Research by Pro-

[1] See also her article "Comparative Developments in Social Work, Medicine,and Law," in The Family, November, 1943, pp. 243–255.

fessional Associations, reference was made to a few of these developments.

NURSING AS A PROFESSION

The third volume of the Studies in Professions was issued in October, 1936. Miss Brown's Nursing as a Profession followed the general pattern of its predecessors in presenting something of the history of the profession concerned, the status of professional training, national organizations, statistical data on number and distribution of nurses and their salaries, and recent trends. Emphasis was placed upon the still "appallingly large" number of nursing schools—no fewer than 1,300—the majority of which were connected with hospitals too small to provide adequate education in clinical subjects or funds sufficient for maintaining sound professional training. She stressed the fact that relatively few schools of nursing have come under university control, as have most schools of other professions. Instead, they continue to be operated by hospitals which, as service institutions, inevitably tend to make nursing service for patients their first consideration and the education of nurses a secondary function.

Special sections of the book dealt with the dynamic growth of public health nursing and industrial nursing, and attention was given to the forward-looking programs of the several nurses' associations. Miss Brown saw the problem of nursing services at a fee the patient is able to pay as insurmountable for many sick persons of moderate income, unless such services were provided as part of prepayment insurance plans or tax-supported health programs.

Her book achieved a large, immediate sale, particularly in schools of nursing, and had to be reprinted within three months. She continued advisory and other activities in the field of nursing, though not to the same extent as in social work. In March, 1940, a second edition, brought to date and considerably expanded, was published. The book was allowed to go out of print in 1944, the Department being then too deeply involved in other projects to undertake the needed further revision.

In 1946, however, Miss Brown became consultant on a survey looking toward the structural reorganization of six national organizations of nurses. She also spoke before some 10,000 nurses assembled in biennial convention on who should bear the expense of and the responsibility for nursing education.

Physicians and Medical Care

The concern for health care for all the people which found partial expression in the book on nursing was more fully developed in her next study, Physicians and Medical Care, published in May, 1937. This 202-page book discussed the reforms which had taken place in medical education; the present adequacy of medical schools; work of national associations in raising standards of professional training; the number, distribution, and incomes of physicians; some of the newer forms of furnishing medical service; and included considerable sections on the problem of more and better medical care for the entire nation. Miss Brown saw this problem as "primarily an economic one which must be solved, not by placing further burdens upon the medical profession and charitable health agencies, but by finding more systematic methods for paying for health service."[1]

Both in the period of its preparation and after its publication, this study involved its author in a series of related conferences, addresses, and activities. In 1935 Miss Brown led a series of round tables at the Wellesley Summer Institute on ways of bringing medical care to all the people. In 1937 she accepted membership on the advisory committee of the Bureau of Cooperative Medicine, which in 1941 became Medical Administration Service. Until June, 1946, she served on the board of Medical Administration Service, whose chief function has been the promotion of group medical practice. Other activities in this general field included assistance in developing the Optical Membership Plan in New York City as a non-profit organization, of which she became one of the trustees in 1944.

[1] Physicians and Medical Care, p. 149.

Lawyers and the Promotion of Justice

But just as professional social work was the dominant interest in the early period of these studies, the law—in its social and public aspects—became a central concern in the latter period. The first published expression of this interest was the book, Lawyers and the Promotion of Justice, issued in November, 1938. It was the fifth and last of the regular series of Studies in Professions, and by a considerable margin the longest of them. As in its predecessors in the series, Miss Brown presented a rounded view of the status of the profession, including emphasis on legal education; she added extensive sections on outstanding weaknesses in the administration of justice and on new trends within the legal field. Dealing with the profession which plays, perhaps, the major role in forming our social and governmental institutions, the book emphasized the need of participation by both the legal profession and the public in bringing legal service to persons of small economic means, in increasing the efficiency and raising the moral tone of the bar and the courts, and in the general promotion of justice.

The study was based on extensive investigation of law schools and interviews with authorities on legal problems. Though Miss Brown had pointed in her Preface to "the multiplicity of problems" encountered by one who attempts to write about a group of which one is not a member, her book received wide and favorable attention from the legal profession as well as from the general public, and involved her in many invitations to speak, to confer on law-school curricula, and to write articles. In September, 1939, her article on "Legal Aid and the Promotion of Justice," was given first place in a special issue of The Annals of the American Academy of Political and Social Science. In late December of that year she arranged at the University of Chicago Law School an all-day conference of a selected group of professors concerned with how to introduce pertinent social science materials into their law-school courses, and how to make training for public service a more significant responsibility of their schools. She also helped, in 1940, to organize a Council for the Furtherance of the Public and Social Aspects of Law which would, it was hoped, stimulate legal education to greater interest in those broad governmental and social problems for the solution of which lawyers need more than technical proficiency. The Council, however, did not survive the war, which reduced law schools to mere skeletons.

FURTHER STUDIES IN LAW

As one result of these studies and activities, Miss Brown felt strongly that legal education in the United States should be so broadened and directed that it could serve usefully not only as training for the private practice of law but for public administration. As a result both of the economic depression and the general trend toward increase in government services and supervision, the public service was expanding rapidly during the thirties. Many administrative positions were in fact occupied by lawyers, although the law schools had centered little specific attention upon preparation either for public legal work or for public administration.

She made extensive field trips in 1940 and thereafter, examining law-school curricula with this need in mind. Eric F. Schweinburg, an American citizen who holds a doctorate in law from the University of Vienna and was an attorney for more than a decade in that city, was added to the staff in October, 1942, to bring to these studies the background and experience of the professional lawyer. His education and training abroad were put to prompt use in preparation of Law Training in Continental Europe: Its Principles and Public Function, which was issued in December, 1945, as the first publication of the newly created department. This 129-page study revealed the very significant differences between legal training as it developed in continental Europe prior to World War II and current American practices. It pointed out the extent to which European legal training was designed to serve the needs of the higher civil service as well as bar and bench, and described the division of continental legal education into a broad, non-professional course of university study and a professional apprenticeship training served in law offices, courts, and administrative agencies.

Miss Brown is preparing a companion publication as this record closes, under the working title Lawyers, Law Schools, and the Public Service. In it she is utilizing the extensive materials gathered not only in visits to law schools but to attorneys in federal cabinet departments and administrative agencies, in an attempt to discover how legal education may best be reoriented to serve the needs of the public service.

The Department is also engaged in a study of how legal assistance may be made available to persons financially unable to engage the services of competent lawyers or to meet the expenses of litigation. This study is being made at the express request of the National Association of Legal Aid Organizations and the Committee on Legal Aid of the American Bar Association. Mr. Schweinburg has visited representative legal aid societies, and criminal and small claims courts. He has examined American literature concerning the administration of justice and has obtained extensive information concerning European provisions for persons of limited resources. In October, 1946, he was undertaking the first draft of the book.

XLIII

LIBRARY: 1932-1946

THE FOUNDATION Library underwent no major changes until nearly the end of the period covered by this chapter. Mrs. Bertha F. Hulseman remained librarian until her retirement in October, 1941, continuing the policies which had contributed to its growth in size, service, and esteem during the twenty-seven years of her membership on the Library staff, for fourteen of which she was in active charge as librarian or acting librarian. She was succeeded by Mrs. Mabel Badcock, until she in turn reached retirement age, having concluded over thirty years of service in the Library by the time of her retirement in January, 1946. Mrs. Adams[1] served as acting librarian until the appointment, in September, 1946, of Raymond W. Holbrook as director of the Library. Mr. Holbrook came to the Foundation from a position as associate director of libraries at the University of Georgia; he had previously been an assistant librarian at the College of the City of New York.

The staff grew slightly during these years, and some changes in personnel occurred. Professional appointments of the period, omitting those of brief duration, included William Roblyer as general assistant in charge of serials, September, 1932, to April, 1934; Miss Agnes H. Campbell in the same position, April, 1934, to February, 1939;[2] Allan H. Wagner as her successor from February, 1939; and Miss Felicia Fuss as assistant cataloguer and desk assistant, from October, 1941. Mrs. Margaret M. Otto, who had resigned from the staff at the close of 1932, rejoined it in February, 1936, as reference assistant, and became acting assistant librarian in February, 1946. Miss Grace P. Thornton continued throughout the period her service as assistant cata-

---

[1] Miss Constance Beal until her marriage in April, 1936.

[2] When she resigned to organize and administer the new library of the Federal Council of the Churches of Christ in America.

loguer and desk assistant, begun in 1930. The addition of a page to the staff, initiated in 1933, proved so successful that this service was maintained, even through the difficult war period.

Members of the staff continued the policy of affiliation with professional organizations in their field, being represented at meetings of the American Library Association and taking active part in the Special Libraries Association, particularly the civic-social group of the New York chapter, later named the social science group. Mrs. Hulseman served on the publication and the hospitality committees of the Special Libraries Association for several years, and Miss Thornton was vice-president in 1936–1937. At different periods Mrs. Badcock, Mrs. Otto, and Miss Fuss have served as chairmen of the social science group. Mrs. Adams' active participation has included service as secretary-treasurer of the New York chapter, Special Libraries Association, member of the subject headings committee of its social science group, and member of the regional catalogue group of New York City and its environs.

The Clientele

It had early been decided that the Library should serve principally four groups: the Foundation staff, students and faculty of the New York School of Social Work, social workers, and the general public who might be interested in its specialized collection. Use by the Foundation departments remained at a fairly steady level, though subject interests changed with the nature of the research projects. The Library built up special collections to meet such needs, and sometimes found its own collection greatly increased at the conclusion of a project, when it inherited much of the material the department had gathered.

Service to the New York School of Social Work was a problem of another sort. The School had grown rapidly.[1] Newer trends in education required wider reading of source and supplementary materials in place of chief reliance on single texts. Both of these movements resulted in much increased use of the Library, where

[1] The enrollment for first fall terms varied as follows: 322 in 1910; 112 in 1920; 671 in 1930; 851 in 1940; and 903 in 1945.

by 1934 seating capacity was exhausted, hats and overcoats were piled up on window sills and floors, and lines formed at the charging desk. To relieve this condition the School finally opened a reading room of its own in 1935, stocked with reference copies of assigned readings for the use of students, which shortly became, in part, a circulating library. The new facility reduced the attendance record at the Foundation Library, although the readings for the School continued to be set aside and all possible reference help was provided for the student body[1] and for the New York School faculty. In 1945 Library hours were further extended, chiefly for the accommodation of patrons from the School.

Attendance on the part of social workers and the general public showed long-term gains as the profession of social work expanded its numbers and as the Library became better known in its neighborhood, but in the recent decade and a half of depression and war exhibited severe fluctuations. The earliest recorded annual attendance is that for 1915, when it numbered 14,033. For the next fifteen years, as a previous chapter has indicated,[2] growth was slow and relatively steady, reaching 25,666 in 1930.

Then, with the onset of the depression, the increase in enforced leisure, and more attention to social problems, attendance leaped upward, establishing new records each year, and posing more difficult problems for the hard-pressed staff. In January, 1932, to meet increasing demands, the experiment of keeping open three evenings a week was tried; on varying bases, and usually omitting the summer months, that practice has continued. Moreover, the Library "seemed to be considered headquarters for material for all civil service examinations in our field," and with the approach of examination periods for positions such as social investigator, crowds could reliably be predicted. By 1935 the all-time record in attendance of 50,886 was reported; but by the summer of that year some relief was in sight, due partly to the opening of the New York School of Social Work's reading room. Limited assist-

[1] One service in this direction was creation of a Labor Browsing Room for students in this field. Begun in 1940, it was abandoned a year later because of insufficient use.

[2] See Chapter XIX.

PERIODICAL ROOM, RUSSELL SAGE FOUNDATION LIBRARY

ance was also available, from 1934 through 1937, from workers assigned to the Library by the Civil Works Administration and then by the WPA.

From 1936 through 1941 attendance was almost stationary on a high plateau of about 42,000 a year. In 1942 "a decided decrease" was noted, which soon carried attendance figures to the neighborhood of 32,000, where they remained during the whole period when World War II was pushing all other activities into the background. In 1946, the first peace year, attendance stood at 39,317.

The attendance for the fourteen-year period 1918 through 1931 averaged 22,000 a year, or about 73 persons on the average library day. In the fifteen-year period, 1932 through 1946, it had mounted to nearly 40,000, or about 133 persons on the average library day. The number of Library patrons had nearly doubled.

The Collection and Its Housing

The collection grew steadily, the bound volumes increasing from 31,568 at the close of 1931 to 44,056 by October, 1946; the unbound items from 105,772 to 169,765. Additions came from purchase, from systemized requests, and from voluntary gifts, some of which were substantial in size and importance. For example, in 1941 Lawrence Veiller made valuable contributions, including items a century old. Many other important gifts are recorded.

But the "gift" process went in both directions. As the Library received unneeded duplicates, or for lack of shelf space had to abandon collections marginal to its interests, the Library in its turn offered its books where they might be most needed—106 books and pamphlets to the Cairo (Egypt) School of Social Work, and substantial contributions to many other libraries abroad and at home, particularly those associated with schools of social work, operating on inadequate budgets, or sufferers by enemy action.

One of the gravest problems was finding room for the growing collection. In 1933 the former drafting room of the Regional Plan of New York and Its Environs on the tenth floor was taken over.

This was not convenient, but it was greeted with much satisfaction "as there will remain space for growth." The space for growth was something of an illusion; by 1936 crowded shelves and lack of space were again a problem, which increased throughout the period recorded by this chapter. Resolute weeding out of files of periodicals and other materials of marginal importance in the social field was one solution; but by 1945 more drastic steps became necessary. Among these steps was disposal of the greater part of the report collection in public health, except for files relating to New York City and State. Discarded material went to the New York Public Library, the New York Academy of Medicine, and items of British interest to the bombed libraries of Bristol, Liverpool, and Glasgow. As a temporary expedient, in 1946 the Library began to expand down into the sixth floor. Space was found, however, for a unique collection— two units of photographic studies by Lewis Hine, one on immigrants and the other on child labor.

Continuous efforts were made, so far as crowded schedules permitted, to increase the Library's service. Revisions were made in the catalogue to bring it abreast of changing terminologies in social work. Exhibits were set up from time to time on subjects of popular interest, gathering together the Library material in those fields, sometimes augmented with special photographs, maps, and charts. In connection with study of foundations undertaken by Russell Sage Foundation, the Library built up a special file on all known foundations, and has become a principal resource in this field. In addition to serving patrons within the Library, the research librarians answered many questions over the telephone and by mail, questions which varied from inquiries as to the psychological effects of baptism and initiation to the more usual areas of social research. In a single year, as many as 200 special bibliographical lists were typed and sent out in answer to specific requests.

PUBLICATIONS

Through the first part of this period, the Library continued preparation and publication of its Bulletin series of bibliographies on a bimonthly basis. As in the past, these covered subjects of current interest in the social field, with an annual selection, Books on Social Subjects. Problems of the depression were necessarily prominent in the bibliographies for this period.

The development of national organizations in most of the special fields of social welfare, and their resulting publications, decreased the need for this service, and with the end of 1939 regular bimonthly publication was discontinued, though occasional special numbers were issued as need arose.[1] The final regular number, issued in December, 1939, was the 158th in its series, which had started in 1913. In addition to unrecorded distribution,[2] these bibliographies reached a total recorded sale of 174,627 copies by September, 1946.

In 1938 Mrs. Hulseman and the Library staff completed a new revision of American Foundations for Social Welfare, which the Library had started in 1915 as a combined bibliography and directory, listing 23 foundations in that first number. The 1938 edition listed 156 foundations and 31 community trusts. A revision of A List of Directories of Social Agencies followed, in 1941.

THE FUTURE

When the war ended and plans looking toward the future could be entertained, it was obvious that the work of the Library needed prompt consideration. If its scope and clientele were merely to remain the same, the inevitable continued growth would require greatly expanded and more convenient quarters. But plans for larger service had been constantly in mind, on the part of the Library staff and the Foundation administration. In late 1945 a survey was begun by Paul North Rice, chief of the reference department of the New York Public Library, into the present position and the possible future of the Russell Sage Foundation Library.

[1] In 1942, when the National Conference of Social Work was held in New Orleans, The South: Its Social and Economic Aspects; in 1943, The War and Social Problems; also, Rehabilitation of the Disabled Serviceman, in two editions; in 1945, Organized Labor's Participation in Social Work.

[2] Free distribution has always been considerable. Figures are not available on either sales or free distribution prior to 1917.

With the Rice report for guidance, Raymond W. Holbrook began to develop his own plans for Library expansion, on assuming directorship in September, 1946. As this record closes it is too early to report on definite developments. However, the Library has already expanded into rooms on the sixth floor, to help meet the immediate space emergency.

Architectural detail from the north façade,
Russell Sage Foundation Building

XLIV

PUBLICATIONS: 1932-1946

THE Publication Department remained under the direction of F. Emerson Andrews throughout the period covered by this chapter. General policies for the wider distribution of Foundation studies which had been earlier instituted were further developed, with adaptation to the special conditions of depression, and then of war.

In the fifteen years of this period the Foundation published 42 cloth-bound books; under many definitions, four of the more lengthy and substantial pamphlets of the period would be added to this book total. All but five of these books were issued under regular departmental auspices, and the conditions surrounding their preparation and publication have been discussed in preceding chapters. Only these five, not elsewhere covered, receive detailed treatment in this section, otherwise devoted to general publishing history.

A Period of Expansion

The depression, which was for most of America a period of slackened activity, had an opposite effect on the publication program. At first book sales, particularly of titles costing more than a dollar, did drop sharply, reflecting the leanness of depression purses. The year 1932 was the low point, but was quickly followed by a period of expansion which brought demand for publications to the highest level in the Foundation's history. This was a natural result of several factors: activity on the part of various departments in supplying materials needed in the relief emergency; and the great expansion of social work itself, adding to its personnel tens of thousands of previously untrained workers and volunteers.

Such titles as Emergency Work Relief, The Incidence of Work Shortage, Cash Relief, Unemployment Relief in Periods of De-

635

pression, and The Public Assistance Worker appeared in rapid succession, dealing so directly with the problems of the moment that many of them became "must" books in their field and garnered substantial sales. But it was not only the new books which felt these effects. In Social Diagnosis, Public Employment Offices, What Is Social Case Work?, and some other older titles the Foundation had provided tools of lasting usefulness which, it was believed, could now be placed in new hands. "Vigorous campaigns were conducted," reported the director, "especially among the newly organized state and national relief agencies." Results were substantial. Public Employment Offices, a highly specialized study for which no great sale had developed, sold 217 copies in its twelfth year, and continued in such demand that a reprint was made by photographic methods. Social Diagnosis, published in 1917, achieved its largest single-year sale eighteen years after publication—2,504 copies in 1935.

Materials other than books were similarly affected. Pamphlets could be issued more quickly to meet emergency needs, and several of those prepared by the Charity Organization Department received wide distribution; in large part, however, in the form of free distribution to special organizations and committees. Forms and record sheets, particularly those used for registration of the unemployed, rose to the unrivaled total of 476,000 in 1932, later to fall when the Charity Organization Department series was transferred to Family Welfare Association of America in October, 1937. Activity in this field then became negligible, except for a substantial increase in the most recent year, when a series of forms prepared for medical social work by the Department of Statistics brought the total for 1946 above 60,000.

Meetings of the National Conference of Social Work, through the depression years, were usually well attended, and at all such meetings the Publication Department maintained its display. State conferences could not usually be covered by the Department, but Foundation books were displayed by the Family Welfare Association of America and The Survey; in 1935 these agencies accounted for more than a thousand books, well above any previous record.

The accelerating demand was met by increased efforts along all lines. Booksellers were visited, and by various other means[1] impressed with the growing importance of publications in the social sciences. Mail campaigns were expanded, and when the limited budget and the low price of the books made ordinary mailings too expensive, postcard mailings were tested, and succeeded. Advertising in periodicals was never extensive, but covered with some thoroughness the journals in the social field, with a few insertions in more general publications. News releases were prepared for nearly all new titles, and for other Foundation events of public interest.

The Standing Order Plan formed the backbone of the Department's book distribution. In his preliminary survey in 1928, Mr. Andrews had said: "The Standing Order List represents, in the opinion of your investigator, the most promising means of distribution of RSF publications now available to you. It has, in the history of the Foundation, reached very nearly to 500, and it could probably be built up to a total ranging between 1,200 and 2,000." The initial goal of 1,200, as already noted, was nearly reached in 1930; but the first depression years brought a decline. With increases in social work personnel, new efforts were made to build the list. It passed the 1,200 goal in 1935, and stood in October, 1946, at 2,460, well beyond the prediction. So large a group of libraries, organizations, and individuals, receiving on publication all but the most highly specialized books and pamphlets, represented a substantial guarantee toward large first printings, making possible the low prices which characterize Foundation publications.

In 1932 the Department began to issue the RSF Bulletin, an internal house organ designed both as an informal record of events of personal and organization interest and as a means of keeping the various departments informed of one another's activities. After several issues on a monthly basis it was made a quarterly, and for fourteen years has been continuously edited by

[1] Including articles by the director in Publishers' Weekly on such topics as "The Awakening Social Field" (June 2, 1934).

the department director, with in recent years an occasional guest editor from another department.

CITY PLANNING PUBLICATIONS

Of the four books during this period written by persons not members of the Foundation staff, three were in the field of city planning. The Foundation had a continuing interest in this subject, stemming from the planning and development of Forest Hills Gardens, a book by Flavel Shurtleff, and the sponsorship of the Regional Plan of New York and Its Environs.[1] Thomas Adams was general director of plans and surveys for the Committee on Regional Plan, and when he desired to prepare and publish a historical survey of city planning it was natural that he turned to the Foundation as publisher. He had the assistance of the Editorial Department in preparation of his book, but it was independent of any research department sponsorship. The Outline of Town and City Planning was published in 1935. It found a good general market, and was for some time a leading college text in its specialized field. A British edition was brought out by J. and A. Churchill of London, who imported sheets; British publication was particularly appropriate since Mr. Adams was a British citizen and a large portion of his practice as city planner had been in England. After destruction of a large part of London and other British towns in the Nazi air attacks of World War II, The Outline of Town and City Planning and the Regional Plan volumes were in great demand in England.

Edward M. Bassett, the "father of zoning," had been associated with the Regional Plan studies with relation to zoning problems. He asked the Foundation to publish under its auspices the definitive volume on zoning which he proposed to write, and in 1936 his book, Zoning, was duly published. It speedily became the chief authority in its field and has wielded a wide influence in what has been called "one of our most useful social inventions in preserving human and economic values in cities." Subsequently, Mr. Bassett arranged with the Foundation to publish his brief treatise on The Master Plan, which was issued in 1938.

[1] See pp. 49–51, 215, 438–451.

A fourth book in the field of city planning was issued in 1939, Mr. Perry's Housing for the Machine Age; it was prepared under departmental auspices, and has already been discussed.[1]

WARTIME DIFFICULTIES

The period of expanding demand for Foundation publications reached its peak by 1938–1939. After that time the depression had spent its force, and the whole category of books in the relief field found few buyers. Other influences were already at work. As early as 1932 Mr. Andrews had pointed to reduced foreign sales because of "war conditions in the East, and unfavorable foreign exchange"; in 1938 the Department suspended all credit to Japanese accounts. The opening sentences of his report for 1942 epitomized the succeeding period:

> Early this fiscal year, bombs bursting on Pearl Harbor blasted us into war. Active participation not only created a market unfavorable for publications not directly war-centered, but it further siphoned into defense and war activities the energies of many staff members. We went through the year without a single new book publication. . . .

Difficulties arose not only in getting books written, but in finding the means to publish any which were written. Metal for wire staples, "gray cloth" for bindings, chlorine to whiten paper, all had essential wartime uses, and were in short supply. Printing plates for which prompt use was not assured had to be melted down by order of the federal government. Selective Service began to drain printing and binding plants of skilled workmen. Costs rose, work was inferior and painfully slow, and mistakes multiplied. One whole edition had to be turned back because in many of the books pages followed each other in erratic order. Worst of all, in January, 1943, the government imposed a paper limitation order using as the base period a percentage of the paper consumed in 1942—the very year when the Foundation was "without a single new book publication." An appeal was promptly taken to the War Production Board, and partial relief afforded through

[1] See p. 513.

applying a three-year average as a base, in place of the single lowest year of paper consumption in some decades. The Department found itself faced for three years with limitation of its book paper to less than 20,000 pounds a year—for a whole year's publishing program, less than is used by a metropolitan department store to advertise a glove sale.

To meet these restrictions, some publications were delayed or abandoned, others reduced in size; lighter-weight papers were used where possible; type pages were re-designed, margins reduced, more words crowded upon each page. Even after these economies, printings of new books were always of inadequate size, and "promotion" became a selective effort of trying to see that the inadequate supply reached organizations and persons most in need of that particular publication with discouragement of all other orders. Reprintings usually could not be undertaken. In one disastrous year, 1944, eight volumes went out of print while only three could be added to the list.

Nevertheless, throughout the war a publishing program did go on. Seven new books were issued during the war years. Sales volume was bolstered for a time by existing stocks of older books, until many of these went out of print; by 1945 the book inventory was at the lowest point in the Department's records.

Whatever the book shortages in America, in China they were worse. China's plight, in the form of a plea for books in the field of social welfare, was brought to the Foundation in 1943, when that country was completely cut off except for limited air transport over The Himalayas. Mr. Andrews had recently helped arrange a microfilm exhibit for the American Institute of Graphic Arts[1] and realized that the contents of half a dozen normal books could be carried on a single thin roll of microfilm. He made arrangements with the Office of War Information and the State Department whereby some 50 recent social welfare books and documents, selected with the aid of the New York School of Social Work, were flown in the diplomatic pouch to the Ministry of Social Research in Chungking in the form of microfilm rolls. A number of Foundation books were included, sections of which

[1] He has been a director of the Institute since 1941.

were afterward translated into Chinese. This distribution required no American paper.

Paper was likewise no factor in several other special "editions." In 1942 the Braille Institute of America published What Is Social Case Work? in Braille type for distribution to libraries for the blind. In the same year the federal Children's Bureau was granted permission to translate into Spanish and Portuguese considerable sections of the Social Work Year Book for distribution and re-publication in Latin America. The following year advance portions of the Social Work Year Book 1943 were broadcast to occupied France by the Office of War Information.

It also happened that paper limitations did not apply to pamphlets, provided they did not exceed 32 pages. The Foundation could therefore issue more adequate editions of any material capable of being compressed into brief pamphlets. A number of pamphlets were prepared, including a special series of eight dealing with administration of relief abroad, elsewhere mentioned.[1] Pamphlet sales, which for a decade had seldom exceeded 5,000 a year, rose above 26,000 in 1944, establishing the highest record in the Department's history.

One such pamphlet was issued outside the departmental procedure. Shelby M. Harrison, general director of the Foundation, was president of the National Conference of Social Work[2] as America entered World War II. His presidential address, "Attacking on Social Work's Three Fronts," was delivered in New Orleans, as darkened ships dropped down the Mississippi and a German submarine was reported at its mouth. This address was issued as a pamphlet, distributed free at the Conference but elsewhere sold. Some 6,000 were thus distributed the first year, together with 5,000 additional copies in abbreviated form prepared at the request of the National Social Work Council and Community Chests and Councils.

In 1944 appeared the final publication of the period under other than Foundation authorship. As a result of homes broken by the war, working mothers, and overcrowded housing, more chil-

[1] See p. 528.
[2] See p. 488.

dren were needing care outside their own homes, with fewer foster homes or boarding homes available. Institutions had to fill in the gap, and the quality of institutional care, a matter of grave concern before World War II, attained a new wartime importance. The person who was perhaps best informed as to the situation in institutions was Howard W. Hopkirk, executive director of the Child Welfare League of America, which had offices on the tenth floor of the Foundation building and was receiving Foundation grants. He had proposed to the Foundation a book that should serve as a practical guide for all those concerned with child-care institutions. He was commissioned to write it, and given the assistance of the Editorial Department. Institutions Serving Children was published in May, 1944, and has already required three printings.

As the war approached an end, a new project was undertaken in which the general director, Mr. Harrison, and the director of the Publication Department served as co-authors. Mr. Andrews, since his employment by the Foundation in 1928, had been officially on half time (in periods of stress it was more than half), devoting his free time to a considerable program of book and magazine writing. Some of this outside work concerned Foundation interests more or less directly,[1] but none had appeared under Foundation imprint. When it came time for the Foundation to consider a revision of its bulletin on American Foundations for Social Welfare, issued at irregular intervals since 1915, Mr. Andrews suggested a much more complete directory section than had previously been attempted, together with substantial introductory text on the history, organization, finances, fields, and general policies of foundations, to be written by the general director. He was invited to share in preparation of such a study.

[1] Out of the Foundation's city planning studies grew his articles on zoning for Rotarian, House Beautiful, his chairmanship of the planning board of his home community, Tenafly, and service as special writer for the Mayor's Committee on City Planning (New York). His concern for effective non-profit publishing was expressed in advisory services to many organizations and individuals in this field, articles in the professional journals, and a staff position with the Twentieth Century Fund as consultant on publications. He has made several addresses at the National Conference of Social Work, a pathfinding one in 1942 on "Family Allowances for America?" resulting in later contributions to Atlantic Monthly and elsewhere on the same topic.

Questionnaires were sent to nearly a thousand foundations, and information for the general text sought from many additional sources. Miss Margaret Hodges, of the Social Work Year Book Department, was drawn in for assistance with the directory section. For two years the Publication Department served in part as a research department, in addition to its usual functions. American Foundations for Social Welfare was published in May, 1946, under joint authorship of Mr. Harrison and Mr. Andrews, required a second printing two months later, and has strengthened the Foundation's position as a center of information and advice for other foundations on this subject.

When World War II ended with unexpected suddenness in August, 1945, a more normal publishing program could be planned. Paper restrictions were soon removed. Supply shortages and production difficulties continued, but it was possible to reprint or bring back into print the books in most serious need of attention.

Summary

At the close of this record, on September 30, 1946, the Foundation has issued 126 publications classified as books.[1] Forty-seven of these were published in the first decade, ending in 1917; 37 in the second period of fourteen years; and 42 in the fifteen years of depression and war recorded in this chapter. Of these 126 books, 42 are still in print, the oldest being Social Diagnosis, first published in 1917. By October, 1946, recorded sales,[2] not including distribution of free and review copies, totaled 303,722 copies. The ten titles which achieved the highest sales in this period were the following:

Richmond: Social Diagnosis	(1917)	29,911
Colcord: Your Community	(1939)	23,378
Richmond: What Is Social Case Work?	(1922)	16,584
Kurtz: Public Assistance Worker	(1938)	9,747
Kurtz: Social Work Year Book 1945	(1945)	7,763

[1] See Appendix C.

[2] The record of sales is incomplete for the period 1908–1917, before organization of the Foundation's own Publication Department.

Brown: Social Work as a Profession	(1936)	7,088
Eaton: Handicrafts of the Southern Highlands	(1937)	6,895
Kurtz: Social Work Year Book 1941	(1941)	6,122
Brown: Nursing as a Profession	(1936)	5,765
Sheffield: Social Case History	(1920)	5,689

Records are even less complete for the briefer publications of the Foundation, with almost none available prior to 1917. Since that date, the sale of pamphlets has totaled 290,480, and these have included a number of pamphlets of substantial size, which under other definitions would be classified as books. In addition, 174,627 Library bibliographies were sold.

Educational scales enjoyed their largest demand in the 1920's, and are now out of print or in relatively small use. Their sale has reached the considerable total of 5,181,255. Forms and record sheets have totaled 3,765,678 since 1917, of which 1,103,000 were sold in the three fiscal years 1931, 1932, and 1933.

Prices charged for Foundation publications are designed to return merely the costs of paper, printing, and binding, without consideration of research and editorial costs, or other overhead. Receipts are therefore in the nature of a publishing revolving fund, returning to the Foundation funds roughly commensurate with its printing expenditures. Income from publications has in this way returned approximately $680,000 for continuance of the publishing program.

One further step, which the department director had been recommending for some years, was expansion of the Department's services in the field of public education. Some of the results of research come to public knowledge directly through the originating department, in consultations, addresses, magazine articles, and through the research process itself; but the main task of dissemination necessarily falls to the Publication Department, which is the principal link between the research departments and the public. In terms of sale and distribution of the publications themselves, the extensive program already described had been conducted. Within the limits of time and personnel, further efforts had been made in the form of news releases; furnishing special information to editors, feature writers, and broadcasters; occasional special articles; representation at conferences and meetings; consultations and correspondence.

Mr. Andrews recommended that his department should additionally function, not primarily as a dispenser of certain specific commodities in book and pamphlet form, but as a center of information in the social field. It should have a total concern for conveying to the public the contents of Russell Sage Foundation books and the findings of research in whatever forms proved most effective, and should be willing to explore new methods toward this end. With trustee approval of this program on an experimental basis, the Department in April, 1946, added to its staff an information secretary, and is currently entering upon this enlarged program of public education.

*Architectural detail from the east façade
Russell Sage Foundation Building*

XLV

GRANTS: 1932-1946

ONLY 19 of the 61 agencies receiving grants in this third period of the Foundation's history were added to the list since 1931, not much more than one a year. The others originated earlier. Thirty-six had begun in the second period, after 1917. Six went back to the earliest days, three of them to the very first year of 1907. A number of these agencies, however, had reorganized their programs in the period, and a few had added important new features to their work.

This was a period of diminishing expenditures for grants. The peak had been reached in 1928–1929, when the total was $440,000, five times as much as the lowest figure, in 1917–1918. It was expected that totals would decline after 1929, as the Regional Plan was finishing its work. So they did, but before that the depression was bringing emergency demands to old agencies and was cutting off some of their usual resources. At the annual meeting in November, 1937, the general director called attention to the situation, and was requested to give special consideration from time to time to this matter of long-standing grants and to suggest reductions "presumably on a graduated basis." A year later a few reductions were made. In each of the following years, as the list was considered, cuts were made with due regard each year to maintaining important work that could not readily find support elsewhere.

OLDEST GRANTEES

The oldest of the grantees, Survey Associates, Inc., returned to the list in 1931–1932, because of the depression, after an absence of eleven years. It received $5,000. Thereafter the grant continued, at an average of $3,000 a year, to the end of this period.

646

At the beginning of the depression there was a special need for the State Charities Aid Association to study and advise state and county officials in regard to unemployment relief throughout the state. In November, 1931, a grant of $2,500 toward a fund of $30,000 for this purpose was given. The grant for carrying on the work for children throughout the state was continued at $20,000 for two more years, then reduced to $18,000 for four more. In 1937, in renewing the application, the Association asked that the grant be transferred to the Citizens' Public Welfare Committee. Recent changes in national and state policy had brought us to the threshold of a new era in public welfare. Informed, independent local citizens' committees throughout the state were needed to assist and advise the state and local departments of social welfare. For this broader purpose, which it believed to be a logical development of its children's program, it asked a grant of $18,000, to be reduced $3,000 each year if it should be renewed. The grant was continued on these conditions for six years. Thus ended the long series of grants to the State Charities Aid Association, which received in all $891,800 in the thirty-seven years.

To the Charity Organization Society of New York, which in 1939 joined with the New York Association for Improving the Condition of the Poor to form the Community Service Society, grants were continued for the Committee on Criminal Courts until 1936, and renewed for the Committee on Housing from 1936 to 1943. The largest amount in this period, however, was for the School of Social Work, to complete the addition to its endowment, to contribute to its general expenses through grants to offset rent for several years and through an annual grant to its budget.

By 1936 Mr. Veiller had become convinced that a body of larger scope than the local Committee on Criminal Courts would require no more time and would be even more rewarding. He therefore proposed that the annual grant to the Committee be transferred to a new organization, to be called the Citizens' Crime Commission of the State of New York.[1] This was done for

[1] See p. 660.

the following year. During the closing years of its life the Committee continued to watch legislation as it affected criminals in the city.

The only grant still in force to the Community Service Society in 1946 was the contribution for the budget of the School, reduced to $5,000. The Charity Organization Society and its successor have received altogether over $1,000,000 since 1907.

The Brooklyn Bureau of Charities, renamed Bureau of Social Services in January, 1945, continued to receive contributions for its work with the blind until 1937–1938; for its Committees on Housing and Courts until 1941–1942 at the same rate as before, and then on a descending scale to $4,000 in 1946.

At the beginning of 1932 the Finance Committee recommended that an additional grant of $5,000 be given to the National Employment Exchange, Inc., for the purpose of seeing it through the depression, provided $15,000 more could be obtained. By April of 1932 the proviso had not been met. To facilitate liquidation $3,000 was then given and in May, 1933, $500 was added, making the total amount granted $23,500. To offset this the Exchange, since its establishment in 1909, had paid to the Foundation $23,940 in dividends. It served a useful purpose for more than twenty-three years.

With the trend toward government aid to slum clearance, and to construction and operation of dwellings, the secretary of the National Housing Association, Lawrence Veiller, was not in sympathy. Through its magazine Housing, however, the Association continued to give its readers an objective account of what was going on, and in its consultation service to put at the disposal of inquirers all the information that was available.

When in 1933 the federal government embarked on active participation in the housing movement, the Association, which had opposed government subsidies, recognized that the public was so sympathetic with the program that opposition would be useless. A memorandum, nevertheless, giving the conclusions of a conference of 38 leaders in the housing movement as to procedure and safeguards required to secure practical results was sent to the Temporary Administrator of Public Works. A comprehensive account—descriptive, not critical—of what was being done in the United States by the federal government, presented at the International Congress on Housing in London in 1935, was printed in Housing.

The October, 1935, number of Housing was the last to be issued. Numerous communications were later received from subscribers in 17 countries, including libraries, editors, and students, expressing regret at its discontinuance. For twenty years it had recorded, accurately and comprehensively, the history of the housing movement in America and other countries.

A statement announcing the decision to disband the Association as of December 31, 1936, contained by implication what its secretary believed it had accomplished in the twenty-seven years. Throughout its existence its reliance for the improvement of housing was on public education, legislation to regulate and control the types of houses that might be built and occupied, establishment of minimum standards of sanitation, safety, and decency, to be achieved within the field of private initiative. The statement added:

> The situation which led to the establishment of the Association 27 years ago no longer exists.
>
> At that time the Nation needed to be aroused to the need of better housing. It was neither informed as to the conditions nor awake to the need. There were no national organizations dealing with the problem—in fact, few local ones outside of New York City.
>
> Today, that is not the situation. The pioneer educational work in this field has been done. There are now a number of national organizations and many local ones and numerous governmental agencies dealing with housing, the latter with vast funds available.

The library and files of the Association, the most complete record of the movement to be found in the United States, were turned over to the Central Housing Committee in Washington. Payments by the Foundation to the Association since its organization in 1909 totaled $295,425.

Continued Briefly or Intermittently

Of the agencies carried over into this period from the preceding one several were for projects that by the end of 1931 were almost completed. A final payment was made on the Regional Plan in 1932. The Cities Census Committee received its final grant in 1932. The next year saw the end of the study on the Costs of Medical Care and completion of the Encyclopaedia of the Social Sciences.

Several others had a natural terminus. The employment bureau demonstration in Rochester was taken over by the United States Employment Service in 1934. The Employment Center for the Handicapped, begun in 1928 as a joint bureau in New York City following a study by Mary LaDame, was absorbed in the new machinery of the state in 1935. East Harlem Health Center was continued, though at less expense, until it was taken over by the Health Department of the city on January 1, 1934. The East Harlem Health Council continued to act as a voluntary advisory and co-ordinating agent for the people of the neighborhood. Small contributions were made for the Council in 1934 to 1937. The Family Welfare Society of Queens, which had received $35,000 in the years 1927–1931 for extension and education, was given another $4,500 in 1937 for the same purpose when the Charity Organization Society of New York agreed to adopt it as a branch of its family service. Provision for the incidental expenses of the office of the volunteer secretary of the Multiple Dwelling Law Committee in New York City, none of the members of which received any remuneration, was continued until nine years later the work of adjusting the new law "to the complicated conditions as they exist in this city" was believed to be substantially completed.

A contribution of $1,500 was made to the budget of the International Conference of Social Work, which met at Frankfurt am Main in 1932. The National Conference of Social Work presented several unusual situations in this period. It had accepted an invitation to meet in Washington, D. C., for its 1936 meeting. Late in 1935, however, the hotels rescinded their guarantee of a "minimum of racial discrimination," and so it decided to go to Atlantic City, thereby forfeiting contributions promised by citizens of Washington. The result was a deficit in the budget of the Conference, toward the liquidation of which the Foundation contributed $1,000. Two years later a "special, non-renewable grant" of $2,500 was made to assist in meeting the financial needs of the Conference, in order that it might start the year 1939, under a new fiscal plan, with no overhanging obligations. In 1941 another special item was made available, if needed, toward the traveling expenses of special speakers to the Conference in New Orleans, but only $400 was called for. And in 1946 $3,000 was promised, payable over three years, to meet the cost of preparing a history of the Conference for its seventy-fifth meeting in 1948.

NATIONAL ASSOCIATIONS

Again in this period the national associations which were formed or first came to the attention of the Foundation after World War I were a conspicuous feature of the grants for these years. Their objects and methods of work have been sufficiently described in Chapter XXXII. With a single exception (regional and city planning) this group received the largest amount of money.

In June, 1946, the Family Welfare Association of America changed its title to Family Service Association of America. It received for expansion of its general work from $15,000 to $25,000 annually until 1946; in grants to offset rent from 1935 to 1943 a total of $33,500; and toward its finance and extension service an average of $7,500 a year until 1944, after which it dropped to $2,500 in 1945. The total amount for this third period was $435,607. In 1946 the only item remaining was the grant for $20,000 toward the general program.

The Child Welfare League of America, beginning the period with a grant of $6,250 and free space, ended it with $7,000 and a grant to offset only part of the rent for space occupied. The American Association of Hospital Social Workers, its name changed in 1934 to American Association of Medical Social

Workers, received $4,500 annually until 1939; after that year it was diminished by $500 each year to $1,000 for 1946. The National Association of Legal Aid Organizations, after receiving annually $2,000 for several years, dropped gradually to $1,500 for the two years 1939 and 1940, then to $1,000 for the next two, and in 1943 to $750, where it stayed for four years. The older National Travelers Aid Association, formed in 1917, had received its first grant of $10,000 from the Foundation in 1929 and the same amount each year through 1932. From 1933 the amount was gradually decreased, ending at $2,000 for 1942.

The American Federation of Arts from 1919 until 1932 had an annual grant of $10,000. After that, when part of the work for which the grant was given had been taken over into the program of the Foundation, smaller and diminishing amounts were needed until 1938–1939 when the grants were discontinued. They reached a total since 1919 of $157,350.

In 1931–1932 the American Country Life Association received $4,500 from the Foundation, compared with $10,000 in 1928–1929. Although the deepening depression prevented hope of a sound financial basis for this agency, small grants were made until 1941. In that year $500 was given to the Youth Section; in 1944, $150 as an aid in printing its conference program.

Until the depression the National Social Work Council kept to its intention of being simply a forum for its members. In 1932 it undertook the United Educational Program, under its own auspices but financed by special contributions, an effort to secure more adequate relief for the unemployed and to keep before the public the needs of other less appreciated forms of social work.

The Committee on Care of Transient and Homeless, appointed by the Council in the fall of 1932, but carried on as an independent committee, made recommendations that formed the basis of the federal transient program of 1933–1935. After the federal program was suspended it kept interest alive and was reorganized in January, 1939, as the short-lived Council on Interstate Migration.[1] An independent committee set up by the Council in

[1] Whose secretary, Philip E. Ryan, wrote Migration and Social Welfare, a 114-page pamphlet published by Russell Sage Foundation in 1940.

October, 1931, and later taken over by the American Association of Social Workers, laid the basis for an effective relationship between social workers and federal officials, and appreciably affected provision for, and administration of, public relief during the depression and later. Another committee of the Council in 1933 helped to bring about better provision by the government for the social needs of the men in Civilian Conservation Camps. An incidental result was the organization (in September, 1933) of the National Education-Recreation Council by the national agencies which had been working together on the committee.

In the fall of 1940 Russell H. Kurtz of the Foundation's staff spent two months, and scattered time later, in helping to prepare a memorandum on Health and Welfare Services in the National Defense, printed and distributed by the Council, and in assembling other material for use in the changing national situation.

After twenty-five years of working within its original framework, as a group of executives and others voluntarily associated for self-education, the National Social Work Council began in 1944 to consider enlargement of its functions.

At the first formal discussion, an all-day session on January 18, 1945, the chairman was empowered to appoint a committee to "draw up some plans to be submitted to the member agencies providing for the enlargement of the functions of the National Social Work Council." Through 1945 this special Planning Committee worked on reorganization plans. They were approved at a meeting held December 7, when the constitution of the Council was amended, and the National Social Welfare Assembly came into being. An interim organization began work. On April 29 the permanent organization of the Assembly took over, under its first president, Charles P. Taft. It included a total membership of 110, reported the director, Robert E. Bondy, representing a "partnership trilogy of lay-staff, governmental-voluntary, national-local cooperation," and looking toward "that goal of human well-being we all like to include in our individual concepts of the American way of life."

Such functional groupings as casework and health councils, the Education-Recreation Council, and the Committee on

653

Service to Veterans came into the organization. Through the
Assembly's Committee on International Social Welfare Organization a plan for the inclusion of social welfare in the organization of United Nations had been presented to the Acting Secretary of State, and at the request of the State Department a panel
of names was submitted to aid in selecting American representatives on the Temporary Social Commission of the United Nations.
The National Committee on Service to Veterans represented 19
organizations giving direct service to veterans, and maintained
liaison with the Veterans Administration and the Retraining and
Reemployment Administration. The Committee on Problems of
Japanese-Americans was preparing information and guidance
bulletins for communities.

These were only a few of the activities in progress. The financing had been proceeding largely according to plan, $45,000 of
the budget of $98,300 to be contributed by affiliate organizations.
Toward the expenses of the first year of "this hopeful enterprise
in good social planning," as its president called it, the Foundation
granted $15,000.[1]

PLANNING

When the Regional Plan Association was incorporated to promote the recommendations of the Regional Plan Committee and
to carry forward its work, it was anticipated that help would be
needed from the Foundation for only a short time, until the
Association could "get a proper start and secure contributions
from other sources." The depression interfered. During the three
darkest years, 1932–1934, grants totaled $146,750. In 1938 and
1939 the amount was set at $25,000 each year on the understand-
ing that later grants would be smaller. In 1946 the amount given
was $17,000, bringing to over $500,000 the total to the Association since its organization in 1929.

During these years of depression and war the Association supplied "continuity of thought and action" in "an environment of
national crises." It spread knowledge of the recommendations of
the Plan and urged their adoption. It made additions to it from

[1] Of which $12,500 fell due and was paid in the fiscal year 1945–1946.

time to time. It issued in 1933, 1937, and 1941 three reports entitled From Plan to Reality showing the progress that had been
made in carrying out the recommendations of the Plan. Its
Bulletin Number 7 was an analysis of the 1930 population figures
for the Region. Slum clearance was studied. Rebuilding of
Blighted Areas, by Clarence A. Perry, was published in 1933.
With the help of the Works Progress Administration it endeavored to organize the counties "for the promotion of planning
projects, helping them to qualify for federal aid, and to establish
planning as an integral part of the county government" until
planning should be "an official matter in every one of our
counties." With workers from WPA a relief model of the Region,
18 by 20 feet in size, was constructed.

The Association assisted in the campaign which resulted in the
inclusion in the New York City charter of 1938 of a permanent
official City Planning Commission. In 1939 sentiment was organized against the proposed Battery-Brooklyn bridge and in
favor of a tunnel, which is now under construction. A study of
existing accommodations in airports was published in 1940 in
Regional Plan Bulletin Number 49. A new traffic and parking
study was begun in 1940. By 1942 temporary relief from traffic
congestion came from the rationing of gasoline and tires, and was
followed by the need for pioneer planning for the transportation
of war-workers to and from the new plants on Long Island.

In 1943 the time had come "to review and re-appraise the
Region's physical development in the light of its postwar economic future." Such a review was therefore made and the results
published the following year. Supplementary studies to it were
Bulletins 64 and 65, Competition in Manufacturing, and Resources and Purchasing Power of the New York Region. At the
end of 1945 Bulletin 66 was published, showing that there was
enough land available—and just where it was—within 25 miles
of the Region's center and one mile from public transportation,
to house 3,000,000 persons in one-family houses. In the fall of
1946 the Association disclosed the results of a two-year study
undertaken at the request of the Civil Aeronautics Authority,
proposing creation by the New York-New Jersey-Connecticut

region of a central airport agency and calling for the construction of 60 new airfields, including a major field in the New Jersey meadows. The governors-elect of the three states would be asked, soon after the coming elections, to confer on a joint airport plan that could be recommended to the legislatures in January. The Civil Aeronautics Authority is using the study as a basis for allocating the metropolitan area's share in the appropriation for airport construction and improvement under the Federal Airport Act of May 13, 1946.

The emergency for the Zoning Committee that brought it to the Foundation in 1931 continued until it disbanded at the end of 1942, having in its judgment successfully completed the purpose for which it was created twenty-five years before. The Foundation kept up its help, without which, wrote its president to Mr. Purdy, "we could never have continued the work to its final success." The total given in the twelve years was $20,050.

Separate grants were given to the American Civic Association and the National Conference on City Planning until in 1935 they merged to form the American Planning and Civic Association, a strong new organization combining the interests and aims of all its predecessors. A better physical environment, "which will conserve and develop the health, happiness and culture of the American people," is its object. Its scope includes national, state, regional, and city planning; land and water uses; the conservation of natural resources; national, state, and local parks; highways and roadsides. Through annual national citizens' conferences on planning, conferences on roadside improvement, through the quarterly magazine, Planning and Civic Comment, and in other ways, it keeps the people informed. It has offices in Washington and New York. Grants have decreased gradually from $15,000 in 1937 to $7,325 in 1946.

Service Agencies

Of the service agencies which were new in the second period the Neighborhood Teacher Association of New York after 1932 received diminishing amounts, from $3,750 in 1933 to $100 in 1937–1938; and Farmers Federation, Inc., after the first contribution of $5,000 for five years was exhausted, received a second of $2,500, which ended in 1937. Contributions to Southern Mountain Workers Conference and to the publication of Mountain Life and Work by Berea College were kept up until 1946.

The American Association of Social Workers received contributions until its analysis of positions in social work was completed in 1934, and free space through December, 1934, then diminishing grants to offset rent through 1946. Joint Vocational Service (Social Work Vocational Bureau from January 1, 1940) had grants to offset rent from 1935 through 1939, an appropriation of $10,000 for a special study of placement and vocational problems in social work in 1938 and 1939, and a contribution to its ordinary budget throughout the period, averaging $7,000 or more in the years 1940–1946.

The annual grant of $2,000 to the National Information Bureau was terminated in 1940. War, however, brought it an "enormous" number of appeals about new agencies, many of them spurious, creating a situation similar to that which brought about its organization in 1917. A "special emergency" grant of $2,000 was made for the year beginning October, 1941. In 1945 the Foundation was one of a number of agencies and foundations that contributed $200 each to make up a deficit in operations, and again in 1946 it gave $200.

In the case of most of the other agencies the Foundation was slow in these difficult years in reducing grants; this was especially true of those dealing with Negroes. The grant to the Federal Council of the Churches of Christ in America, which had been receiving for its Department of Race Relations $5,000 a year since the Department was established in 1922, was decreased after 1940 to $4,500 in 1945, and then to $3,000 in 1946. Atlanta University School of Social Work continued to receive $5,000 annually, except in a single year, 1940; the grant for 1946 was announced as the final one to be made. To the National Urban League $1,000 was given each year until 1946.

When the depression brought new financial problems to the International Migration Service its grant was raised to $5,000. Through the hardest years it also had free quarters. In 1946 it received $5,000. The $5,000 granted to the Common Council for American Unity (formerly Foreign Language Information Service) was gradually decreased in the last few years, and a final grant of $500 was made for 1945. The New York Adult Education Council, which received $500 in 1931 for expenses of its exhibition to be held in the Foundation's halls, was granted $1,000 annually from 1933 to 1946, with an additional $500 in 1937.

Annual contributions were continued to the general budget of the Welfare Council of New York City and a grant to offset rent was given while it remained in the Foundation building. For its Co-ordinating Committee on Unemployment Relief special grants were given until 1937, when the emergency was assumed to be over; and $2,500 a year for two years toward the expense of its Wartime Co-ordinating Committee for civilian protection. The total appropriated for the Welfare Council from the preliminary planning in 1924–1925 to the year 1946 was $182,019.

A contribution to the Social Science Research Council, Inc., for administration expenses, usually $3,750 a year, went on until 1942 when it was reduced to $3,000, and the Council was notified that it would not be continued indefinitely. In 1944 it was again reduced to $2,000. Altogether $87,500 was given to the Council in twenty years.

NEW GRANTS

Most of the new grants made in the years following 1931 were "emergency" measures, in one sense or another. Established agencies found it harder to meet even their minimum budgets and to keep essential parts of their work going. Before long the Foundation's income also was affected, and greater demands were made on it to meet the needs of agencies with prior claims, so that, as had happened in other times, many, for lack of funds, could not be considered by the Trustees.

The Legal Aid Society of the City of New York, more than fifty years old, which was trying to increase its income to enable it to meet the appeals for legal advice from a growing number of poor clients, asked help in 1932 and was given it for the year, and then for the next three, a total of $6,000. The United Parents Associations of New York City, the central organization of the 163 (at the time) local associations connected with public schools, received $3,000 as a "special emergency grant" in 1932. The National Health Council in 1934 "faced an emergency" in continuing its library service, and received $500. Volume 5, House Design, Construction, and Equipment, of President Hoover's Conference on Home Building and Home Ownership, was out of print. It had had a steady demand, and there was no money to reprint it. The Foundation supplied the $750 needed. For incidental expenses of a study of Hospital Statistics in Manhattan connected with a Civil Works Project under the auspices of the Welfare Council $1,000 was supplied. In 1934 $1,000 was given toward a fund of $5,000 to retain the services of Harry L. Hopkins as a consultant for his former organization, the New York Tuberculosis and Health Association, after he went to Washington. In response to a plea from Chicago in the middle of the depression a grant of $1,000 was made in 1933 to the Social Work Exhibits Committee in Chicago, a committee concerned with making a suitable showing of social work at the Century of Progress Exposition.

In 1934 $1,000 was given to the Pennsylvania School of Social Work. This was the "last" $1,000 of a special emergency fund of about $15,000 required by the School for keeping its staff intact and for bridging over the difficult period until new income seemed assured. Five years later another $1,000 was given to a special fund to carry the School through the next year while plans were made to get new money to offset losses in contributions; and $2,500 more was added before 1941.

The American Advisory Council of the Universal Christian Council for Life and Work asked $1,000 or more in the spring of 1937 for expenses of a conference to consider how churches could be more effective in promoting the welfare of their immediate communities and of their nations. In answer $1,000 was granted on condition that the funds be used "in this country to promote a better understanding of social conditions and community problems here."

Hillside, a property at Riverdale in New York City, had been given to the National Bureau of Economic Research early in 1937, for the purpose of developing a center for the planning of economic studies in which other agencies would participate, analogous to Wood's Hole center for the biological sciences. The money needed to equip the building was $15,000. The Foundation contributed $1,000.

The National Organization for Public Health Nursing in 1938 needed a new edition of its manual, of which 8,000 copies had been sold. A competent person was available to make the revision. The amount required, $1,400, was given.

When the Citizens' Crime Commission of the State of New York, made up of leading lawyers and other citizens of the state, was established at the end of 1936, the expectation was that it would soon attract other means of support than the Foundation's grant. In this, however, it was disappointed; so, after four years it was discontinued. The total amount paid to the Commission was $91,000. During its life the Commission exercised an important influence on the treatment of crime through research, publication, and participation in active measures.

In 1941 the American Parole Association, closely affiliated with the American Prison Association, was ten years old. Parole, however, was misunderstood, misrepresented, under systematic attack in some quarters. The Association had plans for an experimental year of exploratory work in improving methods and securing a better and wider understanding of its objects and operation. Estimates of the necessary cost were not large. Toward this effort the Foundation gave $1,000. Later, partly as a result of this study, the Association engaged an executive secretary, started a quarterly bulletin, and was planning a report on current parole legislation and a parole directory. In response to a request from Sanford Bates, its president, a grant of $1,000 for 1944 was made.

Negro colleges and universities always had a hard time raising money. In 1944, in the midst of the war, they joined in a United Negro College Campaign. To this the Foundation contributed $1,000, in view of the inclusion of the Atlanta School of Social Work.

The Social Work Publicity Council[1] had grown since 1929 with the informal help of the Department of Social Work Interpretation, and had expanded its scope and purposes. It had had a substantial part of the time of Mrs. Routzahn and of other members of the staff, and for several years had received grants to offset rent, besides payment of some expenses, at a total cost to the Foundation of about $6,600 a year. By the fall of 1941 it had secured a good board and a small but efficient staff, and was publishing Channels and technical bulletins, maintaining a critical editorial service for its members, and supplying stimulation and guidance to local publicity councils. It had also developed financial support. The time had come when it should be set going more independently and on a larger budget. Furthermore, Mrs. Routzahn needed more of her time for Foundation work. A grant accordingly of $10,000 was given for the year 1942 and the budget of Mrs. Routzahn's department at the same time was considerably reduced. The grant has been repeated in the following years. The name of the Council was changed in 1943 to National Publicity Council for Health and Welfare Services.

A grant of $5,000 was made to the American Association of Schools of Social Work for the year beginning July, 1941. It had just finished a three-year study of education for positions in public social work with a grant from the Rockefeller Foundation. The schools would have to provide new courses, it was expected, and to meet other demands as a result of the study and in connection with the developing defense program. They would need the counsel and leadership of a national organization in which common problems could be considered jointly. In the expectation that the need was only temporary the grant was approved with the presumption against renewal the following year. For several years, however, the income of the 42 schools making up the Association was diminished, while demands for the planning and organizing of institutes and other services increased. Accordingly the grant was renewed each year up to and including 1946.

[1] See p. 368.

In 1946 two new organizations entered the list, in addition to the National Social Welfare Assembly, which replaced the National Social Work Council. The reorganized National Association of School Social Workers, formed in 1919 as the American Association of Visiting Teachers, needed funds for staff assistance to meet increasing demands for service. A grant of $5,000 for the ensuing year was made,[1] on the understanding that it would be $4,000 if renewed.

Finally, in May, 1946, the Committee on Neighborhood Health Development asked $3,000 for its work. This committee was an outgrowth of the East Harlem Health Center, to which the Foundation had contributed while it existed, and the Bellevue-Yorkville Demonstration of the Milbank Memorial Fund. The Committee on Neighborhood Health Development, established by the Commissioner of Health in 1929, planned the citywide system of local health centers, on the basis of these two demonstrations, working out plans for the development of community health organization and education around each one, and providing a link between the official service and the residents of the neighborhood. It initiated action looking toward a Health Council of Greater New York, into which it expected to be absorbed. Meanwhile, funds were needed to carry on its program of co-operation with the Health Department's district system. The $3,000 asked for 1946 was granted.

SITUATION IN 1946

On the list in 1946 were 26 agencies, which received $132,651. This compared with $349,000 in 1931, the year when the Foundation's income began to show the effects of the depression. It compared with a high of $440,000 in 1928–1929 and a low of $82,675, to nine agencies, in 1917–1918. During the years 1932–1946 about $3,250,000 was paid for grants. The total amount given in grants since 1907 was over $9,000,000, about 45 per cent of the total expenditure. Of the 26 grants made in 1946, two originated in the calendar year 1907 and one in 1908.

[1] Of which $1,250 fell due and was paid in the fiscal year 1945–1946.

The largest amount paid on account of a grant in the year ending September 30, 1946, was $22,000, one-sixth of the whole amount for that year, to the Family Service Association of America. Following, in order of amounts paid, were the Regional Plan Association, the National Social Welfare Assembly, the National Publicity Council, the Child Welfare League of America, the American Planning and Civic Association, and the Welfare Council of New York City. These seven account for $71,000 of the expenditure for grants. They include three agencies that developed from departments of the Foundation.

APPENDICES

APPENDIX A

LETTER OF GIFT

To the Trustees of the Russell Sage Foundation:

I HAVE transferred to the Russell Sage Foundation securities and cash aggregating in value ten million dollars. A schedule of the securities and cash so transferred accompanies this letter.

I give them to constitute a fund, the principal of which, as the same is now or may hereafter be invested according to the terms of this letter, shall be held, and the income thereof applied to the improvement of social and living conditions in the United States of America.

The act incorporating the Russell Sage Foundation was drawn under my direction. I refer to it as expressing the purposes for which I have made this gift and the powers which I intend the Foundation to have in its disposition.

I do not wish by this letter to enlarge or limit the powers given to the Foundation by its act of incorporation, or to impose any other or different duties upon its trustees than are put upon them by this act. It has seemed to me, however, appropriate to express certain desires to which I would wish the trustees of the Foundation to conform so far as they may from time to time deem expedient.

While the scope of the Foundation is intended to be national, it is my wish that special consideration should be given to the needs of my own city and its vicinity. I therefore request that at no time shall less than one-quarter of the income of the fund be applied exclusively to the benefit of the city of New York and its vicinity, and I also wish that at no time shall less than one-quarter of its income be applied generally to the United States at large or to the parts of it outside of the city of New York and its vicinity.

The scope of the Foundation is not only national but is broad. It should, however, preferably not undertake to do that which is now being done or is likely to be effectively done by other individuals or by other agencies. It should be its aim to take up the larger and more difficult problems, and to take them up so far as possible in such a manner as to secure co-operation and aid in their solution.

In some instances it may wisely initiate movements, in the expectation of having them maintain themselves unaided after once being started. In other instances it may start movements with the expectation of carrying them on itself.

667

I have had some hesitation as to whether the Foundation should be permitted to make investments for social betterment which themselves produce income, as for instance small houses or tenements, in distinction from investments in securities intended only to produce income. I realize that investments for social betterment, even if producing some income, may not produce a percentage as large as that produced by bonds or like securities, and that the income of the Foundation might be therefore diminished by such investments. On the other hand, if I fail to give the Foundation powers in this respect it may be unable to initiate or establish important agencies or institutions.

I decide to authorize the trustees of the Foundation to invest the principal of the fund, to the extent of not more at any one time than one-quarter of its entire amount, directly in activities, agencies, or institutions established and maintained for the improvement of social and living conditions, provided that such investments shall, in the opinion of the trustees, be likely to produce an annual income of not less than three per cent.

I also wish to authorize the trustees to invest and reinvest the principal of the fund given by me in any of the following manners:

a. In any of the kinds or classes of securities included in my gift.

b. In the mortgage bonds of any railroad or other corporations which have continuously paid dividends on their common stock at the rate of not less than four per cent per annum, for a period of not less than five years preceding the investment.

c. In the preferred stocks of any such companies.

d. In any stocks of companies guaranteed by any such companies.

e. In any securities in which savings banks or trustees may be authorized to invest at the time of the investment.

The authority to invest given by this letter is a condition attached to my gift and is intended to vest that power in the trustees of the Foundation without reference to any law or laws which may now or hereafter limit the power of trustees or charitable corporations in this particular.

I am conscious of the burden necessarily placed upon the trustees in accepting office, and I do not wish to add to that burden by involving them in any expense. I therefore direct that travelling and hotel expenses incurred by the trustees in the performance of their duties shall be paid from the income of the fund.

Yours sincerely,

MARGARET OLIVIA SAGE.

NEW YORK, April 19, 1907.

APPENDIX B

TRUSTEES

The first nine in the list were the incorporators of the Foundation. The others follow in order of their election. In March, 1934, membership of the Board was increased from nine to twelve.

Margaret Olivia Sage	April, 1907 to November, 1918
Robert W. de Forest	April, 1907 to May, 1931
Cleveland H. Dodge	April, 1907 to November, 1920
Daniel C. Gilman	April, 1907 to October, 1908
John M. Glenn	April, 1907 to May, 1907
	re-elected April, 1913
Helen M. Gould (Mrs. Finley J. Shepard)	April, 1907 to February, 1936
Robert C. Ogden	April, 1907 to August, 1913
Gertrude S. (Mrs. William B.) Rice	April, 1907 to March, 1926
Louisa Lee Schuyler	April, 1907 to October, 1926
Alfred T. White	February, 1909 to January, 1921
John H. Finley	October, 1913 to March, 1940
Charles D. Norton	November, 1918 to March, 1923
Fredric A. Delano	February, 1921 to November, 1939
Dwight W. Morrow	February, 1921 to October, 1931
Lawson Purdy	June, 1923
Laura B. (Mrs. Frederic S.) Lee	November, 1926 to November, 1938
Harold T. White	November, 1926
Johnston de Forest	May, 1931
Lindsay Bradford	November, 1933
Joseph P. Chamberlain	March, 1934
Morris Hadley	May, 1934
Harry Woodburn Chase	February, 1936
Arthur H. Ham	November, 1939
Robert M. MacIver	November, 1940
Dave H. Morris, Jr.	November, 1940
Eli Whitney Debevoise	May, 1945

669

OFFICERS

PRESIDENT

Margaret Olivia Sage	April, 1907 to November, 1918
Robert W. de Forest	November, 1918 to May, 1931
Lawson Purdy	November, 1936 to May, 1944
Morris Hadley	November, 1944

VICE-PRESIDENT

Robert W. de Forest	April, 1907 to November, 1918
Gertrude S. Rice	November, 1918 to March, 1926
Lawson Purdy	November, 1926 to November, 1936
Morris Hadley	November, 1936 to November, 1944
Joseph P. Chamberlain	November, 1944

TREASURER

Cleveland H. Dodge	May, 1907 to December, 1917
Henry L. de Forest	December, 1917 to November, 1918
Charles D. Norton	November, 1918 to March, 1923
Lawson Purdy	July, 1923 to May, 1937
Morris Hadley	May, 1937 to November, 1944
Arthur H. Ham	November, 1944

SECRETARY

John M. Glenn	May, 1907

GENERAL DIRECTOR

John M. Glenn	May, 1907 to September, 1931
Shelby M. Harrison	September, 1931

670

DIRECTORS OF DEPARTMENTS

The dates in this list include only the periods during which the individuals named served as directors. They do not include previous years during which some of them were employed by the Foundation.

Hastings H. Hart, Child Helping, May, 1909 to September, 1924
Delinquency and Penology, October, 1924 to May, 1932

Mary E. Richmond, Charity Organization, October, 1909 to September, 1928

Luther H. Gulick, Child Hygiene, November, 1909 to December, 1912

Helen Moore, Editorial, December, 1909

Arthur H. Ham, Remedial Loans, October, 1910 to October, 1918

Frederick W. Jenkins, Library, May, 1911 to November, 1929
Publications, November, 1916 to November, 1929

Shelby M. Harrison, Surveys and Exhibits, July, 1912 to October, 1942

John C. Campbell, Southern Highlands, October, 1912 to May, 1919

Leonard P. Ayres, Statistics, October, 1912 to November, 1920
Education, January, 1913 to November, 1920

Lee F. Hanmer, Recreation, January, 1913 to June, 1937

Mary van Kleeck, Industrial Studies, November, 1916

Ralph G. Hurlin, Statistics, December, 1920

William Hodson, Social Legislation, October, 1924 to November, 1925

Leon Henderson, Remedial Loans, April, 1926 to September, 1934

Fred S. Hall, Social Work Year Book, October, 1928 to October, 1935

F. Emerson Andrews, Publications, January, 1929

Joanna C. Colcord, Charity Organization, August, 1929 to July, 1945

DEPARTMENTS OF THE FOUNDATION AND THEIR DIRECTORS

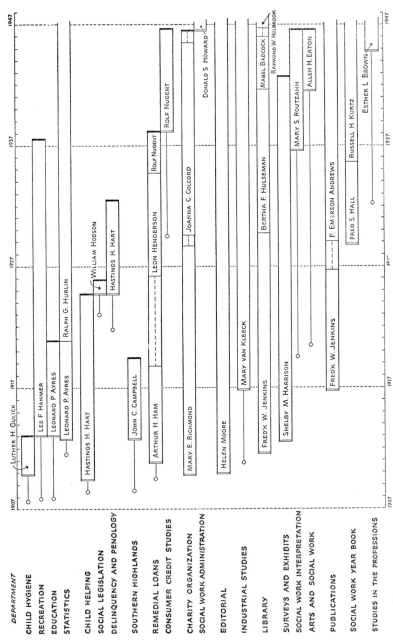

Small circles mark the beginning of work within the Foundation which led to formation of a department. Formal establishment of a department is indicated by double vertical lines at beginning of a bar; termination by heavy vertical line at end of a bar. Broken horizontal lines indicate periods during which a department was without a director.

672

Bertha F. Hulseman, Library, November, 1929 to October, 1941

Mary S. Routzahn, Social Work Interpretation, November, 1934 to September, 1946

Rolf Nugent, Remedial Loans, November, 1934 to February, 1938 Consumer Credit Studies, February, 1938 to July, 1946

Russell H. Kurtz, Social Work Year Book, November, 1935

Allen H. Eaton, Arts and Social Work, May, 1941 to September, 1946

Mabel A. Badcock, Library, October, 1941 to January, 1946

Esther Lucile Brown, Studies in the Professions, October, 1944

Donald S. Howard, Social Work Administration, May, 1946

Raymond W. Holbrook, Library, September, 1946

APPENDIX C

PUBLICATIONS OF RUSSELL SAGE FOUNDATION

The following list includes all books prepared for and published by the Foundation, and a number of pamphlets selected to indicate its main objects and the development of its program. Departmental publications are classified chronologically under the names of the respective departments. Others are listed under the title "Non-departmental." Departments are arranged in the order in which they appear in the text. Letters and numbers, like CO68, are used to identify pamphlets and to facilitate reference to them.

RECREATION

First Steps in Organizing Playgrounds. Lee F. Hanmer. 1908. 36 pp. No. 23.

The Field Day and Play Picnic for Country Children. Myron T. Scudder. 1908. 53 pp. No. 24.

A Safer, Saner Fourth of July. 1909. 31 pp. No. 31.

Wider Use of the School Plant. Clarence Arthur Perry. 1910. 423 pp.

Athletics in the Public Schools. Lee F. Hanmer. 1910. 36 pp. No. 72.

The Exploitation of Pleasure. Michael M. Davis, Jr. 1911. 61 pp. No. 84.

Independence Day Legislation and Celebration Suggestions. Lee F. Hanmer. 1913. 24 pp. Rec129.

Sources of Information on Play and Recreation. Lee F. Hanmer and Howard R. Knight. 1914. 27 pp. Rec136.

———— Revised edition. 1915. 35 pp. Rec136.

———— Revised edition. Howard R. Knight and Marguerita P. Williams. 1920. 46 pp. Rec151.

———— Revised edition. Marguerita P. Williams. 1927. 94 pp. Rec 156.

Play and Recreation in a Town of 6000. Howard R. Knight. 1915. 98 pp. Rec144.

Community Center Activities. Clarence Arthur Perry. 1916. 127 pp. Rec148.

First Steps in Community Center Development. Clarence Arthur Perry. 1917. 31 pp. Rec149.

School Center Gazette 1919–1920. Clarence Arthur Perry (Compiler). 1920. 53 pp. Rec150.

Play for Children in Institutions. Robert K. Atkinson. 1923. 44 pp.
Rec155.

Directory of Training Courses for Recreation Leaders. Marguerita P.
Williams and Lee F. Hanmer (Compilers). 1928. 59 pp. Rec157.

New York School Centers and Their Community Policy. Clarence
Arthur Perry and Marguerita P. Williams. 1931. 78 pp. Rec158.

The Work of the Little Theatres. Clarence Arthur Perry. 1933. 228 pp.

EDUCATION

Medical Inspection of Schools. Luther Halsey Gulick and Leonard P.
Ayres. 1908. 276 pp.

———— Revised edition. 1913. 224 pp.

Laggards in Our Schools. Leonard P. Ayres. 1909. 236 pp.

What American Cities Are Doing for the Health of School Children.
1911. 15 pp. No. 89.

———— Revised edition. 1911. 43 pp. No. 101.

A Scale for Measuring the Quality of Handwriting of School Children.
Leonard P. Ayres. 1912. 16 pp. and scale. No. 113.

———— Revised edition. 1917. Scale. E140.

A Comparative Study of Public School Systems in the Forty-Eight
States. 1912. 33 pp. No. 124.

The Spelling Vocabularies of Personal and Business Letters. Leonard
P. Ayres. 1913. 16 pp. E126.

Fire Protection in Public Schools. 1913. 16 pp. E132.

A Measuring Scale for Ability in Spelling. Leonard P. Ayres. 1915.
56 pp. and scale. E139.

An Index Number for State School Systems. Leonard P. Ayres. 1920.
70 pp. E141.

Trends of School Costs. W. Randolph Burgess. 1920. 142 pp. E142.

The Measurement of Silent Reading. May Ayres Burgess. 1921. 163 pp.
and scales. E143.

CHILD-HELPING

Cottage and Congregate Institutions for Children. Hastings H. Hart.
1910. 136 pp.

Juvenile Court Laws in the United States. Hastings H. Hart (Editor).
1910. 150 pp.

Care and Education of Crippled Children in the United States. Edith
Reeves. 1914. 252 pp.

Elements of Record Keeping for Child-Helping Organizations. Georgia
G. Ralph. 1915. 195 pp.

Child Welfare Work in Pennsylvania. William H. Slingerland. 1915.
352 pp.

A Child Welfare Symposium. William H. Slingerland (Editor). 1915. 138 pp. CH 18.

Child Welfare Work in California. William H. Slingerland. 1916. 247 pp.

Child-Placing in Families. William H. Slingerland. 1918. 261 pp.

A Social Welfare Program for the State of Florida. Hastings H. Hart and Clarence L. Stonaker. 1918. 44 pp. CH35.

Dependent, Delinquent, and Defective Children of Delaware. C. Spencer Richardson. 1918. 88 pp. CH36.

The War Program of the State of South Carolina. Hastings H. Hart. 1918. 61 pp. CH37.

Social Problems of Alabama. Hastings H. Hart. 1918. 87 pp. CH38.

Child Welfare in the District of Columbia. Hastings H. Hart. 1924. 150 pp.

Recent Progress in Child Welfare Legislation: Six papers, with Foreword by William Hodson. 1924. 32 pp. CH52.

Southern Highlands

The Southern Highlander and His Homeland. John C. Campbell. 1921. 405 pp.

Charity Organization

The Formation of Charity Organization Societies in Smaller Cities. Francis H. McLean. 1910. 51 pp. CO6.

Inter-Relation of Social Movements. Mary E. Richmond. 1910. 32 pp. CO8.

What Social Workers Should Know About Their Own Communities. Margaret F. Byington. 1911. 32 pp. CO7.
——— Revised edition. 1912. 42 pp. CO7.
——— Revised edition. 1916. 43 pp. CO7.
——— Revised edition. 1924. 66 pp. CO66.
——— Revised edition. 1929. 71 pp. CO66.

The Confidential Exchange. Margaret F. Byington. 1912. 30 pp. CO28.

Social Work in Hospitals. Ida M. Cannon. 1913. 257 pp.
——— Revised edition. 1923. 247 pp.

A Study of Nine Hundred and Eighty-Five Widows Known to Certain Charity Organization Societies in 1910. Mary E. Richmond and Fred S. Hall. 1913. 83 pp. CO34.

Social Diagnosis. Mary E. Richmond. 1917. 511 pp.

Disasters. J. Byron Deacon. 1918. 230 pp.

Household Management. Florence Nesbitt. 1918. 170 pp.

Broken Homes. Joanna C. Colcord. 1919. 208 pp.

American Marriage Laws in Their Social Aspects. Fred S. Hall and Elisabeth W. Brooke. 1919. 132 pp.

The Social Case History. Ada Eliot Sheffield. 1920. 227 pp.

What Is Social Case Work? Mary E. Richmond. 1922. 268 pp.

The Burden of Unemployment. Philip Klein. 1923. 260 pp.

Child Marriages. Mary E. Richmond and Fred S. Hall. 1925. 159 pp.

Medical Certification for Marriage. Fred S. Hall. 1925. 92 pp. CO67.

Marriage and the State. Mary E. Richmond and Fred S. Hall. 1929. 395 pp.

Marriage Laws and Decisions in the United States. Geoffrey May. 1929. 476 pp.

The Long View. Mary E. Richmond. Joanna C. Colcord and Ruth Z. S. Mann (Editors). 1930. 648 pp.

Emergency Work Relief. Joanna C. Colcord, William C. Koplovitz, and Russell H. Kurtz. 1932. 286 pp.

Community Planning in Unemployment Emergencies. Joanna C. Colcord (Compiler). 1930. 86 pp. CO68.

Community Programs for Subsistence Gardens. Joanna C. Colcord and Mary Johnston. 1933. 74 pp. CO72.

Work Relief in Germany. Hertha Kraus. 1934. 93 pp. CO73.

Cash Relief. Joanna C. Colcord. 1936. 263 pp.

Unemployment Relief in Periods of Depression. Leah Hannah Feder. 1936. 384 pp.

Your Community. Joanna C. Colcord. 1939. 249 pp.

——— Revised edition. 1941. 261 pp.

Civil Service in Public Welfare. Alice Campbell Klein. 1940. 444 pp.

The WPA and Federal Relief Policy. Donald S. Howard. 1943. 879 pp.

REMEDIAL LOANS

The Salary Loan Business in New York City. Clarence W. Wassam. 1908. 143 pp. RL1.

The Chattel Loan Business. Arthur H. Ham. 1909. 60 pp. RL2.

The Co-operative People's Bank (La Caisse Populaire). Alphonse Desjardins. 1914. 42 pp. RL16.

A Credit Union Primer. Arthur H. Ham and Leonard G. Robinson. 1914. 79 pp. RL15.

——— Revised edition. 1923. 81 pp. RL37.

——— Revised edition. Rolf Nugent. 1930. 149 pp. RL42.

General Form of Uniform Small Loan Law. 1918. 7 pp. RL34.

Draft of Proposed Uniform Pawnbroking Bill. 1924. 11 pp. RL39.

The Regulation of Pawnbroking. R. Cornelius Raby. 1924. 63 pp.

Ten Thousand Small Loans. Louis N. Robinson and Maude E. Stearns. 1930. 159 pp.

The Constitutionality of Small Loan Legislation. Frank R. Hubachek. 1931. 50 pp. RL43.

Small Loan Legislation. David J. Gallert, Walter S. Hilborn, and Geoffrey May. 1932. 255 pp.

The Provident Loan Society of New York. Rolf Nugent. 1932. 24 pp. RL45.

Moneylending in Great Britain. Dorothy Johnson Orchard and Geoffrey May. 1933. 185 pp.

Regulation of the Small Loan Business. Louis N. Robinson and Rolf Nugent. 1935. 284 pp.

Annotations on Small Loan Laws. F. B. Hubachek. 1938. 320 pp.

Consumer Credit Studies

Consumer Credit and Economic Stability. Rolf Nugent. 1939. 420 pp.

The English Hire-Purchase Act, 1938. John E. Hamm. 1940. 59 pp. CC1.

Women's Work—Industrial Studies

Saleswomen in Mercantile Stores. Elizabeth Beardsley Butler. 1912. 217 pp.

Women in the Bookbinding Trade. Mary van Kleeck. 1913. 270 pp.

Artificial Flower Makers. Mary van Kleeck. 1913. 261 pp.

Working Girls in Evening Schools. Mary van Kleeck. 1914. 252 pp.

The Longshoremen. Charles B. Barnes. 1915. 287 pp.

A Seasonal Industry. Mary van Kleeck. 1917. 276 pp.

Women as Munition Makers *and* Munition Workers in England and France. Amy Hewes and Henriette R. Walter. 1917. 158 pp.

Industrial Disputes and the Canadian Act. Ben M. Selekman. 1917. 41 pp. IS5.

Italian Women in Industry. Louise C. Odencrantz. 1919. 345 pp.

The Coal Miners' Insecurity. Louis Bloch. 1922. 50 pp. IS7.

Public Employment Offices. Shelby M. Harrison and Associates. 1924. 685 pp.

Sharing Management with the Workers. Ben M. Selekman. 1925. 142 pp.

Employes' Representation in Coal Mines. Ben M. Selekman and Mary van Kleeck. 1925. 454 pp.

Employes' Representation in Steel Works. Ben M. Selekman. 1925. 293 pp.

Employment Statistics for the United States. Ralph G. Hurlin and William A. Berridge. 1926. 215 pp.

Postponing Strikes. Ben M. Selekman. 1927. 405 pp.

The Filene Store. Mary LaDame. 1930. 541 pp.

Labor Agreements in Coal Mines. Louis Bloch. 1931. 513 pp.

Statistical Procedure of Public Employment Offices. Annabel M. and Bryce M. Stewart. 1933. 327 pp.

Miners and Management. Mary van Kleeck. 1934. 391 pp.

The American Miners' Association. Edward A. Wieck. 1940. 330 pp.

Preventing Fatal Explosions in Coal Mines. Edward A. Wieck. 1942. 156 pp. IS8.

Technology and Livelihood. Mary L. Fleddérus and Mary van Kleeck. 1944. 237 pp.

STATISTICS

Salaries and Vacations in Family Case Work in 1929. Ralph G. Hurlin. 1930. 24 pp. St6.

The Incidence of Work Shortage. Margaret H. Hogg. 1932. 136 pp.

The Number and Distribution of Social Workers in the United States. Ralph G. Hurlin. 1933. 11 pp. St7.

Salaries and Qualifications of Child Welfare Workers in 1941. Ralph G. Hurlin. 27 pp. St11.

The Recent Trend of Salaries in Child Welfare Agencies. Ralph G. Hurlin. 1944. 14 pp. St13.

Definitions of Terms and Instructions for Reporting Monthly Statistics of Family Casework. 1946. 26 pp. St17.

Operation Statistics of Selected Family Casework Agencies, 1945. Ralph G. Hurlin. 1946. 30 pp. St19.

SURVEYS AND EXHIBITS

The Newburgh Survey. Zenas L. Potter and Others. 1913. 104 pp. SE2.

Topeka Improvement Survey. In four parts.

A Public Health Survey of Topeka. Franz Schneider, Jr. 1914. 98 pp. SE3.

Delinquency and Corrections. Zenas L. Potter. 1914. 64 pp. SE4.

Municipal Administration in Topeka. D. O. Decker. 1914. 43 pp. SE5.

Industrial Conditions in Topeka. Zenas L. Potter. 1914. 56 pp. SE6.

The Springfield Survey. Shelby M. Harrison, Director.

Vol. I. 1918. 516 pp.

Vol. II. 1918. 675 pp.

Vol. III. 1920. 439 pp.

The A B C of Exhibit Planning. Evart G. Routzahn and Mary Swain Routzahn. 1918. 234 pp.

The Poor and Alms Department, and the Almshouse, of Newark, N. J. Francis H. McLean. 1919. 71 pp. SE28.

Traveling Publicity Campaigns. Mary Swain Routzahn. 1920. 151 pp.

Publicity Methods Reading List. Evart G. Routzahn and Mary Swain Routzahn. 1924. 48 pp. SE31.

Publicity for Social Work. Mary Swain Routzahn and Evart G. Routzahn. 1928. 392 pp.

A Bibliography of Social Surveys. Allen Eaton and Shelby M. Harrison. 1930. 467 pp.

The Social Survey. Shelby M. Harrison. 1931. 42 pp. SE32.

Immigrant Gifts to American Life. Allen H. Eaton. 1932. 185 pp.

Social Work Interpretation

How to Interpret Social Work: A Study Course. Helen Cody Baker and Mary Swain Routzahn. 1937. 79 pp. SWI1.

A Study in Public Relations. Harold P. Levy. 1943. 165 pp.

Building a Popular Movement. Harold P. Levy. 1944. 165 pp.

Arts and Social Work

Handicrafts of the Southern Highlands. Allen H. Eaton. 1937. 370 pp.

Delinquency and Penology

Plans and Illustrations of Prisons and Reformatories. Hastings H. Hart. 1922. 62 pp.

United States Prisoners in County Jails. Hastings H. Hart. 1926. 64 pp. DP1.

Training Schools for Delinquent Girls. Margaret Reeves. 1929. 455 pp.

Training Schools for Prison Officers. Hastings H. Hart (Compiler). 1930. 70 pp. DP3.

Plans for City Police Jails and Village Lockups. Hastings H. Hart. 1932. 27 pp.

Social Work Year Book

Social Work Year Book 1929. Fred S. Hall (Editor). 1930. 600 pp.

Social Work Year Book 1933. Fred S. Hall (Editor). 1933. 680 pp.

Social Work Year Book 1935. Fred S. Hall (Editor). 1935. 698 pp.

Social Work Year Book 1937. Russell H. Kurtz (Editor). 1937. 709 pp.

The Public Assistance Worker. Russell H. Kurtz (Editor). 1938. 224 pp.

Social Work Year Book 1939. Russell H. Kurtz (Editor). 1939. 730 pp.
Migration and Social Welfare. Philip E. Ryan. 1940. 114 pp. YB1.
Social Work Year Book 1941. Russell H. Kurtz (Editor). 1941. 793 pp.
Social Work Year Book 1943. Russell H. Kurtz (Editor). 1943. 764 pp.
Social Work Year Book 1945. Russell H. Kurtz (Editor). 1945. 620 pp.
Community Centers as Living War Memorials. James Dahir. 1946. 63 pp. YB2.

STUDIES IN THE PROFESSIONS

Social Work as a Profession. Esther Lucile Brown. 1936. 120 pp.
——— Revised edition. 1938. 118 pp.
——— Revised edition. 1942. 232 pp.
The Professional Engineer. Esther Lucile Brown. 1936. 86 pp.
Nursing as a Profession. Esther Lucile Brown. 1936. 120 pp.
——— Revised edition. 1940. 157 pp.
Physicians and Medical Care. Esther Lucile Brown. 1937. 202 pp.
Lawyers and the Promotion of Justice. Esther Lucile Brown. 1938. 302 pp.
Law Training in Continental Europe. Eric F. Schweinburg. 1945. 129 pp. SP1.

LIBRARY

Social Workers' Guide to the Serial Publications of Representative Social Agencies. Elsie M. Rushmore. 1921. 174 pp.
American Foundations for Social Welfare. Bertha F. Hulseman (Compiler). 1938. 64 pp. L3.

NON-DEPARTMENTAL

The Campaign Against Tuberculosis in the United States. Philip P. Jacobs. 1908. 467 pp.
The Standard of Living Among Workingmen's Families in New York City. Robert Coit Chapin. 1909. 372 pp.
Report on the Desirability of Establishing an Employment Bureau in the City of New York. Edward T. Devine. 1909. 238 pp.
The Pittsburgh Survey:
Women and the Trades. Elizabeth Beardsley Butler. 1909. 440 pp.
Work-Accidents and the Law. Crystal Eastman. 1910. 345 pp.
——— Revised edition. 1916. 335 pp.
Homestead: The Households of a Mill Town. Margaret F. Byington. 1910. 292 pp.

The Steel Workers. John A. Fitch. 1911. 380 pp.

The Pittsburgh District. Paul Underwood Kellogg (Editor). 1914. 554 pp.

Wage-Earning Pittsburgh. Paul Underwood Kellogg (Editor). 1914. 582 pp.

Housing Reform. Lawrence Veiller. 1910. 213 pp.

A Model Tenement House Law. Lawrence Veiller. 1910. 142 pp.

Among School Gardens. M. Louise Greene. 1910. 388 pp.

Workingmen's Insurance in Europe. Lee K. Frankel and Miles M. Dawson. 1910. 477 pp.

Correction and Prevention Series. Charles Richmond Henderson (Editor):

Prison Reform. Frederick Howard Wines and Others. 1910. 168 pp. *and* Criminal Law in the United States. Eugene Smith. 1910. 119 pp.

Penal and Reformatory Institutions. 1910. 345 pp.

Preventive Agencies and Methods. Charles Richmond Henderson. 1910. 419 pp.

Preventive Treatment of Neglected Children. Hastings H. Hart. 1910. 419 pp.

Civic Bibliography for Greater New York. James Bronson Reynolds (Editor). 1911. 296 pp.

One Thousand Homeless Men. Alice Willard Solenberger. 1911. 374 pp.

The Almshouse. Alexander Johnson. 1911. 263 pp.

Handbook of Settlements. Robert A. Woods and Albert J. Kennedy. 1911. 326 pp.

Fatigue and Efficiency. Josephine Goldmark. 1912. Part I, 302 pp. Part II, 591 pp.

———— Revised edition of Part I. 1912. 342 pp.

The Delinquent Child and the Home. Sophonisba P. Breckinridge and Edith Abbott. 1912. 342 pp.

Co-operation in New England. James Ford. 1913. 237 pp.

San Francisco Relief Survey. 1913. 483 pp.

A Model Housing Law. Lawrence Veiller. 1914. 343 pp.

———— Revised edition. 1920. 430 pp.

Carrying Out the City Plan. Flavel Shurtleff and Frederick Law Olmsted. 1914. 349 pp.

West Side Studies:

Boyhood and Lawlessness. Pauline Goldmark (Editor). 1914. 215 pp. *and* The Neglected Girl. Ruth S. True. 1914. 143 pp.

The Middle West Side. Otho G. Cartwright. 1914. 67 pp.

Mothers Who Must Earn. Katharine Anthony. 1914. 223 pp.

The Settlement Horizon. Robert A. Woods and Albert J. Kennedy. 1922. 499 pp.

Education and Training for Social Work. James H. Tufts. 1923. 240 pp.

Outline of Town and City Planning. Thomas Adams. 1935. 368 pp.

Music in Institutions. Willem van de Wall. 1936. 457 pp.

The Transportation Problem in American Social Work. Jeffrey R. Brackett. 1936. 38 pp. G1.

Zoning. Edward M. Bassett. 1936. 275 pp.

———— Revised edition. 1940. 275 pp.

The Master Plan. Edward M. Bassett. 1938. 151 pp.

Housing for the Machine Age. Clarence Arthur Perry. 1939. 261 pp.

Attacking on Social Work's Three Fronts. Shelby M. Harrison. 1942. 30 pp. G2.

Institutions Serving Children. Howard W. Hopkirk. 1944. 244 pp.

American Foundations for Social Welfare. Shelby M. Harrison and F. Emerson Andrews. 1946. 249 pp.

Music in Hospitals. Willem van de Wall. 1946. 86 pp. G4.

APPENDIX D

GRANTS BY RUSSELL SAGE FOUNDATION FROM
APRIL 19, 1907 TO SEPTEMBER 30, 1946

IN CHRONOLOGICAL ORDER ACCORDING TO DATE OF FIRST PAYMENT

(Grants for activities later incorporated in direct work of the Foundation and a few that
were made to offset rent for offices in the Foundation building are not included.)

Item	First payment	Grantee; fiscal years in which payments were made[a]; purpose of grant	Total paid
	1907		
1.	May	International Children's School Farm League; 1908–1918. For exhibits at Jamestown Exposition and at International Tuberculosis Congress; and toward expense of summer course at New York University for training school-garden teachers.	$19,500
2.	June	Charities Publication Committee of New York Charity Organization Society and its successor, Survey Associates, Inc.; 1908–1921, 1932–1946. For investigation in Pittsburgh ($27,000) and development of periodical, Charities and the Commons, renamed The Survey in 1909.	355,100[b]
3.	June	State Charities Aid Association of New York; 1908–1943. Chiefly for anti-tuberculosis campaign in the state of New York outside of New York City; and for development of agencies for dependent children and (after 1937) citizens' public welfare committees in counties of the state. Also for sundry special purposes.	891,800
4.	June	Charity Organization Society of New York City (Community Service Society of New York from 1939); 1908–1946. Chiefly, and in approximately equal amounts, for Department for Improvement of Social Conditions, including Committees on Tuberculosis, Housing, and Criminal Courts; and for New York School of Philanthropy (New York School of Social Work from 1918).	1,079,471[c]

For footnotes see end of table.

GRANTS TO SEPTEMBER 30, 1946, *continued*

1907

5. July   National Association for the Study and Prevention of $114,550
Tuberculosis (National Tuberculosis Association from
May, 1918); 1908–1917, 1926. For collection of data
on campaign against tuberculosis in the United
States; press service; traveling exhibit and field work
in southern and western states; contribution to ex-
penses of a conference of the International Union
Against Tuberculosis held in New York City, 1926.

6. July   New York Association for the Blind; 1908–1914. For   47,400[d]
demonstration in New York City of training blind
persons for self-support; exhibit of their work; statewide campaign for prevention of ophthalmia neona-
torum.

7. July   National Child Labor Committee; 1908–1912. For   21,000
exhibit at Jamestown Exposition; digest of laws and
literature; establishing office in Cincinnati; investigations and campaigns in the South.

8. July   Playground Association of America; 1908. For ex-   3,000[d]
hibit at Jamestown Exposition.

9. Oct.   Boston School for Social Workers; 1908–1915. For   70,100
Bureau of Research.

10. Oct.   International Congress on Tuberculosis; 1908. Con-   5,000
tribution to general expenses of Congress held in
Washington, September, 1908.

11. Oct.   Chicago Institute of Social Science (School of Civics   71,100
and Philanthropy); 1908–1915. For Bureau of Re-
search, including $1,000 for study of housing data col-
lected by fellows of Bureau.

12. Dec.   St. Louis School of Social Economy; 1908–1915. For   50,500
Bureau of Research.

13. Dec.   Saranac Lake Industrial Settlement; 1908. For experi-   1,610
ment in providing remunerative work for patients
convalescing from tuberculosis.

For footnotes see end of table.

GRANTS TO SEPTEMBER 30, 1946, *continued*

1908

14.	Jan.	Inter-Municipal Research Committee; 1908. To complete studies of abuses practiced on immigrants by notaries public and of conditions under which young immigrant women traveled.	$3,000
15.	Jan.	Grosvenor Atterbury; 1908–1910. For pioneering experiments in prefabricated housing.	32,000
16.	Jan.	Manhattan Trade School; 1908. Contribution for a single year, to enable School (under private auspices at that time) to demonstrate more thoroughly the value of trade training for girls.	10,000
17.	Feb.	Southern Education Board; 1908–1914. To enable the Board to extend its work for improvement of public schools into Kentucky and Arkansas.	55,000
18.	Apr.	President's Homes Commission; 1908–1909. For investigation of housing conditions in Washington, D. C.	5,000
19.	May	Typhoid Fever Commission of Pittsburgh; 1908–1911, 1913. For study of relation between incidence of typhoid fever in Pittsburgh and filtration.	15,100
20.	June	New York Probation and Protective Association (Girls' Service League from 1923); 1908–1926, 1929. Toward establishing temporary home for women on probation from Magistrates' Courts; and for general protective and advisory service for girls.	55,100[d]
21.	Oct.	American National Red Cross; 1909–1913. To make possible employment of a general director at a critical period.	21,500
22.	Oct.	Commission on Country Life; 1909. For traveling expenses, to enable Commission to hold hearings in different parts of the country.	5,000
23.	Nov.	Fairview School Gardens Association of Yonkers; 1908–1912. To provide favorable conditions for a demonstration of the value of school gardens.	60,122[e]
24.	Dec.	Brooklyn Bureau of Charities (Bureau of Social Service from January, 1945); 1909–1946. For Committees on Tuberculosis, Housing, and Criminal Courts; and to provide teachers for blind women in their homes.	350,133

For footnotes see end of table.

GRANTS TO SEPTEMBER 30, 1946, *continued*

1909

25. Feb. White House Conference on the Care of Dependent Children; 1909. Contribution to general expenses. — $1,500

26. Mar. Pittsburgh Civic Commission; 1909. To start contributions for work of Commission, appointed by Mayor to follow up findings of Pittsburgh Survey. — 5,000

27. Apr. Homer Folks; 1909, 1911. For study of juvenile court laws by Bernard Flexner and drafting of a model law. — 766

28. Apr. National Employment Exchange, Inc.; 1909, 1932–1933. Subscription of $19,000 to capital stock, and $3,500 for assistance in the depression. — 22,500[f]

29. May Survey Exhibit Campaign; 1909–1912. Toward expense of showing Pittsburgh Survey Exhibit in other industrial cities. — 1,181

30. June Social Halls Association; 1909. Subscription to capital stock of Association, formed to provide suitable meeting places on Lower East Side. — 15,000[g]

31. Oct. Homer Folks; 1910–1912. For study of fiscal methods of New York State institutions by Henry C. Wright. — 10,847

32. Oct. American Association for Labor Legislation, New York State Branch; 1910. For salary of secretary for State Commission to study Employers' Liability and Unemployment. — 1,000

33. Nov. Alliance Employment Bureau; 1910–1911. To assist Bureau in getting on a firm financial basis. — 3,000

1910

34. Feb. Prison Association of New York; 1910–1911. For study of men discharged from Elmira Reformatory. — 4,100

35. Mar. National Housing Association; 1910–1936. To promote movement for improvement of housing conditions on a national scale. — 295,425

36. Apr. American Association for Study and Prevention of Infant Mortality; 1910–1911. To help launch the newly organized movement. — 3,000

37. June Committee of Fourteen; 1910. To enable the Committee to publish its special report on prostitution in New York City, including codification of laws. — 1,000

For footnotes see end of table.

GRANTS TO SEPTEMBER 30, 1946, *continued*

1910

38.	July	American Institute of Criminal Law and Criminology; 1910. To help the newly founded Institute launch its Journal.	$2,000
39.	July	Central Bureau of Colored Fresh-Air Agencies (Committee on Urban Conditions Among Negroes); 1910–1911. To promote co-operation among fresh-air agencies for colored children in New York City.	2,000

1911

40.	Jan.	New York Child Welfare Committee; 1911. Toward expense of exhibit held in New York City, November, 1910.	7,982
41.	May	American Association for Labor Legislation; 1911–1913. For expansion of program.	8,500
42.	June	American Association for Conservation of Vision and its successor, National Committee for Prevention of Blindness; 1911–1913, 1915–1922. To promote establishment of a national agency for prevention of blindness.	43,833[d]
43.	Nov.	International Congress on Hygiene and Demography; 1912. Contribution to general expenses of the Congress.	5,000

1912

44.	Nov.	Committee on Industrial Relations; 1913. To make up deficit in treasury of Committee, which had conducted successful campaign for appointment of federal commission to study industrial conditions in the United States.	500

1913

45.	Mar.	Intercollegiate Bureau of Occupations; 1913–1914. Toward expense of establishing department for social workers.	1,000[d]
46.	June	Conference on Relief of Dependent Widows and Children; 1913. Toward expense of investigation of need for "widows' pensions" in New York.	2,000

For footnotes see end of table.

1914

47. Dec. Public Education Association of New York; 1915. To continue salary of a visiting teacher, in further demonstration of value of such work. $900

48. Dec. National Social Workers Exchange and (from 1921) American Association of Social Workers (see item 83); 1919–1933, 1935–1946. Chiefly toward expense of employment exchange and for study of positions in social work.   141,653[d]

1919

49. Mar. American Federation of Arts; 1919–1936, 1938, 1939. For purpose of "bringing good art into the homes of the people and to communities that now have little access to it," by traveling exhibits and other means.   157,350

50. Apr. National Conference on City Planning, American Civic Association (American Planning and Civic Association from 1935), and Federated Societies on Planning and Parks; 1919–1922, 1925–1946. To promote interest in city and regional planning, beautification of towns and highways, and development and use of local and national parks.   267,551[d]

51. Apr. New York Committee on Aftercare of Infantile Paralysis Cases; 1919. For work of Committee and in hope that a federation of agencies for care and treatment of crippled children in New York City would result.   5,000

52. July Robert A. Woods; 1919. To provide a guide and interpreter during his visit to China and Japan at instance of Young Men's Christian Association in China.   1,000

53. Oct. American Association for Organizing Family Social Work (Family Welfare Association of America 1930–1946; Family Service Association of America from June, 1946); 1919–1946. Chiefly for expanding field service, launching a monthly publication, and developing office of financial secretary.   740,322[d]

For footnotes see end of table.

GRANTS TO SEPTEMBER 30, 1946, *continued*

1920

54.   ...   Conference of Southern Mountain Workers and $30,505
Berea College (for Mountain Life and Work); 1920–
1946. To continue aid to projects sponsored by Southern Highland Division of Russell Sage Foundation.

55.   Feb.   National Information Bureau; 1920–1925, 1927–   38,400
1942, 1945–1946. Contributions, chiefly in form of
membership fees, to work of the Bureau in investigating national agencies that appeal to the public for
support and reporting on them to its members, and in
providing advisory service to agencies on standards of
administration and financial control.

56.   Oct.   Raymond Pearl; 1921. Toward cost of completing a   8,000
study of influence of social and physical environment
on spread of tuberculosis.

1921

57.   Mar.   Federated American Engineering Societies; 1921.   10,000
Contribution to investigation of causes of waste in
industry, under supervision of Herbert Hoover.

58.   May   Regional Plan of New York and Its Environs; 1921–   1,186,768[d]
1932. For expenses of survey of the Region and prepa-
ration of the Plan.

59.   Nov.   New York Federation of Agencies for Homeless Men;   2,672
1922–1924. Toward expense of a central bureau to
register and classify homeless men and youths applying for help and refer them to the appropriate agency.

60.   Dec.   Committee on Music in Institutions; 1922–1924. To   9,000
make possible further demonstration by Willem van
de Wall, under supervision of Lee F. Hanmer, of
therapeutic value of music in institutions for delin-
quents and hospitals for mental patients.

1922

61.   Feb.   Federal Council of the Churches of Christ in Amer-   121,150
ica; 1922–1946. Largely for work of Department of
Race Relations.

62.   Mar.   American Association of Hospital Social Workers (of   84,250
Medical Social Workers from 1934); 1922–1946. Con-
tribution to work of Association in stimulating establishment of departments of social work in hospitals
and in improving standards of medical social work.

For footnotes see end of table.

GRANTS TO SEPTEMBER 30, 1946, *continued*

1922

63. Apr. Better Times; 1922–1925. To aid in establishing this $6,000
new monthly periodical reporting news about social
agencies in New York City.

64. Nov. National Conference of Social Work; 1923, 1937,   14,900
1939, 1942, 1946. $10,000 toward expenses of fiftieth
anniversary meeting in Washington, 1923; the rest in
small amounts for special requirements.

65. Dec. National Research Council; 1923–1925. For pre-   9,297
liminary work of committee on study of human
migration.

1923

66. Feb. Foreign Language Information Service (Common   103,000
Council for American Unity from 1939); 1923–1945.
To promote assimilation of immigrants and mutual
understanding among the various elements of the
American people.

67. Aug. American Country Life Association; 1923–1942,   108,150
1944. To aid Association in its work for improving
social and living conditions in rural districts; by contributing to cost of publishing Proceedings and Bulletin and building up membership.

68. Dec. Committee on the Education of Non-English-Speak-   53,100
ing Women (Neighborhood Teacher Association from
1927); 1924–1938. To develop more effective methods
of instruction for immigrant women and demonstrate
their effectiveness.

1924

69. Mar. New York State Association; 1924. Toward cost of   500
printing and distributing report on a comprehensive
and unified plan of state parks.

70. May National Social Work Council; 1924–1946. To pro-   162,632
vide for a center for exchange of information and
opinion among national social agencies and discussion
of their common problems. (See item 117.)

71. Sept. Cities Census Committee, Inc.; 1924–1932. Toward   44,000
cost of tabulating and publishing federal census of
New York City by small areas.

For footnotes see end of table.

GRANTS TO SEPTEMBER 30, 1946, *continued*

1924

72. Oct. East Harlem Health Center; 1925–1937. Contribu- $31,000
tion to cost of continuing the demonstration until it
was taken over by New York City.

73. Nov. Welfare Council of New York City; 1925, 1927–1946.   182,019
For general work of the Council (including prelimi-
nary planning) and for various special purposes.

1925

74. Jan. International Migration Service; 1925–1946. For   88,846
work of American Branch.

75. May International Planning Congress; 1925. Contribution   2,500
to expenses of conference and exhibit held in New
York City, April, 1925.

76. June Social Science Research Council; 1925–1946. Con-   87,500
tribution to general administrative expenses.

77. Oct. Atlanta School of Social Work (a department of   105,000
Atlanta University from 1938); 1926–1946. For educating Negro social workers.

1926

78. Jan. National Municipal League; 1926–1927, 1931. For   10,000
study of "regional government."

79. May Child Welfare League of America; 1926–1946. Con-   176,789[d]
tribution to budget of the League, which originated
in Child-Helping Department of Russell Sage Foundation.

80. May Parents' Publishing Association, Inc. (Parents' Insti-   5,000[h]
tute, Inc.); 1926–1927. For purchase of stock in this
limited-dividend corporation, formed to publish a
new magazine, Children.

81. May Caroline Country Club; 1926. Contribution toward   2,500
cost of repairs and alterations at this social workers'
club.

82. Nov. Citizens Committee on Teachers' Salaries; 1927.   1,000
Toward cost of obtaining action on recommendations
made by Committee in its report.

_____

For footnotes see end of table.

1927

83. Jan. Joint Vocational Service (Social Work Vocational $160,722
Bureau from 1940); 1927–1946. Toward cost of operating employment exchange for public health nurses and social workers (see item 48 above) and for special study of placement problems in social work.

84. May Encyclopaedia of the Social Sciences; 1927–1933. 27,500
Contribution to cost of preparation and production.

85. June Family Welfare Society of Queens, Inc.; 1927–1932, 39,532
1937, 1938. For cost of an extension department, to develop interest in the Society and financial support.

86. July National Association of Legal Aid Organizations; 34,000
1927–1946. To promote objects of the Association.

87. Dec. Nassau Industrial School; 1928. Toward increase of 7,500
endowment given by Mrs. Sage in 1907, which no longer yielded sufficient income for current expenses.

1928

88. Jan. Committee on the Costs of Medical Care; 1928–1933. 27,300
To help finance studies looking toward devising of measures to provide competent medical service for all income groups.

89. Jan. Commission to Examine and Revise the Tenement 4,000
House Law of New York; 1928. For printing Commission's report.

90. Feb. Farmers Federation, Inc.; 1928–1931, 1933–1937. 7,500
For developing co-operation among farmers of Appalachian Mountain region.

91. Feb. International Conference of Social Work; 1928, 11,500
1930–1932. Contribution to budgets of first and second International Conferences of Social Work.

92. Mar. Employment Center for the Handicapped; 1928– 37,500
1935. Toward expenses of joint bureau formed by merger of four agencies following study by Russell Sage Foundation for Welfare Council.

1929

93. Jan. National Association of Travelers Aid Societies (Na- 77,000
tional Travelers Aid Association from 1938); 1929–1942. Contribution to budget of Association, with special reference to work for increasing income from other sources.

For footnotes see end of table.

694

GRANTS TO SEPTEMBER 30, 1946, *continued*

1929

94. Mar. National Interracial Conference; 1929. For expenses connected with Conference held in Washington, December, 1928. — $1,000

95. May Multiple Dwelling Law Committee; 1929–1938. For incidental expenses of Committee. — 13,150

96. June Regional Plan Association, Inc.; 1929–1946. To promote adoption of recommendations of Regional Plan Committee and continue its work. — 513,250

1931

97. Apr. Employment Bureau Demonstration in Rochester; 1931–1934. Toward cost of studies, under State Advisory Council on Employment Problems, to discover desirable procedures and qualifications needed in personnel. — 13,500

98. July National Urban League; 1931–1946. For general work of the League in furthering activities for improving conditions among Negroes in cities. — 14,500

99. Aug. Zoning Committee of New York City; 1931–1942. To promote understanding and adoption of the principles of zoning. — 20,050

100. Sept. Council on Adult Education for the Foreign-Born (New York Adult Education Council from 1932); 1931, 1933–1946. Toward cost of preparing exhibit of teaching material and other work of the Council. — 17,750

1932

101. Apr. United Parents Associations of New York City; 1932–1934. To help in financial emergency caused by depression. — 3,000

102. Dec. Legal Aid Society of the City of New York; 1933–1936. To help in financial emergency caused by depression. — 6,000

1933

103. May Social Work Exhibits Committee; 1933. To aid Committee in its work for exhibit of social services at the Century of Progress Exposition in Chicago, 1934. — 1,000

For footnotes see end of table.

1934

104. Jan. New York Committee on Study of Hospital Statistics; $1,000
1934–1935. For incidental expenses of Civil Works
Project 256, conducted for the Committee by the
Welfare Council.

105. Feb. Conference on Home-Building and Home-Ownership;   750
1934. To reprint volume 5 (supply exhausted but in
great demand) of Conference Report.

106. Mar. National Health Council; 1934. For maintaining   500
library service in financial emergency caused by depression.

107. Mar. Pennsylvania School of Social Work; 1934, 1939–   4,500
1941. To help the School through period of financial
stringency.

108. Sept. New York Tuberculosis and Health Association;   1,000
1934. Contribution to expense of consultant service
by Harry L. Hopkins.

1937

109. Jan. Citizens' Crime Commission of the State of New York;   91,000
1937–1941. To continue, on a statewide basis, such
work as had been carried on in New York City for
twenty-five years by the Committee on Criminal
Courts of the Charity Organization Society.

110. Apr. American Advisory Council of Universal Christian   1,000
Council for Life and Work; 1937. For promoting better understanding in America of social conditions and
community problems.

111. Nov. National Bureau of Economic Research, Inc.; 1938.   1,000
To assist in development of a co-operative research
center.

1938

112. Feb. National Organization for Public Health Nursing;   1,400
1938. For revising Manual on Public Health Nursing.

113. May Social Work Publicity Council (National Publicity   53,407[d]
Council for Health and Welfare Services from 1943);
1938–1946. To establish the Council (developed, and
still partly supported, by the Russell Sage Foundation
Department of Social Work Interpretation) on a more
independent basis.

For footnotes see end of table.

GRANTS TO SEPTEMBER 30, 1946, *continued*

1941

114. Sept. American Association of Schools of Social Work; $25,000
1941–1946. To help Association meet increasing needs
of the schools resulting from wartime conditions.

1942

115. Jan. American Parole Association; 1942, 1944. To explore   2,000
possibility of enlisting more substantial support for
work of Association.

1944

116. Sept. United Negro College Campaign; 1944. Contribu-   1,000
tion to fund for Negro colleges.

1946

117. Jan. National Social Welfare Assembly; 1946. Successor to   12,500
National Social Work Council, reorganized to include
national public health agencies and groups of agencies in special fields, and to take an active part in
dealing with social problems (see item 70).

118. June Neighborhood Health Development, Inc.; 1946. To   3,000
continue co-operation with city health centers.

119. Aug. National Association of School Social Workers; 1946.   1,250
For staff assistance to meet increased demands.

ᵃ Years are Foundation fiscal years, ending September 30. For purposes of this table the period April 19, 1907, to September 30, 1908, is treated as the first "year." Fiscal years are designated by the calendar year in which they end: "1946" means the fiscal year 1945–1946; "1945–1946" means the two fiscal years 1944–1945 and 1945–1946; "1931–1946" means all fiscal years from 1930–1931 through 1945–1946.

ᵇ $127,000 to Charities Publication Committee; $228,100 to Survey Associates after independent incorporation in 1912. The $21,500 given to Charities Publication Committee for its Field Department is not included here, but is classified as preliminary expenditure for the Charity Organization Department of the Foundation.

ᶜ Not including $148,500 to Charities Publication Committee. (See item 2 and footnote b.)

ᵈ Plus free office space in Foundation building.

ᵉ Additional expenditures were made after 1912, but they were considered incidental to ownership of the property, which was sold by the Foundation after 1921. (See p. 235.)

ᶠ Dividends amounting to $23,940 were received by the Foundation to May, 1930, which more than replaced original subscription and grants of 1932–1933 combined.

ᵍ On liquidation of the Association between 1922 and 1929, the Foundation received $5,500 as its share of net proceeds from sale of the property. (See p. 241.)

ʰ In 1937 Parents' Institute, Inc. began paying dividends to stockholders and in 1944 a recapitalization plan was adopted whereby the shares of Founders' stock were replaced by twenty-five-year income bonds. By 1946 the Foundation had already received substantial pecuniary returns on its original contribution and its "grant" had become an income-producing asset.

INDEX TO TABLE OF GRANTS

APPENDIX D

INDEX

INDEX

Pages 1–350 are in Volume I

American Association of Visiting Teachers, 662. *See also* National Association of School Social Workers

American Bar Association, Committee on Legal Aid, 627

American City, The, 509

American Civic Association, 464, 656. *See also* American Planning and Civic Association; Federated Societies on Planning and Parks

American Council on Education: American Youth Commission, 504–505; Committee on Education and the Public Social Services, 621–622; Committee on Education and Social Security, 621

American Country Life Association, 325, 471–472, 590–591, 652, 692

American Craftsmen's Cooperative Council, 590

American Federation of Arts, 462, 652, 690

American Folk Dance Society, 77n

American Food Journal, 261

American Foundation for the Blind, 616

American Foundations for Social Welfare, 200, 539n, 633, 642–643, 682, 684

American Friends in France, 1917–1919, The, 528n

American Friends Service Committee, 528n

American Hospital Association, 458–459

American Industrial Lenders Association, 337, 342, 344, 346, 347. *See also* American Association of Personal Finance Companies; American Association of Small Loan Brokers

American Institute of Criminal Law and Criminology, 241, 689

American Institute of Graphic Arts, 373, 589, 595, 640

American Journal of Public Health, 184, 190n, 366, 571

American Library Association, 250

American Marriage Laws in Their Social Aspects: A Digest, 315n, 678

American Medical Association, Public Health Education Committee, 97

American Miners' Association, 552

American Miners' Association, The, 552n, 680

American National Red Cross: civilian relief, 245, 254, 255; disaster relief, 237, 311; East Harlem Health Center, 478; grants to, 236–237, 687; home service, 254, 255; nursing service, 121; overseas service with, 253–254; service in military camps, 529

American Park Society, 464. *See also* Federated Societies on Planning and Parks

American Parole Association, 660, 697

American Planning and Civic Association, 656, 663, 690. *See also* American Civic Association; National Conference on City Planning

American Prison Association, Committee on Jails, 299–301, 306, 308

American Public Health Association, 362, 573. *See also American Journal of Public Health*

American Red Cross. *See* American National Red Cross

American Red Cross Famine Relief in China, 1920–1921, 528n

American Red Cross in the Great War, 1917–1919, The, 528n

American Relief in Russia, 1921–1923, The, 528n

American School Board Journal, 87n, 90n, 174n, 404n

American School Hygiene Association, 98

American Statistical Association: Committee on Governmental Labor Statistics, 389, 405–406, 419, 554; Committee on Measurement of Employment, 388–389, 405; Committee on Social Statistics, 411n. *See also Journal of the American Statistical Association; Quarterly Publications of the American Statistical Association*

American Youth Commission, American Council on Education, 504–505

Americanization, exhibitions promoting, 371

Among School Gardens, 215, 683

Anderson, Elizabeth Milbank, 13n

Andrews, F. Emerson: xvii, consultant on publications for Twentieth Century Fund, 642n; director, Publication Department of Foundation, 433–434, 635–645, 671, 672; member of board of directors of American Institute of Graphic Arts, 640; publications, 539n, 637n, 642–643, 684

Annalist, The, 174n, 404n, 405n

Annals of the American Academy of Political and Social Science, 522, 540, 599, 625

Annotations on Small Loan Laws, 533, 679

Annual Reports and How to Improve Them, 580n

Anthony, Katharine S., 218, 683

Appalachian Mountain region, cooperation among farmers of, 472–473. *See also* Southern Highlands

Pages 1–350 are in Volume I

Pages 1–350 are in Volume I

Pages 1–350 are in Volume I

Pages 1–350 are in Volume I

Pages 1–350 are in Volume I

Feeble-minded, care of, 110, 191
Feeble-minded Children, 200
Feeble-mindedness, 200
Fels, S. S., 193
Festivals: America's Making Exposition and Festival, 372; Festivals of Nations, St. Paul, 586; Folk Festival, St. Paul, 586; National Folk Festival, Washington, D. C., 586
Fetter, Frank A., 15*n*
Field Day and Play Picnic for Country Children, The, 71*n*, 675
Fifty Years of Prison Service, 206*n*
Filene, A. Lincoln, 383
Filene, Edward A., 339, 383
Filene Store, The, 383*n*, 549*n*, 680
Filene, William, 383
Financial federations, 132–133, 310, 569
Financial Federations, 132
Financing the Consumer, 350
Finley, John H.: death, 486; Regional Survey and Plan, 441; trustee, 42, 485, 669
Finley, W. N., 66
Fire Protection in Public Schools, 88, 676
First Steps in Community Center Development, 82*n*, 675
First Steps in Organizing Playgrounds, 71*n*, 675
Fisher, H. H., 528*n*
Fisher, Irving, 22*n*
Fishman, Joseph F., 303, 308
Fitch, John A., 213, 683
Fitz Henry, Louis, 302
Fleddérus, Mary L., 396, 397; associate in research and administration, Department of Industrial Studies, 557, 562–565; publications, 558, 562, 563, 680
Flexner, Abraham, 95
Flexner, Bernard, 105
Florida, social survey of, 252
Folk Dance Society, American, 77*n*
Folk dancing, 76–77
Folk festivals. *See* Festivals
Folk songs, 123–124
Folks, Homer, 14*n*, 105, 106, 688
Food Administration, U. S., 196, 261
Food Administration, U. S. War, 547
Food, Clothing and Textile Industries, Wholesale Markets and Retail Shopping and Financial Districts, 446*n*
Food Conservation Exhibits for Fairs and Expositions, 261
Food Conservation Train, 261
Forbes, John Van Gelder, 528*n*
Ford, James, 218, 683

Foreign born: contributions of, 371–372, 585–586; grants to agencies serving, 474–475. *See also* Immigrants
Foreign-Born, Council on Adult Education for the, 474, 695
Foreign Language Information Service, 474, 658, 692. *See also* Common Council for American Unity
Foreign relief and rehabilitation, 499–500, 527–528, 528*n*, 530
Foreign Relief and Rehabilitation—A Bibliography, 528*n*
Forest Hills Gardens: development of, 42, 43, 49–51, 228; sale of Foundation's interest, 272–273
Formation of Charity Organization Societies in Smaller Cities, 126, 677
Fosdick, Raymond B., 140
Foster care for children. *See* Child-placing, study of; Institutions for children
Foundations: Library bulletins on, 200, 633; Library file on, 632; study of, 642–643
Founder. *See* Sage, Margaret Olivia
Founding, date of, 17
Framingham (Mass.) Community Health and Tuberculosis Demonstration, 193–194
France, 203, 390, 501, 529, 641
Frankel, Lee K., 14*n*, 15, 210, 215, 683
French, George, 596
Fresh-Air Agencies, Central Bureau of Colored, 241, 689
Friendly Visiting Among the Poor, 312
Friends Service Committee, American, 528*n*
From Mountain Cabin to Cotton Mill, 124
From Plan to Reality, 655
Fuss, Felicia, 628, 629
Future of the Church and Independent Schools in Our Southern Highlands, The, 124

G

Gallert, David J., 336, 532*n*, 679
Gardens: school, 234–235; subsistence, 518–519
Gardens Association, Fairview School, 235, 687
Gary (Ind.) school survey, 82, 95
Gebhard, Bruno, 368, 570
Geddes, Anne E., 398, 417, 607, 608
General assistance programs, studies of, 529, 530
General director. *See* Glenn, John M.; Harrison, Shelby M.; Russell Sage Foundation, General director

Pages 1–350 are in Volume I

Pages 1–350 are in Volume I

Howard, Donald S.: assistant director, Charity Organization Department, 528; background, 521–522; director, Department of Social Work Administration, 529–530, 672, 673; executive secretary, Mayor's Board of Survey on the Transfer of Relief Administration, 522; on leave with UNRRA, 499; publications, 524, 525, 528, 678

Hubachek, F. B., 533, 679

Hubachek, Frank R., 679

Hulseman, Bertha F.: director, Library, 422, 628, 672, 673; publications, 633, 682; Special Libraries Association, 426n, 629

Human migration, study of, 393, 477

Hurlin, Ralph G.: chairman, Committee on Social Statistics, 411n; chairman, Committee on Statistics of the Blind, 421; director, Department of Statistics, 398–421, 493, 605–617, 671, 672; publications, 404–406, 409–417, 421n, 609n, 611–615, 680; Regional Survey and Plan, 355, 449–450; secretary, Committee on Governmental Labor Statistics, 405–406; secretary, Committee on Measurement of Employment, 388; Social Science Research Council, 403, 415

Hutcheson, Joseph C., Jr., 301, 302n

Huyler, John S., 100

Hygiene and Demography, International Congress on, 240, 689

I

Illinois, study of administration of labor agreements in coal mines of, 384–385

Immigrant Gifts to American Life, 372, 375, 585–586, 681

Immigrants: cultural contributions of, 371–372, 585–586; photographic studies of, 632. *See also* Foreign born

Improved Housing, 200

Incidence of Work Shortage, The, 419n, 605, 635, 680

Income Reserve Account, 459, 460

Independence Day Legislation and Celebration Suggestions, 675

"Index Number for Educational Progress, An," 174n

Index Number for State School Systems, An, 284n, 676

Indian, arts of the American, 591

Indiana, child welfare study, 103

Industrial Causes of Congestion of Population in New York City, 206n

Industrial Conditions in Topeka, 183n, 680

Industrial Conference Board, National, 541n

Industrial Disputes and the Canadian Act, 167n, 679

Industrial Fatigue, 200

Industrial fatigue, study of, 215, 216, 564

Industrial Investigations of the Russell Sage Foundation, with bibliography, 163n

Industrial Lenders Association, American. *See* American Industrial Lenders Association

Industrial nursing, 623

Industrial relations, 379–385, 549–550, 558–561

Industrial Relations Association, International, 396, 397, 557n

Industrial Relations, Committee on, 689

Industrial Relations Institute, International, 396n, 551, 554, 555, 557–558

Industrial Relations and Living Standards, 561, 564

Industrial Relations Series, 379–385, 549–550, 558

Industrial representation, studies of Rockefeller Plan, 379–381

Industrial Studies, Department of: activities 1920–1931, 378–397; activities 1932–1946, 493, 549–565; publications, 679–680; title adopted, 378n. *See also* Industrial Studies, Division of; Women's Work, Committee on

Industrial Studies, Division of: activities 1916–1917, 152–170; activities 1918–1920, 357–359, 377–379; activities, World War I, 256–258; publications, 679–680; title adopted, 161. *See also* Industrial Studies, Department of; Women's Work, Committee on

Industry, Pennsylvania Department of Labor and, 392

Infant mortality, 105–107, 230

Infant Mortality, 218n

Infant Mortality, American Association for the Study and Prevention of, 105–106, 230, 688

Infant Welfare, 200

Infantile Paralysis Cases, New York Committee on Aftercare of, 462, 690

Information Bureau, National, 471, 657, 691

"Initial Activities of the Russell Sage Foundation, The," 36n

Installment sales, regulation of, 544–545

Institute of Family Social Work, 310, 318. *See also* Institutes, Charity Organization

Pages 1–350 are in Volume I

Pages 1–350 are in Volume I

Pages 1–350 are in Volume I

Pages 1–350 are in Volume I

Pages 1–350 are in Volume I

Pages 1–350 are in Volume I

Pages 1–350 are in Volume I

Pages 1–350 are in Volume I

Recreation, *continued*
81, 181, 182, 188, 332; workers, study of standards and salaries of, 334. *See also Public Recreation;* Recreation, Department of; Recreation, Division of
Recreation Alliance, The, 79, 80, 81
Recreation Association of America, Playground and. *See* Playground and Recreation Association of America
Recreation Association, National. *See* National Recreation Association
Recreation Branch, U. S. War Department, Education-, 251, 323
Recreation Committee, New York City, 322, 332, 503
Recreation Committee, Welfare Council of New York City, 322
Recreation Council, National Education-, 653
"Recreation for Crippled Children," 334
Recreation, Department of, 70, 76; activities 1913–1917, 70–84; activities 1919–1931, 321–335, 360n, 376; activities 1932–1937, 490, 502–513; activities, World War I, 84, 249–251; discontinuance, 492, 511–513; origin, 65; publications, 675–676; Regional Survey and Plan, 446–449; Sag Harbor, 269. *See also* Playground Extension, Committee on; Recreation, Division of
Recreation, Division of: activities 1909–1913, 70–84; origin, 72; publications, 675–676. *See also* Playground Extension, Committee on; Recreation, Department of
Recreation Leaders, Training School for, 505–506
Recreation in Springfield, Illinois, 81
Recreation Institute, 83
Recreation, National Conference on Outdoor, 325
Red Cross. *See* American National Red Cross
Reeder, Nell M., 548
Reeder, R. R., 206n
Reeves, Edith, 107n, 220, 676
Reeves, Margaret, 291, 681
Regional Council, 445
Regional government, study of problems of, 464
Regional Plan, 279, 638; volumes, 446n
Regional Plan Association, 495, 510; grants to, 464, 491, 654, 663, 695; origin, 451; reports published by, 511, 655
Regional Plan Bulletin, 655

Regional Plan, Committee on. *See* Committee on Regional Plan
Regional Plan of New York and Its Environs: contributions by Foundation staff, 446–450; Economic and Industrial Survey, 447, 449; executive secretary, 440, 442; general director of plans and surveys, 442; grants to, 278, 463–464, 650, 691; list of Survey and Plan volumes, 446n; organization, 441–443; origin and preliminary work, 438–441; presentation of Plan, 451; Regional Plan Association launched, 451; scope, 444
Regional planning, 463–465, 654–656. *See also* Regional Plan of New York and Its Environs
Regional Planning, Round Table on, 447
Regional Survey, 279, 449n; list of volumes, 446n
Regional Survey and Plan. *See* Regional Plan of New York and Its Environs
Regulation of Pawnbroking, The, 339n, 349, 532n, 678
Regulation of the Small Loan Business, 142n, 533n, 679
Regulation W, 500, 546–547
Rehabilitation of the Disabled Serviceman, 633n
Rehabilitation and relief, foreign, 499–500, 527–528, 528n, 530
"Relative Values in Public Health Work," 190n
Relief, 126n
Relief: civilian, 255; disaster, 28, 214, 237, 311; expenditures, index of, 415–418; and rehabilitation, foreign, 499–500, 527–528, 528n, 530; statistics, 607–608, 609–611; unemployment, 418, 475, 514–524, 647, 652, 658. *See also* Work relief
Relief Bureau, New York (City) Emergency, 490, 541, 607–608
Relief Expenditures by Governmental and Private Organizations, 1929 and 1931, 418n
Relief, President's Organization on Unemployment Relief, 418
Relief and Rehabilitation Administration, United Nations, 499, 500, 501, 547–548
Relief Resources, National Committee for Mobilization of, 418
"Relief Statistics of the Children's Bureau, The," 418n
Relief Statistics, Joint Committee on, 610–611

Pages 1–350 are in Volume I

Pages 1–350 are in Volume I

Pages 1–350 are in Volume I

Pages 1–350 are in Volume I

Pages 1–350 are in Volume I

738

Social workers: employment and vocational bureaus for, 238, 461–462, 576, 616, 657; enumeration and classification of, 409–411, 611–612; estimated number of, 411; recognized as occupational group by Census Bureau, 411, 611; salaries, studies of, 612–614
Social Workers, American Association of. *See* American Association of Social Workers
Social Workers' Exchange, National, 461
Social Workers' Guide to the Serial Publications of Representative Social Agencies, 423n, 682
Solenberger, Alice Willard, 215, 683
Some Conditions Affecting Problems of Industrial Education in 78 American School Systems, 89n
Some Problems in Sickness Insurance for Women, 162
"Some Results of Two Years' Study of Family Case Work Statistics," 413n
"Some Shortcomings of Socio-Sanitary Investigations," 190n
Songs of American Sailormen, 525n
"Sources of Error and Incomparability in Employment-Unemployment Surveys," 419n
Sources of Information on Play and Recreation, 321n, 675
South Carolina, social survey of, 252
South: Its Social and Economic Aspects, The, 633n
Southern Education Board, 229, 687
Southern Highland Division: activities 1908–1917, 115–124; discontinued, 281–283; origin, 62; publications, 677
Southern Highland Handicraft Guild, 282, 374, 587
Southern Highland Schools Maintained by Denominational and Independent Agencies, 282n
Southern Highlander and His Homeland, The, 282n, 677
Southern Highlanders, Inc., 588
Southern Highlands: handicrafts, 282, 374–375, 586–590; health, 120–121; John C. Campbell Folk School, 282; schools, 117–119, 282n. *See also* Appalachian Mountain region; Southern Highland Division
Southern Highlands, The, 124
Southern Mountain Workers, Conference of, 122, 282, 374, 479, 657, 691
Special Libraries Association, 426n, 629
Spelling scale, 92, 286n, 436

Spelling Vocabularies of Personal and Business Letters, The, 676
Spelman Fund, 470
Sportsmanship Brotherhood, 325, 504
Springfield (Ill.) Survey, 81, 93–94, 186–190
Springfield Survey, The, 188n, 189n, 353, 680
Standard of living, studies of, 28, 209–210, 559, 560–561, 563
Standard of Living Among Workingmen's Families in New York City, The, 682
Standing Order List (Foundation publications), 433, 437, 637
State Charities Aid Association (New York), 197–198; Bureau for Exchange of Information, 287; child welfare, 233–234, 455, 647; Committee on Dependent Children, 234; grants to, 27, 30, 223, 226, 233–234, 454–456, 647, 685; library of, 197–198; tuberculosis, 27, 30, 226, 455; unemployment relief, 647
State Department, U. S., 255, 640, 654
Statistical Association, American. *See* American Statistical Association
Statistical Procedure of Public Employment Offices, 390n, 554, 680
Statistics: blindness, 616; child welfare, 414; cost of living, 421; crime, 390; employment, 388–389, 390, 404–406; family casework, 412–413, 414, 614–615; hospital social work, 413, 414, 615; hospitals, 659; medical social work, 413, 414, 615; mothers' aid, 413, 414; prisoners, 401; public employment offices in Europe, 390; public health, 404; relief, 609–611; social casework, 411–415; unemployment, 419, 554; wages, 389. *See also* Statistics, Department of; Statistics, Division of
"Statistics in the Administration of a Public Welfare Program," 609n, 611
Statistics of the Blind, Committee on, 421, 616
Statistics Branch, U. S. War Department, 247–248
Statistics, Committee on Registration of Social, 414, 415
Statistics, Council of National Defense, Division of, 246
Statistics, Department of, 324, 400n, 436, 447, 490, 493; activities 1920–1931, 398–421; activities 1932–1946, 605–617; publications, 680; title adopted, 398. *See also* Statistics, Division of

Pages 1–350 are in Volume I

Pages 1–350 are in Volume I

Pages 1–350 are in Volume I